MW00448703

My Grandfather's Hat

The Travels of Habib Fakih – A Memoir

As told to

Karen L. Fullerton

Copyright © 2012–2021 by Karen L. Fullerton

Cover and interior design by Masha Shubin | Inkwater.com
Photos © Habib Fakih

All rights reserved. No part of this book may be reproduced or transmitted in any form or by any means whatsoever, including photocopying, recording or by any information storage and retrieval system, without written permission from the publisher and/or author.

ISBN 978-1-0879-8287-8

1 3 5 7 9 10 8 6 4 2

DEDICATIONS

I DEDICATE MY MEMOIR TO MY LOVING WIFE, SIHAM, AND TO ALL OF THE family that we started together and that will come after us. I want to acknowledge the diverse people who accepted me into their communities as I moved to various countries. Their support and efforts in helping me start my businesses are greatly appreciated. I hope that my experiences and thoughts in this book encourage and inspire my children and all the next generations to be honest and be an example to others, to work hard and be productive, and be happy.

HABIB FAKIH
APRIL, 2012

I HAVE BEEN LUCKY ENOUGH TO HAVE VERY SPECIAL PEOPLE FROM MANY different countries in my life from an early age, and this book is dedicated to them. Their friendship and willingness to share with me their experiences, foods (especially Lena's!), and customs have broadened my own life. I appreciate and thank LeeAnn Gauthier for her editing and help to conclude work on the book. My husband, Les, deserves a thank you for supporting me in this project—although I think it was not too tough, as he also enjoyed Lena's dinners!

KAREN FULLERTON
OCTOBER 2020

TABLE OF CONTENTS

FROM THE AUTHOR

WHILE I WAS AT THE COUNTER IN HIS DONUT SHOP SELECTING A DONUT, another customer asked Habib where he got his knitted hat. Habib explained that it was his grandfather's, and told a fascinating little vignette about his grandfather's life.

That hooked me! I asked Habib if I could write the story of his life. It has been a wonderful experience that I would not trade for anything. It was an honor for me to have Habib and his family share so many personal stories and experiences—they were entertaining, funny, happy, and sad. I learned much about the beautiful Lebanese culture and customs.

I thank Habib and his family for allowing me to do this—and for all those delicious dishes Lena prepared!

Thank you also to Inkwater Press for patiently guiding me through the publishing process.

KAREN L. FULLERTON, M.B.A., B.S.
JULY 28, 2012

PREFACE

To my family:

This is the story of my life. I wanted this written so that you, my family, my children and my grandchildren, who lived parts of it with me, and your children later, would know about our family. My grandparents and parents were wonderful people, highly respected in our town and by everyone who knew them. My grandfathers and father were very important to me in my young life, and I remember them with love. They taught me about our religion, and our appreciation of our Lebanese history and culture. I formed all of my values from the examples of how they lived, through all the family stories they told me, and the principles they taught me that have guided me throughout my life.

I hope that you can read our story and use it as a foundation for your own successes, so that you live happy, productive lives. I hope that you can reflect in the future the same strength our family has always shown when situations were tough. I hope that you can reflect the consistent love for each other that is obvious in this story. Enjoy!

LEBANON

I SPENT A LOT OF TIME WITH MY GRANDFATHER WHEN I WAS YOUNG, AND I still wear the knit cap he gave me. When I was around eight years old, we would go to the market together, and I would help him because he was partially blind. He told me about my family's history. Our last name, Fakih, means "expert in religion," and "interpreter of the Koran." My grandfather taught me the values of our religion and family. I learned respect for other people, the importance of family, and the value of hard work from the conversations we had when I was young.

My grandfather was a shoemaker. He had a shop and people working for him. He had the wooden patterns for shoes of all sizes and designs. He would have his workers make fifty pairs of men's boots, fifty pairs of women's shoes, and fifty pairs of children's shoes. He would put them all in bags and travel with his mule from place to place, selling them in the markets. Each village and town had a certain day of the week that was market day, and that's when he would arrive to sell his shoes. He would be gone for a whole week, selling even on Saturday and Sunday. He carried his money in a belt hidden under his clothes. When he had sold all the shoes, he would come home and rest. He would travel for one week, and stay home one week, getting the goods prepared for the next trip. When he returned from the trips, he exchanged the Turkish money for gold. He only kept small change in his pocket, and always traveled by day and with other people so that he would not be robbed.

My grandfather did very well in his job. He made money and bought houses and land. But my father wasted it all. My grandfather spoiled my father. My father told my grandfather that he wanted to open a candy store. But my grandfather told him that he should learn to make and sell shoes. My father refused and still wanted to have a candy store. My grandfather opened the candy store for him. He called all his friends and people he did business with, inviting them to the store and giving them candy. The store didn't last more than six months!

My father ended up becoming a saddle maker because my grandfather had a neighbor who made saddles for horses, donkeys, and mules. My father saw that that family was doing very well in their business. On market day, ten donkeys would be in a line waiting for saddles. My father said, "I don't want to be like my father, making shoes and going to the villages to sell them." He told his father that he wanted to learn saddle making. My grandfather agreed, and went to the market to talk with the most experienced saddle maker. He asked if his son could learn saddle making with him, and the saddle maker agreed. He taught my father how to do it. Within one year, he had learned the trade and could work on his own. But he didn't want to open his own store. He wanted to either work for the saddle maker or be a partner with him. He didn't want the responsibility of hiring people. He was a handsome young man, with blue eyes, and people liked him. He was so clever; he could tell stories, he could sing and he was so nice.

He loved my mother. One day he hid so he could see her coming out of the house. He was wearing a nice silk shirt, and he hid in the chicken cage. That evening, as usual, my grandfather locked the gate of the chicken cage to keep people from stealing the chickens. My father had to remove rocks from under the gate and squirm under to get out. His older sisters saw him come in all dirty. He said he had fallen down, but later he told them what really happened.

I spent a lot of time with my grandfather when I was around eight years old. We went to the market together, and I would help him because he was partially blind. He talked to me about my family history. My grandmother died when my father was just four years old. But my grandparents had two daughters, and then a first son before my father was born. That first son, my uncle, was named Moshen. Moshen was young during the time when the Turkish were taking young people away to help them in war battles. My grandfather sent Moshen away on a ship to fight alongside the Turks. He went to Mexico and never came back. He died there. Our family was spread around Lebanon at that time. Some were living in the mountains and some in Beirut City. My grandfather's relatives came to the southern Lebanon and stayed there, which is why our family grew up in Nabatieh. So our closest relatives were scattered all over that part of the country, where over the generations they found jobs and made their homes.

Since my grandmother died when the children were so young, our relatives encouraged my grandfather to remarry, so that he could have help with the children. My grandfather didn't want to remarry. However, a wife was found for him. She was divorced, and had a little baby the same age as my father. My grandfather and his new wife always fought. One day he came home from work and discovered that she had beaten my father. He asked her, "Why are you beating up my son?" She replied, "Because he was beating up my daughter." My grandfather said, "Okay. Take your daughter and go home. I don't want you anymore." He did not remarry again. He took care of the children himself, and with the help of friends, neighbors, and family. During that period, he only traveled to the towns selling shoes about one week out of each month. He also tried to hire someone to make some of the trips for him because he didn't want to leave the children for so long.

My grandfather on my mother's side maintained property for the schools in the area and did other things to make money. He cut tobacco. Old-time tobacco was very thin—as thin as hair strands. The men cut the tobacco with big knives. It was very precise work, and when they wrapped it in the cigarette paper, it looked very nice, exactly even, better than the commercial cigarettes. My grandfather taught two of our relatives, my uncles. One of the uncles, Mohammed, also sold vegetables at the village market. A town close to the sea grew many nice vegetables. It was about forty kilometers away, and there weren't very many cars at that time. Mohammed would hire a horse or mule with a cart on Sunday afternoon, travel to get the produce, and bring the vegetables back in time for the 6:00 a.m. opening of the market on Monday. He would ask me to help him. In the afternoon, after school, I would go to help him unpack the fruit as he ran out, and pick out bad grapes from the good. At the end of the market day, around 5:00 or 6:00 p.m., he would divide up all the remaining fruit and vegetables and I would be able to take them home to my mother. Sometimes there was so much, my brothers would have to help me, and we were supplied for the whole week. My uncle didn't ever pay me money, but he gave me all that food for my family.

Another of my uncles, Ali, painted buildings. Later, he opened a store to sell paint, and then became a building contractor. Our neighbor had a nice, good-looking girl who he saw when he would visit his sister, my mother. He loved that girl and married her and had a few children.

One time some building materials that he had ordered were being delivered. The load included some heavy window glass. He was injured when they were pushing the glass from the truck, and became paralyzed. His son took over the business.

A fourth boy, Ahmad, had children who all became teachers. Some of them gave private lessons in their homes. They were all quite successful. One of my aunts, named Khairriyeh, was about ten years younger than me. She married a painting contractor. They had about four boys and three girls. All the boys were in the painting business, and very successful. I visit Ahmad and my relatives whenever I return to Lebanon. Ahmad is about ninety now. His wife had a stroke recently.

In the 1940s, war came. I was almost 12 years old, and my town, Nabatieh, was very slow, economically. The people in South Lebanon were very poor. At that time, the war was between the French and the Allies, and the French army stayed in our town. De Gaulle wanted to join the Allies, which he later did. There were about 1,000 soldiers standing in line, and de Gaulle was doing an inspection. I saw him pass through town; he was so tall. He was going south to Palestine to join the Allies. There were so many soldiers because the town was near the border. The people in the town had little food and few supplies, and were very scared because of the presence of the soldiers. The Allies were coming from Palestine to take Lebanon from Vichy forces, who were allied with the Germans.

My father did not know what was happening to our family during the war at first, because he was out of town. He made and repaired saddles, *jellal*, for farmers' mules and donkeys. He had to travel from village to village and would be gone two to three weeks, then return one week and then go again. I was the oldest child, and had three brothers and three sisters. After me, they were born in this order: Fatimah, Najat, Hassan, Mohammed, Hesniyeh, and Yussef. As the eldest, I felt it was my responsibility to take care of my brothers and sisters. During this time the army took all the food from the stores and markets. It was a scary time, because if you argued with the soldiers, they would beat you up. Since I was so young, I was able to get food and supplies for the family because the soldiers ignored me.

The rains were very heavy in the rainy season and it was too cold to go outside. Our family prepared by storing supplies of beans and meats and other foods. My father would buy a sheep and slaughter it. My mother would partially cook all the meat with the fat. They then stored it with potatoes and other vegetables, also buried in the fat (*awarma*) in a large clay pot (*jarrat*). The fat sealed the food, protecting it from the air, and preserving it so we could eat it all during the cold season. We would sit around the warm fire and my grandfather would tell stories about his life and the country while smoking his cigarettes. My father smoked his hubbly-bubbly (water pipe), and my mother drank her tea. Many times, cousins and friends would also be there, listening.

Our town was arranged with a park in the middle, surrounded by stores and houses. Beyond that was farmland and orchards. Because my grandfather was old by then, he was living in a little house with one of my uncles. But about one kilometer (three-quarters of a mile) away was an orchard of fig trees that he owned.

In the summers, rich people moved to second or rented homes in the mountains. Middle-class people, like my father, had land, and would go there to build temporary huts. Many neighbors did this in the summer. Each summer, after school was out, we set up camp in my grandfather's fig orchard. My mother and father would make a hut out of branches, grasses, and mud, which acted like cement. My mother would plant flowers all around, and we would stay there enjoying the fresh air and the breeze. My brothers and sisters and I would play in the orchard and climb the trees. We had a little stream on the land, so we had fresh water. We would carry mattresses, blankets, and supplies to the hut. My father would walk to work each morning and then bring a basket of meat and vegetables from the town each evening. My mother would cook, and we would have dinner together. After dinner my father would build his hubbly-bubbly. My grandfather would smoke his cigarettes and they would put a teapot on the charcoal fire, talk about the day and enjoy the evening. I remember how it seemed like such a long wait until the summertime each year.

We also moved to this fig orchard to be safe during the war, when the soldiers took over the town. The path to the orchard was too narrow and rocky for a car. My brothers, sisters, and I all walked with my mother along a rocky narrow path. We all carried some of the different foods and supplies with us. My mother built the hut and arranged stones to make an area in which to cook, just like we did in the summers. My sisters gathered twigs and branches for the fire. Every few days, my mother sent me back to the house in town to get more beans and cracked wheat. She told me to take a bag and cut some grass to hide the food. Then if soldiers asked what I was carrying, I could say the grass was for my family to eat. The soldiers were taking food from the villages at that time, because the supply routes from Palestine and Beirut were cut. There were very few people in town because of the war; only children like me, returning to get supplies. This was early in the war and the French Vichy soldiers were from Morocco. They were also Muslim, and respected women, children, and old people—so while they would take the food, they would not harm us.

In the middle of the town there was a very big playground. It was just grass and did not have benches or other structures. After school we used it to play ball and running games with our friends. The French soldiers kept their horses on it. One time, when I was walking in town, I saw an officer trying to pick grass along a wall to feed his horses. I remember that there was a rich man in town, a business man, who bought and sold horses and sheep. He was very close to our family, a good friend of my father, and I called him my uncle. He planted pastures for his animals. I saw that the officer needed grass for his horses, and I noticed the piles of empty tins of sardines and meat, so I knew that the soldiers had food for themselves. I went to the pasture, just three or four hundred feet away, and found an old can to use as a knife to cut the grass. I got as much as I could carry on my shoulder and went back to the officer. He was sitting on a boulder with a few horses close to him and many horses farther away. I spoke to him in French because we learned a little French in school.

"Do you want grass for your horse, sir?"

"Oh yes," he replied. "How much do you want for it?"

"Bread and sardines; I have little brothers and sisters that are hungry. Can you give me something to eat?"

He went to his bags and gave me a large loaf of bread and a big can of sardines that would last a week. The officer asked, "It's good?"

"It's good, give me something to put it in because I forgot the cloth bag my mother gave me to carry food."

The officer gave me a hay bag. I said, "Tomorrow I will bring you more grass, if you give me plenty of bread and sardines." He said okay and I walked back to my family in the orchard.

I went to my mother, who was talking with neighbors. Other families were there, doing the same thing. I called to my mother, "Come."

"What's wrong?" she said.

I responded, "Just come." I showed her the food.

"Where did you get these? Did you do something?"

"No, Mama," I said, and told her the story. She just laughed. She called my brothers and sisters over, put the sardines on a plate and cut the bread. Everyone was so surprised and happy.

In a few days, I asked my sister, Fatimah, who is two years younger than me, to go with me, back to the pasture. The town remained deserted, as everyone was afraid to be around the soldiers. I cut one bundle for Fatimah and one bundle for me. We went back to the officer. It looked like he had been waiting for me, as he had several loaves of bread and canned meats. We did this for a while, every day or every other day. Then one day, we went with some grass, and the soldiers had gone away. We were very sorry, because we did not have access to the food anymore.

Surrounding the town one-half to one mile away, were orange, fig, and olive orchards. After the French soldiers left, the Australian army, as part of the Allies, came into the town and camped in these orchards, using the foliage as camouflage.

One day I was going to visit my "uncle" Saleh (the cousin of my father; his father is the brother of my grandfather). My grandfather lived with Saleh as he got older. They lived at the end of the town. My father moved my grandfather to this uncle's house because he had to work away from the town and could not as easily watch over my grandfather.

My father was unaware at first that the war had started, because he was out of town working. He had appointments and had promised people he would be there. He was in villages, and was safe, because the soldiers were only interested in the opposing soldiers, not the civilians. Very few people were injured. Occasionally, a plane would be shot down that would kill civilians accidentally. But that war was mostly soldier to soldier, and army to army.

One day in the 1940s, during the war, when I was about twelve years old, my uncle Saleh sent for me. I did not know why. He said, "Your grandfather is very ill—he wants to see you, to talk to you." My mother and brothers and sisters were living in the fig orchards. I was the only one who sacrificed to go on dangerous errands. I tried to find food for them. My brothers were too young, and my sisters could not go because of the soldiers. I felt like I was the head of the household. I was taking good care of my family because I could get food. My mother always told me, "You are the man of the house …" You are this, you are that. When my brothers talked to me, my mother said, "He is taking your father's place." I laugh, remembering—I enjoyed that!

When I went to my uncle's house, I saw my grandfather lying on his mattress. He asked, "What is the news of your father?" I told him, "Maybe he is trapped because of the fighting between the French and the English." My grandfather said, "Okay, my grandson, come near me." I did. Then he started to sing in Arabic, something like, "If somebody loves me and when I need him I couldn't see him." I was nearly crying, but I told him, "My grandfather, I am near you here. Anything you want—you want food, you want money ..." I was just trying to make him happy. For five years he was almost blind. He would put his left hand on my right shoulder and walk with a stick. I used to take him from place to place, to visit cousins, and other relatives. I was so happy when I took him to the relatives because they gave me so much candy. I was always happy to take him when he asked me to go out with him. I remember those days; they were so nice. He always impressed me, and I admired and respected him so much. He told me the night that he called me to come to him, that if he passed away, "I want you to read the Koran for me." I slept with him that night. The next day he passed away.

My uncle Saleh said, "You promised your grandfather that you would read the Koran for him." This was a great honor for me. Saleh had a great big fig tree in his yard. My grandfather was taken outside and he was washed and dressed. Then my uncle gave me the Koran and said, "Now you start to read the Koran." I read the Koran. I read it very well for my grandfather, because I had learned it well and finished it in school. It was a very sad time for me.

Normally, because Nabatieh was small (about 10,000 people) and everyone knew each other, most townspeople would attend the funeral ceremonies. My grandfather's family was very large, including both his father's and mother's side. Everyone called him "Uncle." However, there were very few people at the ceremony because of the war, and very few people even knew that he had died. My father was not there. We gave one of the town's taxi drivers a note to give to my aunt to inform her, as she was in Beirut. Another aunt lived in a village close by and we waited for her to arrive. In the afternoon, we buried my grandfather. There was just my aunt, my uncle, and a few friends. We were on the road carrying my grandfather's coffin to the burial ground, when my aunt from Beirut arrived. She stopped the funeral procession and we put the coffin on the floor of the taxi. She cried. Even though I was very young, I was allowed to ride in the car with my grandfather's coffin. If you had seen me then, you may have laughed or cried—I don't know! It was an honor for me to stay with my grandfather's coffin. Usually when we bury the dead, everyone offers condolences and sympathy to the head of the family at the gravesite. My uncle again made me the head of the family and everyone shook my hand. After the funeral ceremony, I returned to my family in the fig orchard, and told my mother, crying, that my grandfather had died. My little brothers and sisters cried, and my mother fed them flour and water with sugar. Even getting sugar during that time in the war was difficult. Some families ate soup made of grass, water, and salt.

After a few months, everything started to return to normal in Nabatieh. People were returning to live in their houses. We finally did not see soldiers all over the town. The army stayed in their camps away from the town, and everything remained calm. If the soldiers needed supplies, they came into town in their trucks, made their purchases, and treated the townspeople with respect.

I would soon be starting school again, as there were a few desks open. I used to go visit my aunt in Beirut every summer, and so that summer, she invited me for a visit before starting school again. My aunt was a very good tailor. Her husband bought and sold eggs and poultry and gave her money to buy yards of cloth in Beirut. She sewed clothes for my family. I always returned home with a big bag of new clothes!

One day while visiting her, I took a towel and walked about a mile or mile and a half to the beach to meet my friend to go swimming. It was Sunday and the markets were closed, so it was quiet in the town. Suddenly a jeep with Australian soldiers stopped next to me on the road. They started talking to me in English, but I didn't know English at the time. We always just said "Hello George!" to any English-speaking person, referring to King George! So, I said, "Hello, George!" The sergeant driver and another soldier stepped out of the jeep. They had guns with them and I was scared. They assured me, "It's okay, it's okay," and started to talk to me. I didn't understand anything. The sergeant looked up and down the road and saw that no one was around. He put his hand behind him and then brought it in front of him with his fingers curled upward, making a sound like, "khee-khee-khee-khee." I realized he was asking for eggs. So in Arabic I asked, "*Baddak bied*?" ("You need eggs?") He said, "Yes, yes!" So I started to tell him where to go in Arabic, and he was trying to talk to me in English. Suddenly he grabbed me by the shoulders, lifted me up in the air and set me down in the jeep. I took him to a special, huge market place in Beirut that sells chickens, turkeys, and eggs. When we stopped, he looked and yelled, "Oh George, George." He was very excited and he shook my hand. He gave me £1 and said thank you very much.

I looked at that English pound and I forgot to go for my swim; I forgot to play. I had an English pound! Too much money. So I went to my aunt and said, "Look what I got." She asked, "Where did you get that? Did you get it from the ground?" I said, "No, wait. Let me tell you what happened." She just laughed and said for me to keep it for my father. We changed the £1 for ten Lebanese pounds. My father earned one Lebanese pound for every day he worked, so that was worth ten days' pay. With that money we bought lots of food, meat, shoes—lots of everything. Everything was very cheap then. You could buy candy at the store for one penny.

For myself, I learned that word "egg." The next day, I went for a walk near the Australian soldiers' camp. I was about thirteen years old. Near the road I could smell the food, and kept walking until I got near the kitchen. I saw the cook and said, "Hello, George." He said, "Hello, George" back, and grinned. The Australian people liked to smile and were very friendly. I saw the cook take a big spoon and ladle some yellow powder into oil and it became eggs! I asked, "Eggs?" and he said, "Yes, eggs—do you have some?" I said, "No, I will come back." I went to my aunt Amni in a village about half a mile away. Her husband was a farmer. I asked if I could have some eggs and she assumed they were for my family. She said she could give me ten or twelve eggs. She placed them in a little basket made of grass, and covered it. Then she warned me not to fall down and let them break. I laugh when I remember that I was insulted. I told her not to give me that warning: "Don't you listen to my mother? She says I am the man of the house!" She offered me money, too, but I told her I just wanted the eggs.

I went back to the Australian cook, carefully carrying the eggs. He was very excited and offered me money. But I told him, I did not want money. I wanted some empty petrol containers made of tin that I saw stacked up against a wall. He said to take them all. He called a driver over and told him to put the cans in the van and take them where I wanted them. The driver was happy to do it, since the cook promised him a fresh egg. I signaled the direction that I wanted to go in, and we took off. I directed him to the man who made my father's hubbly-bubbly. He cut and soldered tin to form the tea kettles, water pipes, and other items. When we drove up to his shop, I went in and told him that the man I was with wanted to sell the tin cans. He asked how much for the eighteen or twenty cans, and I said he wanted one pound for each, but that I needed to be the one giving him the money so that I would get a tip. That made sense to the shop owner, so he paid me the twenty pounds. Then he offered me a tip for getting the tins for him—but of course, I refused it. I told him that next time he had to repair my father's hubbly-bubbly, he could do it for free, and he agreed to that. Of course the driver was not expecting to be paid for the cans, so he said goodbye and drove off. I had just made twenty pounds!

I found my father in the shop in town working on his saddles. I told him, "Let's call it quits for today and go home." He said, "What do you mean? Leave the work!" I took him off to the side and told him the story of all my lies to earn the twenty pounds. He said, "These are not lies, these are good!" I gave him fifteen pounds and told him I wanted to keep five pounds for capital to start my business.

We bought food on the way home with the other money. I told him not to tell anybody, to keep it secret. I told him, "I want to make you rich, Daddy!" He laughed and said okay. My family was so happy with all the good food. Other people were not aware of the extra food that my family occasionally had. People were so busy keeping their own families from starvation that they did not involve themselves in other people's business. People had respect for others and did not judge their activities.

So now I had five Lebanese pounds for capital to start my business. I walked to another village, close by, with a basket and towel. I saw a house with chickens around it. I went to the door and a woman came out and asked, "What can I do for you, sonny?"

"I need some eggs," I said. "My father is not feeling well and the doctor is telling him to eat eggs. So I want to buy some eggs, and I will give you money."

At that time a Lebanese pound would buy forty or fifty eggs, and I had cashed the pound in for small change.

"Yes, son—I have about ten eggs for twenty piasters." (About 20 cents).

I said, "I will give you whatever you want; I love my father."

In sympathy, she said, "Oh, sonny, I will give you one free, take one free."

I took about twenty eggs and put them in the basket. Then, to hide the eggs, I picked up figs and placed them on top in the basket. On the way home, somebody asked me what I had in the basket, and I said, "Figs, to take to my brothers and sisters." He said that was okay; that there were too many figs. They were like apples in America; there are so many that people tell you to take as many as you want, because nobody eats all of them.

I went back to George, the cook; he saw me from far away and watched me with the basket as I walked up. I said, "Hello, George."

"Hello, come here. What do you have in that basket?"

"Eggs, George."

"Eggs! Show me. How many?"

I showed him the eggs, and he said, "Oh, I love you, I love you!" So I asked him, "What are you going to give me now?"

"What do you want?" he answered. "I don't have much canned meat, only four or five."

I said, "I will take them. I saw full bags near us. What do you have in those bags?" I laugh when I remember. By then we were talking half Arabic and half English. We became very friendly and he already liked me by the second day. He said, "Look, you are my brother." I felt like he truly meant that I was his brother or his son. He was not very old, in his thirties—a very strong man with blond hair. He told me that the bags contained old army shirts, shoes, and clothes, and I told him that I would take them. So he called the driver like before— his name was Jimmy or something—and the driver came over to us. The cook and the driver talked. The cook must have been a sergeant, because the driver kept saying, "Yes, sir; yes sir." He told the driver to go around and collect all the old clothes. I told the cook that I could use the clothes because I had a big family with no shirts, no pants, no shoes. He gathered the clothes into huge duffel bags and put them on the back of the jeep.

This was a Monday, and on Mondays there was a weekly market in the middle of the town. People came into the town and set up a stall area where they could sell whatever they wished. It was free to do this; the government did not take a fee and a license was not necessary. I went to the stall where may father was working and said, "Come, father, come!" He was barefoot and quickly put his shoes on. We went to the stall where a distant cousin of the family was selling vegetables. The driver unloaded the two duffel bags and we opened them and pulled out the clothes. There were nice pants, jackets, shoes and shirts. My father said, "Where did you get these?" I explained it to him, and then I started to shout, "Any piece for one pound, any- thing for one pound!"

After half an hour, everything was sold, and we had collected forty or fifty pounds. I just took ten pounds and said, "Papa, it's all yours." I laugh when I remember that he said, "Oh, my son, you are my good son! I don't want to go to work anymore! I will work with you, and you just tell me what you want me to do—I will work with you." I just wanted to cry when my father said this, because I respected him. Then he told my mother, "Habib, he is the savior." My father worked so hard. He had to work all day to finish just one saddle, cutting the leather and sewing with needles, from eight in the morning until three or four o'clock, just to earn one pound. Imagine him buying food for ten family members (and then nine after my grandfather died), with three of us attending school.

I continued to get food for the army every day, and they continued giving me supplies for my family. It remained a secret. I used to go to the camp and help the cook clean the pots and tables and do other work in the mess for the officers. One day an officer asked George, "Who's this?" George explained: "A little native brother for me. He is very honest. I want you to respect him." After the soldiers were there about three months, George told me that they were pulling up camp and leaving. He saved lots of clothes, jam, food, and other supplies for me. He said, "Habib, I am going to miss you." Believe me; he felt like a father to me, he was so nice. I thought about going with them. But I couldn't go because I did not know the Arabs in the area to which they were moving, and I would not have had any place to sleep, as I could not sleep with the soldiers.

We continued to use the supplies the army had provided for me. But I kept thinking about what I needed to do next. Although we had returned to the schools, they were very bad. The schools and the mosques were still being used like refugee camps for people who had not yet returned home or who needed to rebuild their homes from the devastation of the war. Progress was slow; the families had to rely on their own at this point because the government didn't have enough funds to even supply its own soldiers.

One day at the end of the war, when I was about thirteen or fourteen years old, I was listening to a neighbor (who was also a distant relative) talking about how he would make trips to Palestine and then return. His name was Abed, and he was about five or six years older than me. He had been to Haifa, and explained that to get there he went through the villages and over a high mountain pass in order to cross the border where the police would not see him. He said there was a lot of money and much work in Haifa. He said he was leaving the next morning at 5:00 a.m. He agreed to let me go with him. I decided to go with him, but I could not tell my family, because they would not have allowed me to go. They wanted me to go back to school as soon as it reopened. I asked him to keep it a secret. He warned me that if I were not at the meeting point right at 5:00 a.m., he would leave without me.

I needed to take money with me for the trip so I went home and opened the cupboard where my mother kept the household money for when my father was out of town. Two pounds were in the cupboard, and I took just one pound and put it in my pocket. I packed two shirts and two pants, and slept in my clothes. Believe me, I did not sleep all night. I watched the big clock on the table and kept hearing the loud tick tock all night. At 4:30 a.m., I got up, and took my shoes and went outside. Because the bathroom was outside, we were accustomed to the family going out the door during the night, so this did not alert my family that there was anything unusual.

I waited about ten or fifteen minutes at the meeting point for Abed and we left. We met up with a taxi that he had arranged to take us to the border in a two to three hour trip. There were five of us, and I was the smallest one. The taxi was like an old Model A with a cloth top. I laugh when I remember how much it shook and chugged when the driver started it with a handle near the steering column. We arrived at the mountain at about 8:00 a.m., and had to climb up the mountain, and go down the other side to a town named el-Bass. The pathway was just wide enough for one or two people, and zigzagged so that we were hidden from view on the curves. There were low grasses and thorny, prickly bushes that caught our clothes along the way. The hike through the mountain took about an hour.

PALESTINE

WHEN WE ARRIVED IN EL BASS AT ABOUT 9:00 A.M., A MAN WAS WAITING for us with a tipper (dump truck). He probably worked in Haifa, about an hour away, and drove back and forth to his job every day. We were able to completely hide in the tipper, as it was very deep. He drove us to Haifa and left us in the middle of the street called Shareh Muluk—King's Street. I knew of a distant relative on my father's side, Ali Fakih, who had a children's clothing store in Haifa. My friend also knew him, and he took me there. When we arrived, Ali asked, "Who are you?" I told him my father's name. I told him that there was no school, that my father did not have work, and that the house was empty—there was no food, no anything. Then I started to cry—I didn't want him to send me back! I was *so* scared that my father would be mad at me. Ali finally sat me in a small chair and said, "Don't worry, I will find you some work that is easy for you. You can make some money and send it to your daddy."

Oh, I was *so* happy! Then Ali took me to his house. He was from South Lebanon, and had only been in Palestine since the war. He knew people who were able to help him get a permit to work there.

The next day Ali took me to a restaurant to wash dishes. I didn't make very much money, only about five pounds a month. The restaurant owner was a Palestinian, and he was very rude. If I made a mistake or left a dirty spot on the floor, he would push me or yell at me and say bad words. One day he cussed my father and my mother. I was so angry that I didn't say anything. I took my pack and I left. He called me back, but I told him, "I am not like you; I don't want you to cuss my mother and my father. I have had good training and it is okay to tell me what to do, but not to say bad words or shout at me." I explained what happened to Ali, and he said he would find me a different job. After Ali's friends made some trouble for the restaurant owner, the Palestinian begged me to come back to work for him, but I said no.

Then Ali found me work with an old Turkish man who had a restaurant. The Turkish man said he wanted a boy from Lebanon, not a boy from Palestine or any other place. When I met him, he asked why I wasn't going to school. I told him my father was poor, that my family did not have food. He gave me the job and told me he would pay me ten pounds a month. The Turkish people keep to themselves and don't easily trust people outside the family. They don't want others to mix with them. The restaurant owner showed me his house, which was close to the restaurant. When he needed anything from the house, or he bought something for his wife, he trusted me to deliver the purchases. He was so happy with me. I worked for three months there, and saved twenty or thirty Palestinian pounds, which were then equivalent to English pounds. Every Palestinian pound was worth ten Lebanese pounds, so I had saved about three hundred Lebanese pounds. Sometimes I would not eat for one day—just drinking water, saving money for my family.

Back in my hometown after the war, food was rationed based on the number of family members. The government established rules for the rationing and had distributors assigned by areas in each town. The families paid the distributors who would then provide the food. One of my father's relatives was a distributor, but he didn't care about the family; he was more interested in the money. The way he operated was that if you had money, you got the food, regardless of the rules. He provided food to whoever paid the most. So I needed to get the money that I had earned in Palestine to my family so they could replenish food and supplies.

I had sent word earlier to my parents with someone traveling to Lebanon that I was working in Palestine, but I never sent money by messenger because people would take it. I needed a way to take the money back to my parents. I bought a mattress and pulled out most of the cotton. Then I went shopping for pants and shirts for my brothers and head ties for my sisters. I hid most of the money in the clothes, and stuffed them all into the mattress. People told me ways to hide the money in the clothes, and not just put it in pants hems. Then I sewed the mattress closed again. I kept out a few pounds for expenses and carried the money in my pocket on the trip. I thought that if the police found it, they would think they got everything I had.

Then I told my Turkish boss that I wanted to go to visit my family for two or three weeks. He thanked me and said, "You go, and come back." He liked my work. When I reached the border, I recognized the driver of the bus. He told me that I would have to have papers to cross the border—otherwise I would be put in jail. He said that if I would give the police at the border a Palestinian pound, they would let me cross. I gave the driver one pound for the information and gave the police one pound to let me through. There was a neutral zone of a few hundred feet between the Palestinian and Lebanese borders, and I put the mattress on my shoulder and walked with two or three friends, carrying it through. After a long time, a taxi drove up. I was so happy because the driver was a neighbor and my father's good friend. I had played with his children when I was younger. He took the mattress from me and put it between the headlights and radiator of the car, balanced on the bumper. The car was made for about five people, but he had about fifteen people in it. During the trip, I stood on the running board on the side and he held onto me with his arm.

When you enter Nabatieh from the north, my father's business was the second or third store on the right. The driver stopped and yelled to him, "Abu Habib!"—which means "the father of the first son." He added, "Come take your son, he is here."

My father hugged me and said "Come." I said, "Wait, I need to get the mattress." The driver said, "Why do you need this mattress; throw it away. It is all smelly." I said, "I know it is all smelly, but you don't know what is inside." My father said, "Why do you want this? Let's give it to somebody." I whispered to my father, "Lots of things and money are inside." At that, we went straight to the house; he left his work for that day.

I asked my father how the rationing was going. Sometimes my mother's brothers were able to help feed the family. But my father explained to me that they had not had the money to buy their rations that month. There was no food in the house, so the timing of my arrival was good; God had told me to get to my family. Things were very bad after the war—not just for my family, but for all families. People had to take care of just their own families, because there was no work, and people could not buy food to eat. People had a lot of pride and would offer someone less fortunate one loaf of bread if they had two, for example. Usually the offers were rejected, because that meant that another person would go hungry; people were ashamed and had too much pride to take something from another person who was no better off than they.

When we arrived home and I had greeted the rest of the family, I took scissors and cut open my sewing in the mattress. I distributed the pants and shirts to each brother and my father, and gave the dresses to my sisters. I came to my dirty, smelly socks, which I had packed in case the police started looking in the mattress. One of my sisters took the socks, and started to throw them away. I said, "Don't take them away! Bring them here." I opened the socks and pulled out very beautiful silk head ties. I asked for my shoe and pulled out money. Then I said to Hassan, my brother, "Give me your pants!" He didn't want to give them back to me, but I took them, and pulled out money that I had stuffed into the waistband.

After that, my father and I went to exchange the Palestinian pounds to Lebanese pounds. Then we visited the man who distributed the rations. We paid him about twenty-five pounds for what my father owed him for food. Then I asked him what he had for sale. He said, "Everything!" I said, "Then give me some sugar, rice salt—whatever you have." He said, "Do you have the money?" I said, "Yes, of course I have the money." Imagine—twelve or thirteen years old and I am talking to this man this way! He gathered the supplies and said it came to 105 pounds.

I said, "Okay, here is 150 pounds. Put the extra forty-five pounds in your book"—that is, on credit. "If my father wants anything, you give it to him." The man said to my father, "Oh, I wish my sons were like your son. You take all my sons, and give me Habib."

On our way home a neighbor saw us with all the supplies we had purchased. He asked where we had gotten the money. He told his son, "You go to Palestine. Look at Habib. He went to Palestine and worked for three months, and came back and made his family rich!" They all started to get jealous.

I stayed with my family for two weeks, and then went back to Palestine. I made the trip the same way that I did the first time—by taxi, then walking over mountains to get across the border. I went back to our relative, Ali Fakih, the children's clothing store owner. I visited the Turkish man that same day also. Ali said he could get the registration (like a US green card) for me that would permit me to work legally anywhere in the country, just like a Palestinian. Ali knew the police and immigration officials that could help me get the permit. I told him I needed to work a couple of months to earn the five pounds to pay for the permit. I wanted to be able to make more money than I had before, so I went to the Labor Office (like an unemployment office) where companies advertise available jobs. The worker asked me if I wanted to work in an officer's mess. I asked, "What is an officer's mess?" He explained that it is a restaurant and a place for the British officers to stay and relax during leaves. It was on a mountain, and I would be able to stay at the camp in a tent and eat there. They would pay about £10 per month. I wanted to try a new experience and get away from the town with the same people, and have new experiences. I also thought I might be able to make more money. The camp was above Haifa, in an area called Hadar Kermel. It was just beyond an area where many Jewish people lived. The camp accommodated 50–60 officers.

I met an officer in charge, and he put me in the kitchen to clean plates, knives, forks, etc. It was next to the cooking kitchen. The cooks were old Egyptian men, so I could speak their language. Many people would try to use the Palestinian slang, but I was not afraid to tell them I was from Lebanon. I said, "If you want to kick me out, kick me out." But they said that it was okay, I could work. The officers got fancy food, but the cooks always made simpler food for the staff, gardeners, etc. After I finished cleaning, I would go over to the cooks and talk to them nicely. If I saw them cleaning a big pot, I would say, "Oh, sir, excuse me—let me clean it for you." The cook said, "Habib, you are a good boy. Don't eat with those people next time. When you want to eat, you come to me and let me know." The next time they gave me the officers' food. I stayed outside and would say hello to the officers as they came by. I made it look like I was cleaning something.

Every day, the cook gave an order for vegetables and supplies to a local man who was about twenty-one years old. He was provided a van and driver and was sent the five or six miles to the town to do the shopping. One day that man did not show up; he was sick. The cook called for me and asked me if I knew downtown. I said, "Yes, I know downtown." I told him I had worked for five years in downtown, and that I would have no trouble buying the vegetables. The cook told the officer in charge, "Habib can buy for us, he knows the place."

I spoke French, and the officer could speak a little French. So I started to pick up a little of his English, he picked up some of my French. He liked me for that. So he wrote the list for me: five pounds of potatoes; five pounds of tomatoes; one pound of garlic. Then he called the driver for me. The driver knew the route to the town. When we got there, I took the list and started buying the vegetables. I had the driver follow me and we put everything in the van. I crossed off everything on the shopping list and we drove back to the officers' mess. We arrived back in camp about two hours later.

The cook asked how we got back so quickly. "Did you buy every-thing?" I assured him I did, as the driver took basket after basket out of the van. Referring to the man who usually did the shopping, the cook said, "That silly man, he takes five or six hours to come back!" I said, "Maybe he goes somewhere else." The cook asked if there was enough money. I told him it was more than enough. I bought all the supplies for six or seven pounds and the officer had given me twenty pounds. Also, for example, the list was for five pounds of tomatoes, but I wrote on the list that I had gotten eight pounds. The cook told me to go see the officer and give him back the extra money.

When I saw the officer, I said, "Bonjour, Monsieur!" He said, "Bonjour, Habib. How have you come back so quickly?" I said, "Because I finished!" I had asked the driver to come with me, in case the officer didn't understand me. He asked the driver, "Why is it was so much faster with Habib?" The driver explained that the other man left the driver in the car and went away for a few hours. The officer said, "That SOB is going to be the one washing dishes from now on!"

Because of this, I got a promotion and started doing that job for the officers' mess. I laugh, because I can still hear the officer shouting at the vegetable man when he came back to work from being sick.

I used to get sent with the driver to get cooking gas every morning. One day the driver was late, and there was going to be no gas for preparing lunch. The Egyptian cook asked me if I could get the gas. I said, "Don't worry." I walked to the place where we bought the gas, about a mile away. I put the gas container on my shoulders and started walking back to the camp. An officer driving along the road saw me, stopped and said, "It is so heavy. Here, you can put it in the van." He said, "Habib, you are a *good* boy."

The camp was on the top of a hill and I used to go to the beach for a few hours occasionally. I would stop at a little grocery store and buy candy and snacks to take with me. I became friendly with the man in the store and his young daughter, Naomi. One day, when Naomi saw that I was going to the beach, she asked her father if she could go with me. He said that I was a good boy, and that he would trust his daughter with me. We sat on the beach and enjoyed the water and the air.

Suddenly two boys, about twenty years old, appeared. They were drinking and smoking and behaving badly. They tried to take advantage of Naomi. She was scared and moved to stand behind me. They asked me who I was and I told them it was none of their business. I grabbed a big piece of driftwood and started threatening them with it. They finally ran away. I told Naomi, "Let's go, before they change their minds and come back." I knew her father would kill me if something happened to her! We walked back to her house and told her father what had happened. He said, "I like you, Habib. I trust you, but you won't be taking Naomi to the beach again!"

Generally, the staff stayed in the camp and socialized with one another. However, I didn't join them very often, as I was the youngest one, and our interests were different. So I would get bored. I was young and had a lot of energy. I wandered into the bar area of the officers' camp and said, "Hello, Tetch."

He said, "Hello, young boy. What are you up to?"

I said, "Nothing. Can I help you?" I offered to wash glasses and clean behind the bar.

Some officers came in and said, "Hey, Tetch, I see you have a helper today!" When they asked for a beer I would give them a beer. Tetch asked me if I wanted to work with him. He asked me what I wanted in payment. I responded, "Anything you have." And Tetch asked, "I can give you a beer?" I said, "I don't drink beer." He said, "Okay, we will see about that later."

So I helped Tetch and rearranged the shelves behind the bar. When everybody left, he asked me if I wanted the beer. Instead, I asked for a chocolate and orange juice. But this man was *after me* to drink beer! I said, "Look, if I come here to help you and I drink beer, I will get drunk and won't be able to pay you for the broken glasses. I would be so ashamed to do that. Please, don't let me have a beer. My whole family never drinks. I was bored; I like you and wanted to work with you. Don't let me run away from you, because I want to help you. You look nice."

Tetch said, "Habib, I like you." So, I came every day to help him.

One day while I was helping in the bar, Christmas arrived. Everybody was happy and celebrating. One of the officers opened a beer and said, "Habib, have this drink on me." He was a high level officer with lots of stripes on his shoulder. It was more like an order. The officer who was in charge, Jens, was sitting next to him, and said, "Habib, come on, come on." So I saw that everybody was happy. I took a sip. It's good, it's nice. I take another sip and another sip! The first officer said, "Hey, take it easy, Habib. Don't drink it all at one time."

Maybe I was tired. I started to think to myself, "Everybody drinks. Why don't I drink? It is because of my religion, but my religion is far away right now. All the officers drink. Maybe one day I will be an officer and I will want to do the same." I started talking to myself, saying, "I want to be happy. My family is far away—never mind." I was trying to convince myself—everybody was doing it! It must be good! I should not be afraid. Nothing will happen. I said to myself, "If I feel tired, or start to feel dizzy, I could go home—my tent is not too far away."

I drank from my bottle. So the officer, John, asked me if I liked it. I said that I did. But I told him, "I am scared that if I don't drink it, maybe you won't like me." He said, "No Habib, I like you, you are a nice boy." The beer made me unafraid to say what was on my mind, so I started to talk to him about the money that I had earned. I told him that it was not enough to send to my family. He said, "Is that the beer talking or you talking?" I assured him that it was me talking. He said, "You have never told me that before." I just started to chat with him. The beer was Beck's or Heineken. I liked it very much.

Then I told Tetch, "I think I see the bar turning. Are you making the bar turn?" Tetch laughed and said, "No, Habib, go sit down." I said, "No, before something gets broken, I am going to go to my tent." He offered to help me to my tent, but I told him I would be okay. When I started to get into bed in my tent, the men in there asked me if I wasn't going to get into my pajamas before I laid down. But I got into bed with my clothes on and went to sleep. The next day, I felt nice and good. I went to the kitchen. The people at the kitchen were laughing at me.

I said to them, "Can you keep a secret?" And told them that I had drunk a bottle of beer. They laughed and said, "That is the secret? That is no secret! Everybody drinks."

I asked, "Is it good?" One man said, "It is good if you drink one bottle, or half a bottle—not too much. Don't drink too much, because you are just now learning to drink. Don't have too much, my son." I thanked him. "Come on, let's give you a cup of coffee." I told him that I don't drink coffee. In my family we only drank tea or a little milk. He said, "You have to drink coffee to wake you up." He poured me a cup of coffee and put a little sugar and sweet milk in it, like the British do. I tried it, and it was nice. I said, "Why didn't you tell me about this a long time ago?"

I continued to work in the bar for about two years. The chief and John, who was the officer in charge of the whole operation, were very nice, and they liked me and the work that I did.

During my stay in Palestine, I visited my family about every six months to bring them money. One time I told the officer that I would like to go to visit my family. The officer said, "Two weeks only," and gave me an extra ten pounds. The officers asked me bring things back, but I couldn't bring anything over the border. I again bought a dirty, smelly mattress and put all the things that I was bringing to my family inside and re-sewed it. I said goodbye to Ali Fakih and his wife, and took the taxi with the same driver as before. My family was always very happy to see me.

One time when I arrived, the schools were in session again. My youngest sister, Hesniyeh, wanted to attend classes, but my father would not let her. In those days, the girls usually did not go to school, and they could not read or write.

I told my sister, "Come with me. We are going to the school to see if I can get you in." I talked to the principal and offered to pay twenty Lebanese pounds. But my offer was rejected and we were told that my sister could attend without any payment. So I donated the twenty pounds to the school and they accepted the money that way. They told my sister that she could start the next morning and to be at school at 8:00 a.m.; that all of her books and lessons would be prepared for her.

The next morning we got up, and my sister dressed for school. I told my father that I was taking Hesniyeh to her first day of classes, as I had enrolled her in school. I expected my father to be upset, but he just said, "If you think it is okay, I will accept it." I think my father understood that I was more experienced in the world because of my traveling.

I also think he recognized that he was being very protective of my sisters by keeping them home. I think he had this concern because one time when he was walking in the village there was a teenage boy walking ahead of him. The boy stopped and looked around, but did not see my father. He put a piece of paper under a rock and when he left, my father read it. It was a love letter to a girl. My father hid in the bushes and after about an hour, a girl arrived, took the note, and put hers in its place. My father felt that he was protecting his girls from interacting with boys and worldly dangers by discouraging them from reading.

Finally, on one of my visits home, my aunt, Tifaha, from Beirut, was visiting my family at the same time I was there. She wanted me to return to Beirut with her, rather than to Palestine, because there was beginning to be a lot of unrest in Palestine between the Jews, Arabs, and English. The Jews and Arabs wanted to get rid of each other, and both wanted to get rid of the English. My family felt that it might be getting too dangerous. I had been happy in Palestine, and had planned to go back before my family made me aware of the increasing tensions in the area. So I agreed to accompany my aunt to Beirut.

When we arrived in Beirut my aunt introduced me to her neighbor, who cooked for the Officers' Club in the city. He introduced me to the man in charge there—an English sergeant. He asked if I could speak English. I explained that I had worked in the British Officers' Club in Palestine, and had learned English there. He offered me a job serving British tea in the afternoon. I said, "That's nice," and agreed to take the position. The salary was ten Lebanese pounds per week, plus tips, which would be all mine. So I went off to buy the uniform—black shoes, black pants, black tie, white shirt, and white jacket. They would train me. I worked different shifts, rotating with the other boys.

One day I was serving a nice, good-looking couple. The husband was a high-ranking English officer, and the lady was very nice looking, but I didn't think she looked English or Lebanese. The lady watched me all the time. I served them, they ate, said goodbye, and left. When I went back to the table to clear it, I saw something on the floor under the table. It was a gold bracelet. We always carried a white towel on our arm, so I dropped the towel over the bracelet to cover it; I didn't want the other waiters to see this.

I then picked up the bracelet hidden in the towel and took it to the head steward. He was a tall, thick Lebanese man who never smiled, but he was so nice. I said, "Boss, I want to see you privately." Then I explained how I found the bracelet, and that I thought it belonged to my last customers. He said, "Oh, this is gold; why did you bring it to me?" I said, "Because you are the chief, the boss. I don't trust other people; I trust you and you are responsible here. Maybe the people will come back for it." He put it in the safe in his office. After my shift was over, I went home and told my aunt and uncle (I called him "uncle" because he is my aunt's husband) how I found the bracelet. "Habib, you are very good," they said. "We are proud of you. If the people came back asking for it, and no one had turned it in, the restaurant might have fired everyone."

The next day when I first got to work, the boss called me over. He pointed out that the same woman was there, with her husband. He was a high officer in the Navy, with four or five stripes. They called me over, and the woman said in Arabic, "*Marhaba*" (meaning "hello"). "Did you find this, Habib?" I said yes, and explained how I had found it under the table and took it to the boss. I was surprised when she thanked me in Arabic. I asked if she was Lebanese, and she said yes. She gave me 10 pounds for finding the bracelet. I didn't want to accept the money, but they insisted. The officer said, "My wife didn't sleep all night because she didn't know where she lost it. We went to all the places that we had gone yesterday and when we asked here, they told us that the waiter named Habib found it. So we waited for you to come today."

The next day they came back for lunch, and had tea in my area. While they were eating, the English officer asked me where I learned English. I explained that I had worked in the officers' mess in Palestine. He said he had visited that officers' club during the time I worked, but had not seen me there. I told him that I had worked outside and with the supplies, not in the restaurant. He asked me if I wanted to go back to Palestine and told me that he had a good job for me. His wife, Mariam, said, "Habib, say yes. I am going back with him, and then I will get to see you." He explained that the job would be in the Navy fleet mail office, distributing mail from England to all the Navy ships. I asked if the money would be good, and he said for me not to worry. They were leaving the next day, so the officer gave me his card and told me to contact him if I decided to go back to Palestine. Mariam begged, "Habib, please come, please come. I like you, and want to see you again." Her husband knew a little Arabic, and explained that Mariam had a brother who looked like me, and I reminded her of him.

The officer assured me that he would give me a good job if I came. I started thinking, "I know Palestine so well. I understand the city. I have lots of friends there. I miss Palestine."

That evening I went to my aunt and explained that the officer would give me a good job in Palestine. The work was at the harbor, so it would not be dangerous. My aunt and uncle did not want me to go. I contacted my family and they did not want me to go, but I told them, "You cannot control me. I am working, and I am the boss. I will be able to bring money to you. If you try to control me, I will leave and not come back." My mother finally told me to do what I wanted, but asked me to come back every two or three months.

My aunt had one son who had lived in Nigeria for 15 years, had started a business, married and had children, but had never yet returned to visit her. She wrote her son and said, "If you love your mother, you will start the process for Habib to get a visa to go to Nigeria so that you can take a vacation and visit me." She explained that I knew English and was good at business. She said, "Otherwise, I am not your mother—don't pray for me, and don't talk to me."

At the same time that she was writing to her son, I was arranging to go to Palestine. I packed and left for Palestine. I went to my uncle Ali, who I originally stayed with in Palestine. He said people were asking for me during the six months I had been gone. The next day, I went to the harbor. This would have been about five days after the officer and his wife Mariam would have arrived back in Palestine. A harbor policeman stopped me and asked where I was going. I showed him the business card of the officer I was seeking and he showed me where to go. A big English sergeant with a gun looked at my card and I asked if the officer was there. He said yes. I told him to go tell the officer, "Habib is outside." The officer came right out to me and shouted, "Habib, you did it! Mariam is going to be so happy!"

When he finished greeting me, he called Miriam on the phone, and said, "Guess who's here?" She immediately said, "Habib." He shouted, "How did you guess?" Miriam responded, "I was 100% sure Habib would come. You take good care of him like you promised me, Honey."

He asked me to wait while he finished some paperwork, and then showed me where I would work and told me that I could start the next day. We walked a few hundred feet to the mail distribution office. It was a building made of wood with a corrugated metal roof. The building was divided into three sections. The first section was where the incoming mail was dropped off. Sorting was completed in the second section, and the third section held the sorted mail for distribution to various port offices and ships anchored in the harbor.

There were three men working. The two European men were about 35 and 45 years old, respectively, and the Palestinian was about 25 or 30 years old. I was the fourth and youngest one. We went inside and he said, "Gentlemen, I want you to meet Habib, from my wife's family." Oh, oh! He just winked at me and whispered, "Don't say anything." After all, we are of the same family! All Lebanese and from the same town!

He told the other men that I would be working with them, and to take good care of me. Then he wished all of us good luck and walked out. So I thought to myself that I better give the impression of an upstanding family member related to the officer. So I immediately said, "How is everybody? Do you speak Arabic here?" I explained that I would be starting work the next day, but I asked them to show me around and tell me about their jobs. I saw them whispering in English. They did not know that I also spoke English, and could understand them. They thought that I was sent to work as a spy to see how much work they were doing. So I said, "Guys, don't think I have come here to spy on you. I am a friend. I like to work. I am not from here, I am from Lebanon. I will be honest with you. I came to make a living. I came here because of the officer's wife, my cousin. I came here to work and see the country, enjoy the place." They said, "Oh, okay." Then I came the next day to work and they started showing me the duties.

At noon the officer came to me and asked if I had eaten lunch yet. He asked me to come in his car and told me that we were going to his home. "Mariam has made good Lebanese food. She is waiting for us." He took us to a nice, good, beautiful house on a hill. Mariam was waiting for us at the door. She hugged me and kissed me. She said, "Habib, I smell Lebanon on you." She was *so* nice. She was in her thirties. Her husband was in his forties. She had made kibbee, garbanzo beans, and salad. We ate the delicious food and after about an hour, the officer said he wanted to take a walk. He said, "Habib, if you want to stay with Mariam this afternoon, you can." I said, "What about my own work?" He said, "No problem!" He treated me like his son or brother. They treated me like I was their family, like a big sister and big brother. I declined but said that I would like to come on a Sunday when I was not working. I told them I would call to make arrangements for the next Sunday. Then the officer took me back to the mail office.

A few days later, I asked the other men in the mail office where they bought their coffee. I said, "Look, everybody give £1." Then I bought a coffee pot, coffee, and sugar. "Now, we will make the coffee here ourselves and save money." I told them I would make the coffee. They said, "No, no, boss."

I quickly said, "Don't call me boss." I didn't want the officers to think that I was acting like I was the boss. I showed them how to make the coffee and I made good friends with all of them.

So my life was easy. I had rented a room in a house with a friend from my town, Mohammed Hejaze, for £1 per month. Mohammed also worked at the harbor, as a foreman supervising the dock loaders. He was a few years older than I. We ate outside and slept in the same room.

Mohammed had a Syrian friend who was a tailor. The Syrian lived in the town in a big tent with many other people. He bought a truck to drive between Lebanon and Iraq. It was common for young men to live this way, because they came to Palestine to work to save money for their families, send brothers and sisters to school, and start their fortunes. South Lebanon was a very poor place. It was rural and there were no manufacturing or other big businesses. At the time, the country was under the control of the French. They were improving it in many ways, but were unable to help people start making money for their families. The rich man was rich and the poor man was always poor.

We visited the Syrian friend many times after work and ate dinner together. We would buy a couple tomatoes, some onions and bread. We went to the butcher at the end of the day so that we could get a discount on the meat. To save money, we bought liver and fat and the cheaper cuts of meat that others didn't want. The Syrian had a stove and pot in his tent. We all helped prepare the vegetables and cooked them in the pot. We didn't need to buy oil, because the meat had enough fat in it. The next day we would buy ingredients for falafel and other dishes.

Some days, we would go to a restaurant and buy a large plate of rice and a vegetable stew to pour over it. Then we shared it to save money. We would enjoy the evenings. After dinner, we would make tea and listen to music on the Syrian's little radio. Then we would all walk back to our homes around 10:00 or 11:00 p.m. In the mornings there were sweet shops or bakeries that had puddings and cakes for ten to thirty cents. We would stop on the way to work, and that was enough food until lunchtime. At lunch we would buy falafel or meat sandwiches from the market.

There used to be some trouble between the different national-ities in Palestine. People from the different countries were fighting amongst themselves—the Jews and Palestinians and Europeans. One Friday it was very slow at work. There was really nothing to do. No ships were coming in and it was boring. The weather was very nice that day. There was a public swimming pool near the mail office. People paid 10 or 15 cents and were given a card or number. Then you could change your clothes, get a receipt, and use the pool.

That day, there was an olive green truck parked very close to our building. That was very unusual. When I asked the other workers if they knew anything about it, they said it had been there when they first opened the building. So I decided to ask an officer about the truck. But my co-workers said, "Leave it, it's not disturbing us." I was suspicious of the truck and I did not like the responses I was being given. It was about 2:00 p.m. and I said, "Hey, guys, how about if we close and go home? I want to go to the beach and go swimming. I am bored here. Is anybody with me?" But they said that we were not supposed to close until 5:00 p.m.—three hours more. One of the men said, "If you take responsibility for closing early, we are with you." I said, "Okay, I will take responsibility. I will tell the officer that it was a nice and beautiful day, that we did all of our work, and we wanted to go enjoy ourselves." I asked the big, older man if he was expecting anything else, and he said no. So I said, "Let's close, let's go." I assured them again, "*I'll* be responsible!" I knew that the officer would not deny me, that I could explain, and that my friend, Mariam, would stand by me.

We proceeded to close the office and started walking to the gate, a few hundred feet away. I was talking to my Palestinian coworker, who had become a good friend. Then we heard, "*BOOM!* The olive green truck had exploded.

Everybody was scared. We started to run. We saw that our mail office had completely collapsed. Pieces of the truck were scattered all over. People came running, "What happened, what happened? Are you okay?" Imagine if we had been in the office. That place was flat on the ground. The policemen and officers were arriving at the site. My officer friend brought his wife, Mariam, to the harbor. They were so sad because they assumed I had been in the building at the time of the explosion. Mariam was crying. She felt that she was to blame, because she had convinced me to work there. I was sitting talking with my friends when Mariam and her husband drove up. Mariam looked at me, "Habib, are you okay? How come you are not injured?" I told the big, older man to explain in English to the officer, and I explained to Mariam why we weren't in the building.

"Look, Mariam, I was so bored with no work, there was no air conditioning, and the day was beautiful. I told the other men that I would take responsibility for closing the office early." I told the officer, "I take all the responsibility." The officer responded, "You take all the responsibility? You are magnificent! You are so nice—you saved yourself and all these people!" Mariam hugged me and said, "God loves you, God loves you. How did you get this idea to get out? How did you know why that truck was standing there?" The other workers told her that I kept asking why the truck was there, but no one knew or could do anything because it was an army truck (not navy). So I finally just said, "Let's close and go away."

The police investigated and found that the truck had been smuggled from the army camp to bomb the mail office in hopes of destroying official documents and letters from relatives in England. It was an effort to destroy the morale of the English. We processed the mail from another location after that.

I had been living in Palestine about six months at that time. About a month after the bombing, I received a letter from my father through my uncle Ali in Palestine. It said that I needed to come back home because my visa to go to Africa was ready. This was a result of that letter that my aunt in Lebanon wrote to her son in an effort to get me to oversee his businesses in Nigeria so that he could come back to Lebanon to visit her. The visa was processed through the British Consulate, as Nigeria was then under British rule. I went to tell Mariam the news. She was both sad and happy, and wished me good luck. She did not want to see me go, but she was happy because she said that people made very good money in Nigeria and I would have a good future. The officer hugged me and we all said goodbye. I left my job working in the mail office in Haifa for the English Navy fleet at the end of April.

This was in about 1946, and I was about 17. When I arrived back in Lebanon, my mother and father started crying. When I asked why, they said, "Because you are going to Africa now, and some people that go to Africa never come back." I told them, "I was either going to go to Africa or return to Palestine." My parents finally relented.

"You go to Africa, because it is much safer. We don't care about the money, but for your sake."

When I had visited my aunt during summer vacations in Beirut, I usually had little jobs and I had worked in a canteen near the hospital. It sold sandwiches and drinks like Coca-Cola. I would take orders from the sick people, and then return with their food. They would pay me, plus give me little tips. I would give my aunt the money I earned to send to my family, but we agreed that she would take as much as a third of it out and save it for me. She always told me that if I saved money, I could eventually do some business with it. My aunt was very good at managing money, and she liked me. I really didn't know how much money she had kept for me over the years until she told me that I had 2,000 Lebanese pounds.

Everyone—my brothers, my sisters, my cousins—were happy to see me return from Palestine, but not happy that I would soon leave again for Africa. My mother cried because she was worried that she would never see me again, like my aunt's son. I assured her: "Don't worry, I love my family, I love you. As soon as I get a little money I can make my fortune here. I will come back." Then we had to start preparing for my trip to Africa. First we had to get a passport for traveling. We had to go to the Immigration Office and the British Embassy for the visa. Then I had to buy the ticket. It was too much work, always having to travel back and forth to Beirut from my small town! One day, I went with my father to the Immigration Office; we needed to give them two photographs and a notice from the police that I was clean, had not done anything wrong, and did not have a conviction record. As we were waiting our turn, the Immigration Inspector walked down the stairs. He was our neighbor! He asked what we were doing there, and my father explained that we were making preparations for me to join my cousin in Nigeria. So he said, "Okay—you go get the photographs, the paperwork, and meet me back here. I will get the clearances done from here. I will take care of that. You come back. I will wait for you here." He took the documents when we returned and said he would get the passport and bring it for us to our town.

Oh! My father was *so* happy to save the trouble of going back and forth to Beirut, because each way was two to three hours at that time—a round trip of four to six hours. And this was before freeways were built.

While I was waiting for all the travel documents to be completed, I went to Beirut to visit my aunt. I visited the man who I used to work for at the canteen. He told me he wanted to sell his store for 2,400 Lebanese pounds. I had only 2,000 saved with my aunt, so I said, "I only have 2,000. Will you sell it to me for that much?" The man said he needed 2,000 pounds to buy a travel ticket, and he had a 400 pound debt to pay on the canteen, so he insisted on 2,400 pounds. He said, "If you give me 2,399 pounds, I still won't sell, because 2,400 is what I need!"

I went to my aunt and explained that the man wanted to sell his canteen. I asked her, "Can you lend me 400 pounds? Forget Africa, I want to buy the place!" She shouted, "No you don't! I want to see my son! You have to go. I want to see my son! If you don't go, I will kill you!" I laugh when I think back on this. God bless her soul. She died many years ago and was a very special aunt to me. I said, "Do you really want to send me to Nigeria? If I stayed here, I could make money. I could stay near you here. You love me!" She said, "I love you, but I love my son, too. You go away from here—get your visa and passport!"

The next day I waited for my father to come from our little town. Since I was so young, my father or guardian had to be with me to get the visa from the British Consulate. We showed them my passport, paid about 10 Lebanese pounds, and they gave me my visa. When we were walking out, I said to my father, "That's it, now no more stay in Lebanon." I looked at my father and there were tears running from his eyes.

"Oh, Daddy," I said. "Why are you crying? You want me to go to Africa. You want me to make money. Don't worry. You know me, I can make money. I will make money. I will buy you a house. You won't have to work with the saddles. You will be free." He was crying and he wouldn't look at me.

We walked a long way toward the garage. I said, "Why are we going here? You forgot—we have to go to my aunt's and sleep there tonight." So we turned around and started walking to her house. It was far away and took about an hour, but taxis were too expensive, about one-half pound. It was one pound to one dollar at that time. My father was fair-skinned—a blond with blue eyes. When he was upset, he would easily blush. When we arrived, my aunt looked at my father and saw that he was upset. My aunt assured my father that as soon as her son visited her, he would go back to Nigeria and would send me back to return to Lebanon. My uncle (my aunt's husband) was very happy and said, "Habib, come sit near me. What would you like me to buy for you?"

I said, "What is all this fuss?"

He said, "Because I am going to see my son after 15 years." We spent the night there and went back home to arrange the trip to Nigeria.

Many people came to the end of the town to see me off. My grandfather, my mother and father, my friends and cousins all came. Hundreds of them. There were so many people that it scared me— like I was never coming back. But it was really because my father and grandparents knew so many people in the town. They really came in support of my family. At the end of town, I got in the car with my father and uncle and we rode to the airport in Beirut. There, my aunt met us. Everyone waited in the visitors' section to send me off. I was taken to the plane, and two very large boxes were loaded for me. My relatives had filled the boxes with Lebanese food, cakes and many other snacks. As I walked toward the plane, I looked behind me and all my relatives were waving white handkerchiefs. It was so scary. The plane was a ten or twelve seat, two-engine prop jet with thin aluminum wings. The chairs were wood, and cushions were distributed for them. It took two or three hours to get to Egypt in those days. Now it would take one hour or less.

On the plane I was holding several jars. When we landed, the Customs official asked me what was in the containers. I said, "This jar is olives, this jar is cream cheese, this jar is white cheese." He was surprised to know that I had held them all during the flight. I told him I also had things in my suitcase. He said, "I don't care about the suitcase, I want to know what is in the jars." I said, "I tell you, : olives, they They don't have olives in Nigeria, they only eat peanuts, groundnuts." He opened the jar and smelled. He asked, "Did anyone put any powder in this can?" I said, "Powder! You would spoil the whole thing if you put powder in—what kind of powder? Do you mean sugar or salt?" The man looked at me and said, "Don't worry, my son, don't worry. I will let you go." It was obvious that I didn't know anything about drugs.

We got on a bus and were taken to the best hotel. I remember that the name was Illio Palace Hotel. Very high class people lived in that hotel: ministers and religious people. They put me in a room with a very nice man who, I think, was from South America. He spoke good Arabic with me. We spent the whole night in Egypt. The next day they took us to the plane and we boarded for the next stop, Algiers. Some new passengers joined us. We got to the hotel and we were tired. On the plane I had seen two people who I later found out were an actor and actress in a film, and a rich man from Lebanon who had financed the film they acted in. I had not taken too much notice on the plane, because we were all too scared. We had arrived in Algiers in the evening and they told us to meet downstairs for dinner. I dressed nicely and went downstairs to the room where we were going to be eating. The people involved in the film were all sitting at one table. The actor, Mohammed Salman, asked me where I was from, and I told him Lebanon. When he wanted to know more specifically, I told him the town was Nabatieh. He said he was from a neighboring town. I sat down at a chair opposite from him. The restaurant was arranged with tables on either side of a long narrow aisle.

The steward came by, a good-looking French lady, and told us we should go select our wine. The actor asked me if I knew anything about wine. I said, "No, sir, I only know by name there is a wine but I don't know anything." He said I had to pick a bottle, otherwise people were not happy. "How does it taste?" I asked. He said, "It tastes good—makes you rest, makes you sleep good." I had heard of all kinds of drinks but I never tasted anything other than beer at the army camp. So I thought it was probably like beer. The wine steward came around with the list of about 20 wines. I didn't tell her what I wanted, I just put my finger on one of the wines. The actor asked if I had picked a good one. I told him I didn't know. He suggested that he select one for me, but I said, "Whatever comes, it will be okay. It is all wine, right?" He said, "Yes, for you it is all wine." They brought him a short little bottle of red wine. For me they brought a very long bottle of light red wine, rose.

I enjoyed the wine and drank it all, with the other people at the table. The man, about fifty, who did the financing of the film, left to go to his room. Now, only the actor and actress were left talking with me in the restaurant. Finally, they were tired and decided to go to their rooms, too.

I wanted to go, so I put my hand on the table to stand up, but my foot did not want to move! *What's wrong with me?* I thought. I couldn't control myself. So I sat down and started to think to myself. I waited for the waiter to come to help me, but she didn't come. I also didn't really know what to call her. I only knew to call a waiter *garcon*, but she was a woman. So I thought, *Why worry? I can stand and walk between the tables, going hand over hand, table to table in the narrow aisle.* By the time I got to the door, I could stand a little bit. Then, another problem: I didn't know where I was. How I got to my room, God knows! When I got in my room, I took my clothes off, put them on a chair, and threw myself onto the bed, wearing only my underwear. When I put my head on the pillow, the room started spinning.

I sat up and said, "Shame on yourself, Habib!" I tried to go back to sleep, then: *woop!* Everything came up—I threw up on the bed, and on the floor. I ran to the bathroom and threw up. Finally, I washed my face and wanted to try to go to sleep. But where could I sleep? I couldn't sleep on the bed and the floor was dirty too. The room was such an excellent room—a very nice room, with an excellent carpet. I had never been in such a nice place. I said to myself, *Oh Habib, you have a chance to sleep in a bedroom in a good hotel and look what you have done to yourself! Oh, how come I drank? Shitan made me do that.* (Shitan is the devil.)

I thought, *I shouldn't do this, I shouldn't do that.* I was trying to decide where I could sleep. There was a balcony outside of my room. The pillow and some of the bed sheets were still clean, so I took them to the balcony, rolled myself in them and slept the rest of the night outside my room. In the morning I woke up and went into my room. Oh, the place smelled! So, what should I do? Okay, they are going to make me pay money—that's okay. My clothes were still clean because I had laid them on the chair the night before. I dressed and went downstairs to have breakfast at 10:00 or 11:00 am. I took a walk outside for a while. By then, it was time for dinner. I chatted with the actor and actress during dinner. They asked me how I had spent the previous night and I said, "Oh, excellent, very good!" They asked if anything had happened to me. I said, "Oh, nothing—nothing happened to me." I was ashamed to tell them the truth. They looked at each other. Maybe they got in trouble too. They had each had a full bottle, also.

I still hadn't been back to my room to see what had happened to it. But I finally went back. The maid was just finishing cleaning my room. She was an old, square woman, and very nice. She spoke to me in French. "Bonjour, mon petit. I cleaned your room, don't worry. The old man (the manager), he doesn't know anything." French francs were the common currency, and the smallest denominations I had were twenty franc paper, which was too much money for a tip. But I gave it to her anyway. She came to me and said, "Merci beau-coup." She came over and kissed me! I asked, "How is it inside?" She said, "It is clean, very nice, everything is nice. Don't worry, nobody knows." So I said, "Thank God, my heart rests."

I was so happy. I went in the room and everything looked so nice—the bed, the carpet, the bathroom. Everything was clean and smelled so nice. I said to myself, "Habib, now enjoy yourself. Have a good sleep in a wonderful room, like a king. Make yourself like a king." Thank God I had the money to take care of the room. I spent the evening with my acting friends, but I never drank with them again! When the waiter asked me if I wanted wine, I said, "No, thank you, I will be traveling tomorrow." The waiter asked if I wanted a little glass of beer. I refused, saying, "Nothing! Only a glass of water, thank you!" The waitress laughed; maybe she had figured out what happened to me.

The next day we were taken to the airport to fly to Lagos, Nigeria. My cousin, Hassan, and his friend were waiting for me at the airport. Hassan was thirty-five. He was married and had three girls and one boy. We got in his car, and he drove on the left side of the street. A car was coming toward us, and I shouted, "Hassan, Hassan, you are on the wrong side, and the other car is on the wrong side." He explained that in Nigeria people drove on the opposite sides of the streets compared to Lebanon and Palestine. For a short while after I arrived, there were a few other times when I forgot this practice.

NIGERIA

WE ARRIVED IN LAGOS, AND HASSAN, WHO WAS ABOUT 35 YEARS OLD at the time, took me around, introducing me to his friends and relatives. On the second day, we had to fly south to the town he lived in, Jos. It was the same type of plane that I had just been traveling in, and it took two to three hours to make the trip. It seemed like we were flying low, just over very tall palm trees. Hassan asked me if I liked to fly. I told him not to worry about me. Since I had been flying on all the legs of this trip, I was getting used to it. I asked him how he liked flying, and he said that it scared him. He only had to fly once every five or six years.

We arrived in Jos and went to Hassan's home. I met his wife and children. His wife had a sister in the same town and it looked like a good family to me. My cousin liked me. Hassan asked me about all my family in Lebanon. I brought out all the food and other gifts that my aunt, his mother, had sent with me for the family. I told him, "Now you have to go visit your mother and your father." He said, "We will have to see how good you are in taking care of my businesses."

"Just let me know what to do," I offered.

He owned a transport company. About fifteen trucks, lorries, and related equipment were housed in one building. In another store, he sold spare parts for automobile repair. He lived right behind this property. The next day he took me to a clothing store that he owned. A Lebanese man, about twenty-five years old, managed the clothing store for him. The fourth business was an ore-mining company. He also had a manager for it, as it was far away. The manager was an engineer, and had a very beautiful wife. Hassan's wife was also very beautiful, but Hassan "zigzagged"—meaning he carried on with other women. He was young, handsome, and had money. He had everything he wanted. Because of his businesses, he socialized with a lot of people. They were mostly English businessmen. Because Nigeria was a new country, and the Africans were not yet experienced in government, the British maintained control.

Hassan introduced me to all the elite people in the town. I met with his bank manager. He took me to a men's club where Africans were not allowed, only white men. All the men looked alike to me. I had never mixed with those people, except the officers in the military camps in Palestine. I started to work in the stores and Hassan watched me. I worked in the offices and observed the workers. I asked them to explain their jobs so that I would understand the businesses. I did not speak English real well yet, and the workers did not speak English anyway, so I wanted to learn their language. I wanted to try to communicate and make myself helpful to my cousin, so that he would be able to leave to visit his parents.

In my mind, I was trying to learn enough so that he could leave and return. Then I would return back to Lebanon. I asked him how much he would pay me to do this for him. He thought I should stay eight or nine months. I explained how I had wanted to spend £2,000 to open a store back home, but had spent it instead on the trip to Nigeria—this was so he could leave. I told him how his mother had shouted at me and told me I could not spend the money to buy a business because I had to go to Nigeria. Hassan assured me that he would make it worth my time. He said he would double or triple that money. I agreed to his promises. So for three months, he took me around to all his businesses, and I learned the operations. One day, he took me to see the bank manager. He told the banker, "Now Habib is going to sign for me for any checks in or out—money, everything. Habib is taking over. I am appointing him the manager for all my businesses."

The manager of the iron ore business periodically brought the raw, mined ore to the bank. The bank would weigh the ore, and put its value directly into Hassan's bank account.

There were about 1,000 Lebanese people in this community, and it was organized with an elected head, treasurer, and secretary. They represented the Lebanese people and generally helped intercede and interpret for them. Hassan took me to the head, Mr. Arab. He liked me and trusted me.

Mr. Arab had a very large transport company, with about fifty trucks. They needed to move food and other goods between the French country of Fort Lamy and our town. The supplies originally came into Lagos by ship from Europe. From Lagos they were put on railcars, and would be transported to Jos. From Jos they were loaded on transport trucks and taken to the riverbank. The trucks were put on the ferries to be taken to the village. In the summer, a major river along the route always dried up, so truck transportation was limited to the eight or nine dry months. There was no bridge.

Hassan was getting ready to leave for his three-month visit to Lebanon. He had a huge safe, about five feet tall and three feet wide. He showed me his will and said that if he didn't come back, I should go to Mr. Arab, the community head, and he would know what to do. He then showed me a bag of jewelry and told me it was for his wife. He instructed me to let his wife take pieces of jewelry out of it and put it back, as she wanted to wear them. He said that the safe only had two keys. "One key I will give to you," he said. "And the other key I will give to Mr. Arab. Nobody else will be able to open the safe, not even my wife. You are responsible for everything."

Hassan left to go to Beirut to visit his mother and father. After I had seen him off at the airport, the driver took me back to my cousin's house, where his wife and children would remain during his visit in Lebanon. I remember that my cousin had a new, green Hudson, an American car. It was only about six months old. He also had an army jeep from WWII, painted in the army olive-green color. The jeep was used by the Syrian man who managed the transport trucks. Here I was, the manager of all these businesses, and I didn't have a car—I didn't even have a bicycle!

I spent time with the man who ran the clothing store. He was Lebanese, about twenty-five years old, and his name was Albert. He was such a good friend. He had a bicycle and I bought one. In the evenings, we rode outside the town. He was the only person from my town, and it was pleasant because we could understand each other. He had a very nice family, a father that worked in mines, and two sisters and two brothers. They invited me to their house often to drink tea and visit. His mother was so nice. That was the only way I spent my spare time. My cousin's wife always had her Lebanese women friends over to the house, and she spent a lot of time visiting them. She had her sister in the house to help out. The children were young, and not yet in school. They had a teenaged African nanny to help take care of them.

One day the Sudanese man who ran the spare parts store asked me to watch the store, because he needed to go get his lunch. He said, "Don't worry, all the parts have a price tag right on them." Everything had been priced by my cousin. The sales would be entered into a book each day. The normal process for all three businesses in Jos was that each brought their books and money to me. I checked the books against the money that they brought and then deposited the revenue. Five minutes after the manager had left, a customer, an African boy, came in with a generator/alternator. He wanted to return it. I asked him how much he had paid, and he said, "Six pounds." I looked in the book and saw that in the book was written "Generator—five pounds."

I asked, "Did you pay him five or six?" He said, "No, sir, I paid him six." I said, "Okay, can you sit down and wait on the bench? He just went to eat and he is coming back now." About 15 minutes later, the manager walked in and wanted to know what the customer wanted. The boy explained again that he wanted his money back. I asked the manager, "Wait a minute, how much did the customer pay you?" The man said he thought he had charged five pounds. But the customer said, "No, I gave you six pounds." The manager responded, "Oh, okay—I remember now, six pounds."

He started to open the door to give the boy the money. I said, "Wait, the books say five pounds, and you took six pounds from the man. Have you been doing this a long time in this store?" He said, "Oh, I just made a mistake." I responded, "No, that was no mistake."

I gave the six pounds to the customer and he left. Now, I said to the manager, "You go home. Don't come back again. I'll send the money that you earned to Mr. Arab and he will pay you." The manager was a big, wide man. I thought he could twist me with two hands! Then I took the keys for the shop from him. He complained and begged me to keep him. He went to my cousin's wife's house and complained that I fired him because of his mistake. He explained to her the "mistake." She turned to me and said, "Because of one pound you want to fire this poor man? Leave him alone." She assured him, "Don't worry, you can come back to work."

I said, "No. I said no, this man is a thief! I don't want to leave him in this position. Didn't you hear what your husband told you? Habib is responsible for all my business. You are responsible in the house only, with the children. Your business is in the house and my business is outside."

She said, "No, I am the owner when your cousin is not here, so I am going to be responsible too."

To the man, I said, "Go away." Then I called Mr. Arab and explained what I did. He said, "Well done, Habib. Thank you. Send that bastard to me, and if he wants to talk to you, you let me know." I took fifty pounds to Mr. Arab, as that was what the man made each month. I told Mr. Arab to pay him the whole amount, even though he had only worked part of the month. Mr. Arab said, "Habib, you are a very good man." He prepared a document for the man to sign to confirm when he got his money. The man came the next day asking for his money. I sent him to Mr. Arab.

This situation gave me an idea. I wondered, if this man tried to steal from my cousin, others might be doing that also. My cousin was making so much money he might not be paying attention. His attention was focused on "big money." So I watched the transport, the clothing store, and the mining managers. The mining manager, an English man, came every Saturday in a van carrying the iron ore. He put the ore in the yard. I checked how much ore he brought. The little bag was very heavy. He signed in a book for ore and for the £20 to £100 he needed to buy supplies—such as separating pans, pick axes, and shovels.

Next I focused on the transport company. Where was this truck going? The Syrian manager said he hired the truck out for £30 for a trip for three or four days. He would need two drums of gas at forty-four gallons each. Two drums cost £10. If he needed tires, each would have been £10. The driver would take £5 for expenses. So it would take £15 if the truck came in with no damage. I kept talking to myself with the manager standing next to me. How much would that leave for profit? There needed to be income to cover the usage on that long trip. My cousin had told me that he would have charged £60 or £70 for that length of trip or a little longer. I worked it out, and we would make £30, that was just about equal to the expenses. A profit of about £20 would have been good then, but I didn't think that the truck would make anything for us.

The manager explained, "We let him go, instead of having him stay." I asked, "Why, because we would make no profit?" He said, "Because, those people are friends, they go to the other town, and they are our customers. We would always give it to them." I asked, "My uncle used to do that?" When he said yes, I said, "Well, myself, I don't think I will allow this." The manager shouted, "Who are you? Who are you?" I said, "You don't know who I am? You better ask Mr. Arab who I am."

Then I called the driver, an African, over, and told him to empty the truck and take it back to the man who wanted to hire it. I didn't want to let it go unless the man was willing to pay £50. The driver was so good and very anxious to listen to me, because Hassan had told them, "You better be good to my cousin and listen to him. He is going to be manager. Take care of him, he is a boy but he has sense. Don't play around with him!" The Africans, Hausa people, understood, because they respected their masters. They were very loyal. They had families and houses to support, and my cousin was very good to them.

The Syrian manager shouted to the driver, "You can't do that!" The driver said, "Before you shout at me, he is the owner. His cousin is the master, and he told us to respect him, even though he was small." In the Hausa language it would be said, "My *Gida*"—a sign of respect for bosses, heads of households, etc. So the driver and others knew I spoke a little English and I was starting to pick up a little of the native African Hausa language. The driver took the truck, took the load off, and brought the truck back. The manager was so upset he took the jeep and drove off.

I told Mr. Arab about the situation. What is the use of sending the truck for £30 when that is what the expenses would be? Mr. Arab said he would talk to the manager. He told me to take the wheels off the trucks and put them in storage. Put something under the axles of the trucks. I had the drivers remove the wheels from the fifteen trucks. There was really no significant business during that rainy season for the trucks because they could not move in the muddy roads. The profitable work was during the summer, when the roads were good. Mr. Arab sent his driver to get the manager from his house. The driver brought the man to Mr. Arab. He was paid and told, "Never go near Habib. Hand the jeep over to him."

In a half-hour the man dropped off the jeep, went away, and I never saw him again. I had a worker cover the jeep with a tarpaulin, because there was no roof. I didn't know how to drive and I was scared to try. So I wasn't going to be driving it! I laughed as I said to myself, "Why are you scared, boy?" If I wanted to go someplace I would take a driver with me. But the driver really was connected to my cousin, and because of the poor relationship I had with my cousin's wife, I didn't want to use their driver.

One day I asked a strong boy, from the Hausa tribe, "Why are you sitting like a boss, while your boys that are your drivers are working on the trucks?" He retorted: "Leave me, it is not your business." I said, "You are telling me that I have to leave here! Do you know that I am your boss?" He said, "Oh, oh—you are not my boss. My boss is Hassan, and he is not here! You *yaro*—you get up and go away." (*Yaro* means "boy" in Hausa.) He just turned his head and started to walk away, and he started to say some bad words that I didn't understand.

I looked down and spotted on the ground the crank that we used to start old cars. I picked it up and hit him between the shoulders. *Bam!* I beat him up! I was so upset! After all, I was the boss! All the boys—the drivers—began to laugh. I was insulted. I wanted to keep hitting him on the head. The other drivers took the crank from me, yelling, "My *Gida*! Leave him alone, leave him alone! You'll kill him, you'll kill him!"

Other drivers took him outside and sat him down. I never saw his face. All the boys were so scared, they never even smiled. They all went to work and worked a lot—before that they had only worked a little! I shouted at them, "Everybody, if I see somebody not doing good work, I will beat him—I will kill him!" They all shouted, "No, no." In Africa at that time, the white man was usually in charge, and acting this way was considered acceptable. The police were white, the government was white, and most of the important positions in authority were held by white men.

My cousin's wife was just outside the door and overheard this; she might have been cleaning rice. She looked at me, and was so scared. "Habib, why did you do that? Maybe he will kill you. Maybe he will wait for you." I told her it was not like in Lebanon. Here, when the native people were threatened and afraid, they stayed away because they were scared. I said, "That's the end, everybody go inside." I stayed and worked with the drivers the rest of the day. The boys jacked up all the trucks and put them on blocks in preparation for the rainy season when it was too muddy for transports. I marked each wheel so that I would know which truck it came from. I had fired the manager, and then I locked the store and left.

Now I had fired two managers. The transport company was closed for the rainy season and I was managing the auto parts store myself. I was also overseeing the managers of the clothing store and the mining business. At this time, I was still living in my cousin's house, although my relationship with his wife was not good. She was a very good cook, and I was eating Lebanese food during that time, and she also cooked African food. My cousin's wife and I didn't get along because she didn't want me in charge of the business. If I sat down at the table to eat, she would get up and leave. She was trying to show me that she was upset with me because I would not listen to her.

I was bored one day, so I inspected the trucks that were in storage, and then went out to the jeep that we had earlier covered with a tarp. It was parked next door to where my cousin, his family, and I lived. The tarp had a little hole in it that happened to be just at the driver's side front windshield. I lifted the tarp just enough to get in, and sat behind the wheel. Through the hole in the tarp, I saw the sister of my cousin's wife sitting outside the house in the garden, picking rocks out of the rice. (She stayed in Jos a lot because her husband had gone off to war in Turkey and not come back. No one ever knew what happened to him.) I pushed the button to start the car, and put in the clutch. I had never driven before, but I had watched the driver when he took me places. So I cautiously shifted into first gear, slowly lifted my foot from the clutch and pushed gently on the accelerator. The car slowly rolled forward a little. Then it stopped. I waited a little bit. I got it moving again ... it went forward a little more and stopped. I slowly drove the jeep forward again.

My cousin's wife's sister stared at this jeep moving forward with no driver. It was far enough away that she didn't hear the motor and only saw it moving. She suddenly threw the rice up in the air, "*Baaa!* Sister, I saw that car with the tarpaulin move!"

My cousin's wife came out of the house, answering her. "Can't you see? Is something wrong with you?" When my cousin's wife went back inside the house, I drove the car forward a little again. Her sister yelled, "It moved again!" My cousin's wife said, "You are crazy!" The sister retorted, "I'm not crazy, I saw that jeep move again. I swear to God! It is the devil! It is the devil!"

I was laughing so hard. I went into the house and said, "What's wrong? What's wrong?" They told me, and I assured them that I had been around, saw nothing unusual, and there had been no driver in the area. Later, I went to my cousin's wife and whispered, "That was me."

She said, "You? – Are you trying to kill my sister?"

All during this time, I walked around the town and got to know the area and the people. I went to the market and walked through all the food stalls. I bought a Raleigh bicycle when my cousin left, and Albert, who ran the clothing store, and I would take rides in the evenings. He introduced me to many neighbors in the town. I was becoming familiar with the community in Jos—the Africans and the other Lebanese people living in the community.

During the time my cousin was visiting his mother in Lebanon, I was in control of the whole place, but my cousin's wife and I didn't agree. She didn't want me to do the job and she wanted to be my boss. I was not going to argue with her, but I was doing what was good for the business, because my cousin believed in me and assigned the management of his various businesses to me. Also, the head of the Lebanese community in Jos was very much impressed with me. He said, "Habib, you are doing a good job. At your young age, I am amazed that you can manage to get all these things done, and I believe that you are helping your cousin very well. You're taking good care of his property."

So I didn't care what my cousin's wife thought about me. If she looked nervous when I talked to her, I just kept quiet. I would have a cup of juice or eat what was on the table. When I would go away I would say goodbye, and when I returned I would say hello. Sometimes she answered me, sometimes not. But anyhow, I was doing my job. I had to respect her. I had to be nice, and be very good to her, but she always wanted to give me orders.

One time I went to the clothing shop. It was after WWII, so many things coming into Africa were rationed. Imports from many countries, cloth and clothing, food, whiskey, and other goods from Europe were all under rationing. Large general stores in Lagos received the rationed quantity of goods, and then they would distribute shares to all the small stores. One man got goods for £4,000, another store might get £2,500 worth of goods. We only got £1,500 worth of goods for a ration, every two weeks. We went in our van to get the load for the deliveries every two weeks and I would write a check for £1,500. When we returned to the store, Albert and I would then work to sell the goods. During that time, traders would come into the store. They would buy some of the goods and then go to the villages outside the town to resell them to the bush people. This was all in the town of Jos, in south Nigeria, about 800 miles from Lagos and the ocean.

When I went to the clothing store, I noticed that there was a lot of wool cloth sitting on the shelves, not sold. Albert, the store-keeper, divided his rationed inventory among the bush traders who he knew would be coming to his store. For example, he would put two blankets, two shirts, in each bundle, thus dividing the lot. The traders knew the price, and they paid him and took the bundles to be sold. We would make £100 or £200 profit. It was very hot in Jos, so Albert did not include the wool cloth in the bundles to be resold in the bush, because the people did not need wool coats! But we had to accept the rations from Europe as they came; we could not order or select goods of our choice.

So people were coming to buy the stock, but they did not want the wool. By then there were 40 bundles of wool filling the shelves, because two bundles of wool were included with each delivery. I asked Albert, "Why is this there?"

"It's not selling."

"Okay. It's not selling. Why do you buy it?"

"We must buy it, it is how rationing works."

"All right. Then why you don't sell it?"

"People, they don't want it."

I start to think it over myself. I was smart. I was fifteen, sixteen years old and this stupid boy is in his late twenties, and he had a high school education, and I tell him, "Albert, you have to find a way to get rid of this." He said, "There is no way. Unless, when customers come, we would sell it to them under price. Like half price."

I said, "Then, we lose half price here and we get some of their money. But now we are losing money overall. We're not making too much money. Then how much do you think you would pay? £50 a month? Where's the profit? That's all this big store makes? £100, £200 every month. That's too small for a big store like this. Only £200?"

"Yes, £200."

"No. This is not a good business. You know, next time when the supply comes, you just put all the supply in the store. Don't sell it. Don't do anything with it, and send the supply card (inventory listing) to me. Do you understand?" He said, "Yes." He was starting to be afraid, because I had already fired two managers. I said "Look, if you don't listen to me ..."

"I know, I know, you will fire me. I will never sell it. It is your cloth, your store. You're the boss."

"Okay," I said. "Now, Albert, just when you get the supply, put the supply in the store and send for me. I'll tell you what to do."

"Okay."

So, the supply came and Albert sent for me. When I arrived at the store, I said, "Albert, how do you divide this?" He said, "I divide it into four shares. One, two, three, four." I said, "Okay. How much wool did we receive?" He said, "Two." I said, "Okay. Put in each share, one bundle of that wool. Put the two from the latest shipment in two bundles, and take two off the shelves so that each share has wool in it. So we sell the bundles, then we need to sell the others."

I went on. "Don't charge them extra—don't make a profit on it. Make it exactly the same price that we bought it for. Put it with this one." So we make money on one bundle and the other bundle just allows us to get our cost back. We make no profit. He said, "Okay, but they will not buy the two bundles." I said, "Never mind. Did *you* pay for these?" He said, "No sir. You paid the money." I said, "Okay." So we made four shares, and in each share, we put one bundle of that wool.

The traders came the next day and said, "Albert, where are the goods?" Albert said, "The goods are in the store. Come." So he showed them. They said, "What is that you put inside?" He said, "Well, the boss said I have to put one bundle of wool in each share." They said, "We can't buy it." Albert said, "Well, it's up to you." They argued with Albert and he said, "Well, the boss said you have to pay for the bundles including the wool, or no sales." The people got upset and they left.

Albert called me at the spare parts store and told me that the customers were upset and left, refusing to buy the goods. I said, "Okay. No problem. Just close and go home." He said, "Okay, yes sir." That evening I went to his house with my bicycle. He got his bicycle and we went for a ride. When we came back, he said, "Mr. Habib. These people, they are not going to buy the cloth." I said, "Why are you worried? I am paying the money. I'm taking all the risk." He said, "Okay." So, the next day the customers came. Again on the third day the traders came. For one week they came and went away, but still, I didn't change my mind. All the cloth in the town was gone; the supplies were depleted. Only in my place was there a nice supply of material. The people in the town and bush needed the cloth. I told Albert, "Tell the traders that if they don't buy today, I'm going to break the bundles and put the material outside the store and sell it by pieces to the people in the town. You know if you sell them by pieces, you get more money."

But the traders were friends of Hassan, my cousin. They came to the store, bought fabrics, went to the bush, and sold it by pieces to make a little money. I told them, "You have to buy it. Do something with it. You can sell it in the bush." They said, "The bush where we go has temperatures of over 100 degrees—it's hot!"

"I don't care," I said.

Finally, one trader said, "Okay, Albert, I'll buy my share." He paid and left. Then, the second one came and bought his share. The third one. The fourth one. Then Albert called me.

"Guess what?" he said.

"What?"

"They bought them!"

"Yes."

"How did you know that they would finally come and pay what we were asking?"

I said, "Okay. Now, between me and you ... every time a delivery comes, take some of that old inventory down from the shelf and make the bundles like we did this time. Before the boss comes back, I want you to get rid of all this old bad stuff."

"Okay."

"Keep it to yourself. Before they buy, do not tell the other traders what we did here."

"No, I will never say anything." So, we continued that process and were able to get rid of all the old wool fabric and were making good money by the time my cousin returned. There was no bad stock remaining in the shop.

After that, I felt that I should give my attention to the iron ore business, far away in the bush. The ore was mined just like gold, using a sifter and water to separate the metal from the dirt. I didn't like the way the business was being run. Each week, the English man came and collected his money in payment for himself and to pay the miners, then bought supplies of shovels, picks, and so forth. Every Sunday he brought his wife and they went to my cousin's home. His wife was a nice English woman—a blonde. My cousin's wife would make a delicious barbecued meal every Sunday. They would visit and then leave with the money, the pick axes, and the rest of the supplies.

One Saturday, he sent his driver, saying that he couldn't come that Sunday. He requested payment for the work, mining supplies, and some bags of rice. I told the driver, "Well, I'm going with you. You're going to take me and bring me back." He said, "Where's the money?" I said, "The money is with me." We put the pickers and everything in the truck and left.

It was almost a three-hour drive through the bush. It was raining. The road was bad, with lots of holes, lots of mud. In spite of that, we managed to get there without problems because of the good vehicle. When we arrived, I saw a nice house and a store next door. As soon as we stopped, the English man and his wife came out to greet me. They said, "Come in for coffee." They made coffee and I drank and visited with them.

Then I said, "Let's go down and see the miners who are waiting to be paid." I went with the manager to the office. He had a list of how much every person had worked and needed to be paid. It was usually about £1, £2, or £2.5. I remembered that there used to be twenty or thirty miners waiting for their pay. But now I only saw fourteen or fifteen people. That was about £20 or £25 at that time. I said, "Usually you ask that I give you £50, £60. This time you only ask for £30. Why is that?"

I took the book. "Next time I want to see the book when I send the money with you. You must bring it back with you each time."

I took the current documents with the money and put them in my pocket. Then I went inside the store. I saw lots of pick axes. I said, "Why do you buy more pickers from me each time? Are you selling them here?"

"No, no, no, no!" he said. "I am just giving the men choices."

I said, "Instead of unloading the ones I brought, I am going to take back some from the ones you have!" I put them back in the big van that we drove down. He argued, "We have to keep them here because we need them in the bush."

I took control of that business too, and I recall that the mining manager quit when my cousin returned. I think he thought, "If Habib is going to stay and manage the business, I don't want to stay here."

I finally had control and was managing of all my cousin's businesses. One week before my cousin returned, the English manager of a French company contacted me. His wife was French, and he and his wife loved whiskey. Whiskey was rationed at that time—one bottle for each person every month. The manager for the company who supplied the food and bottles of whiskey had his rationed stock of four or five cases of whiskey for the whole town. There were not too many white people in the town at that time, and the Africans were not drinking the whiskey. Also, it was very expensive—£4 or £5. Since my cousin was a successful business person, he could afford to buy the remaining stock. Not too long before, he had paid him for the two cases, plus paid him a tip on top of the purchase cost. At that point, Hassan had four cases, and every case contained twelve bottles. It was the Black and White Brand, the favorite brand at the time.

The English manager of the French company came to say hello and drank coffee with me occasionally. One time he told me, "Habib, tomorrow I will have a load for you to deliver to Fort Lamy." Fort Lamy was in the town of Chad. It was far away from Jos, toward the boundary of Nigeria, and then another 150 miles across French territory. He wanted to transport fourteen to sixteen French Peugeot cars, and he wanted them to go by truck; driving them on the roads. The roads were not in good condition—there was a lot of rain and mud, and the bridges were very unstable. Bridges were not built like they are in America. They just cut big trees and laid them across the banks of the rivers.

The manager offered to let me transport one load, which was made up of two cars. I asked, "How much money for one or two cars? Does it pay well?" He said that it would pay £150 for each load of two cars.

"And how many loads are there?"

"I have seven or eight loads, meaning fifteen or sixteen cars."

"When are they coming?"

"In a couple days they will be here. They ship them from Lagos, and then come by railway to here."

I thought this over quickly. My brain began to work, work, work. I said, "Hey, I have a good deal for you." I know he loves whiskey, and his wife *loves* whiskey. She would die for it. If you tell her, "I will take you to the bush to get one bottle of whiskey, she would say, 'Let's go!'." She loves her whiskey <u>very</u> <u>much</u>. So I told him, "Look, sixteen cars … I will give you two cases of whiskey—twenty-four bottles—if you will give me the whole load of sixteen cars and let me take them to Fort Lamy."

He said, "Oh Habib, you have to be joking! You're joking! Where can you get that much whiskey?" I said, "I have it." He said, "I don't believe you." I said, "Okay, come with me."

I had the key for the storeroom belonging to my cousin. I took him to where I kept the trucks parked. I took him inside to show him all the shelves. I said, "One, two, three cases. Look at the cases, three cases."

"Habib," he said, "if you give me the three cases, I will give you all of the loads. I do not care!"

"You've got it!" I shouted. "You've got it! But let's keep it a secret."

"But how can we do it without everyone seeing this?"

"Look, when the cars come I will send the lorries to park behind the building." There was an entry behind the street and next to the railroad tracks. To help hide the activity, there were shops and houses in front of the railroad tracks. I said, "I will send all the trucks to be loaded. You load each one, and I will give you all the cases of whiskey.

Once we are loaded, we will drive straight out of here, and never came back through the town."

"Can you do that?" he said.

"Yes."

"Give me the whiskey."

"No whiskey until the last truck leaves from here. Then you get your whiskey."

"Okay, you don't trust me."

"I don't trust my own father, believe me."

"Okay." We made the arrangements. I called the drivers. They went to the store to make the trucks ready and got the drums of gas. I told them to stand by, waiting for the rail delivery of the cars. I paid them some pocket money—good money. Every four-wheel truck had a trailer, so they could each haul one car in the truck and one car in the trailer. Within a day or two, the manager called me, "Send me one." I sent him one. The driver drove behind the building. He did not drive on the main streets to get to the railway. He went behind the town. He finished loading, then left. The manager called to say, "Habib, the first load is already gone. Send me the second." This continued on—the third, fourth, almost the eighth. I sent them all, and they went on their way to Fort Lamy.

During this time, my cousin came back to Nigeria for a week. I told him and Mr. Arab about the transport of Peugeots. Hassan was so happy to see that his businesses were in good condition. Mr. Arab told him, "Habib did good." My cousin couldn't be upset with me for firing his employees because Mr. Arab told him, "If you don't want Habib, I want him from you. I want him to be a manager for me. I will appoint him as manager to work in my business." Hassan said, "Oh, I could not! This is my cousin. You want to take him from me and give him a job? I would be ashamed, for he is my uncle's son. My uncle would be upset if I let his son be alone in Nigeria working outside our arrangement."

Hassan traveled with the respected head of the community, Mr. Arab, to Fort Lamy, where he would make arrangements with the companies that received goods from England, France, and other countries. They came by ship to Lagos, then by railway to Jos. Many Lebanese people had trucks and were in the transport business. Hassan saw his trucks with his company's name, Kissrawani Transport, on their sides, traveling on the roads earlier. When he arrived back in town, he did not see his fleet of trucks, so he thought I had sold them and that was why he saw so many on the roads and none in his yard. Also, his wife had told him that I had given away his cases of whiskey without explaining why. I was out bicycling with a friend, and he sent a driver to look for me. When I returned to the house, my cousin was sitting on the veranda with his wife and friends. We went to his office, and I explained that he hadn't seen the trucks because I had taken them to the river to wash. I explained how I got all the business for transporting the Peugeots. He forgave me for giving away his cases of whiskey and said, "You rascal!"

Hassan contracted to start up the transport business that season. I boarded in a house in the town of Maiduguri, on the way to the border of Chad. An African family took care of it. The house was made of mud and grass, maybe 10 feet by 8 feet, and not very secure. The people slept outside in the warm season and inside in the rainy season. There was a bed outside with mosquito netting around it. The natives wore big knives on their arms. They were the Beriberi tribe from the region of the same name, originally from Libya or Tunisia. They liked horses, were very proud warriors, and did not hesitate to fight. The best thing to do when working with them was to just be respectful. It was very good if you made friends with them, because you did not want to be their enemy. I made friends with them and they protected my truckloads of goods. We never had any trouble or anything stolen.

There were three main tribes in Nigeria at the time. The Yoruba and Ebu tribes to the south, and the Hausa in the North. I was very proud that I learned the Hausa language in just six months. The Hausa were Muslim, the Yoruba were half-Muslim and half-Christian, and the Ebu were Christians, due to the American missionary influence. Sixty or seventy percent of the people in Nigeria were Muslim. I interacted with the tribes in Maiduguri, since I spent the season among them. But it was difficult to stay in that bush area once the rainy season came, because of the roads, and because I had to run inside the house or tent each time it started raining in the middle of the night.

We used to go hunting in the bush. We would see a tribe that ordinarily did not wear any clothing. They were all naked. However, when they wanted to come to town, they were required by law to wear clothes. The men had to wrap a blanket or cloth around their waists to enter the town. They sold charcoal for barbecuing, and they sold some vegetables. In exchange, they would buy matches, salt, and some sugar. They lived in mud or grass huts. They farmed, grew vegetables, and raised some chickens. Their lives were very simple and they produced almost everything they needed for their survival.

One night when I was asleep, I awoke hearing someone yelling, "Kill him! Kill him!" The landlord was shouting, "Kill him!" I tried to get under the bed, but it was too low, so I couldn't. I dreamt that I was fighting. It was cold and scary. When I finally got back to Jos at the start of the rainy season, I told Hassan that I didn't want to stay there again.

The next time I had to go to Maiduguri, I bought beds, mattresses, and sheets, and rented a house with an Ebu cook. The cook was very nice and had a good-looking wife. She cleaned the house and helped in the cooking. I always had to stay there, because that was where we had to stop to transfer goods from the Mack trucks to smaller trucks. Mack trucks could negotiate the road to the end of Maiduguri but not beyond, as they were too big and heavy for the mud in the rainy season. We would have to unload the Mack trucks and put the goods on smaller trucks at Fort Lamy, on the outskirts of Maiduguri. One Mac truckload would fill two or three smaller trucks. We also made money by taking passengers who rode on top of the loads.

There was a river at Fort Lamy that we had to get the trucks across. People from the transport company would employ ten to fifteen workers to reload the goods. The trucks came and we loaded them. I always went to supervise them. I met another young man, about sixteen, whose family was doing the same thing in the transport business, and we met more friends our age. While the boys were reloading, we left them and the drivers, and went across the river on the ferry.

We were hungry so we went to a bar. The bar was cool and relaxing after all the hard work in the hot sun. We were talking as good friends do, eating French baguette sandwiches. We asked for a bottle of wine and three glasses. We were so hungry and thirsty, so we asked for another bottle of wine, and another. I was drunk, but I needed to go check the trucks. We kept chatting about Lebanon. I stood up—uh-oh, no feet! Three bottles, and I could not move! Luckily, my cousin's friend, Abdullah, was in town. He took us, one by one, and shoved us in his car. He took us to his house. We were three skinny guys and he helped each one of us into bed. We woke up the next morning, and washed up because we didn't smell good. The trucks and drivers had already crossed the river and were waiting on the other side when we rejoined them.

The next day we went to the bar again! The wine was nice; it made us happy! After a long visit, I told my friends goodbye, and went home to go to bed. I couldn't sleep; the bed started to turn, and turn, and turn. I woke up. I sat down. I went back. I sat down again. The cook's wife stayed in a room on the side of the house near the kitchen. She was watching me, and finally came to me and said, "What's wrong?"

"I cannot sleep." I said. "I do not know why this bed is turning."

"Oh, what shall I make for you?"

"Can you make me a cup of coffee?"

She went away to make the cup of coffee for me, and then gave it to me to drink. Then I felt like I was going to vomit. So I went out to the other side of the yard, where it was all mud. But I only vomited a little bit. Then I washed and came back inside the house. The woman sat down with me and held me. She said, "Nothing will happen to you. Come on, go to bed." She put me to bed, and I wasn't sure what happened after that.

The next day when I awoke, she asked me, "Do you know what happened?" I said, "No, no, I don't know what happened." She said,

"Oh, oh, we make love." I said, "What! Are you sure?" I didn't take her seriously. I said, "You lie!" She said, "No." I said, "Anyhow, if you are serious, or not serious, don't tell your husband." She said, "Oh no! How can I tell my husband?" I said, "Okay."

I took £1 or £2 and gave it to her so she would keep our secret. I said, "Even if I do believe you, I did it only because I was out of my mind." And I really was out of my mind. I didn't feel anything. Anything!

The next two days in a row, my friends and I drank wine, wine, wine. It's something that had never happened in my life before; it affected me. But I was so happy. I enjoyed it with my friends. I had a good time, after we had worked hard. It was hot, and we were tired ...

On the last day I woke up feeling strong like a horse; I was recovered and felt like nothing had happened. We finished loading, and took the load to the other side of the river. But we didn't go back to the bar anymore because we knew it was a big mistake. I told my friends, "I am going to buy you bread and cheese, and we are going to take it with us. We can eat the food along the way. It is not necessary to eat it in the bar." They said, "Okay."

I went to the store. It was a French bakery and all the staff was French. A girl waited on me, and I asked if the bread was made there. I asked her for the best *fromage*—cheese. She said, "Yes." She went in the back and brought Camembert out for me. I bought the cheese and bread and left. The cheese was packaged in a box of light wood. So I took it to my friends, and everybody took a portion. They each left with their trucks and we all drove away. While we were driving, the sun beat down through our front window. Our cheese was on the front seat between the driver and me. I started to smell something. Maybe the cheese was old, I don't know. It started to smell like (whispering) "shit." So I asked the driver, "Did you put your wooden box somewhere in back?" He said, "No, Master." I said, "Look!" He looked at himself. "Maybe it's me," I said. I looked, but there was nothing. But the smell was awful. The heat of the sun was melting that cheese!

When we reached some nice, shady trees, I told the driver to stop. I was so hungry. I always carried a box with water and beer. I unloaded all this from the truck and got out the box of cheese. I held the Camembert in my hand. It looked like it had already melted. But I had my bread, and I left the car and walked toward the trees. It seemed like the smell was following me! Then I rubbed my nose; the smell was on my finger! What is that? I opened the box and looked at the cheese. I saw a worm squiggling inside! Maybe it was old, or maybe that was normal for Camembert. I threw it away and washed my hands. I ate my bread without anything, just salt. I finally got back to the house. Later I asked somebody about that cheese and they told me, "That's the way to eat Camembert cheese. It smells bad." But I do still like Camembert cheese.

Now it was the first of April. I became acquainted with many people in the Lebanese community. They all lived in the same area—the married and unmarried people. I got to know one or two families very well. They liked me because of my cousin. They knew him because of his businesses and because he was rich. When they came into town they ate lunch at his house. He threw parties for them. He helped them by giving them loads to transport. So they respected me. They gave gifts to me; they liked me. If they did something for me, to please me, it was because of my cousin. It was not for me, but indirectly for my cousin. They were returning, through me, the favors that my cousin had given to them in the past. Before my cousin left for Lebanon, he asked his friends to look after me, to not forget me, to be nice to me, and so on. And they did.

It was April Fool's Day, so I decided to play a joke on them. I did not have a car, but I had a friend with a van. His name was Josh. I said, "Josh, I'm going to play a joke today. What do you think?" He said, "Okay."

"Look, can you lend me your van?"

"Here is the key. What do you want to do?"

"I want to go talk to Lora." Her house was a little far away—half a mile from the house. I explained, "I want to tell her that your wife has fallen down and broken her leg."

"Okay."

"Now, don't you say anything."

"No, I won't."

I took the van, and went to find Lora. I asked her, "Do you know what happened?" She said, "What?" I responded, "Josh's wife was walking on the veranda and stepped on a banana peel or something. She fell down and broke her leg, and now they are taking her to the hospital!" She started shouting, "Oh, oh, oh, why did she do that! Why didn't she look? She's blind! She walks like a blind person!" She started to shout, and was very upset—Josh's wife was a good friend.

Then I went to Josh's wife and told the same story about Lora. She said, "Oh! Oh! What happened?" I said, "They already took her to the hospital. I am going that way. If you want me to, I will give you a lift." She said, "Oh, yes give me a lift." Then she jumped inside the van. I started driving, and in the middle of the road we met up with Lora. When I stopped, Lora shouted, "What's wrong with you!" Then Josh's wife got out of the van and they looked at each other. One said, "Nothing happened to you!" And the other said, "And you, nothing happened to you." I drove away by myself and they followed me. For two or three days I didn't go near those two women!

It had been almost a year since I had moved to Nigeria, and it was 1947. I was about nineteen years old. My cousin, Hassan, was permanently back from Lebanon and I was back in Jos. One day he said to me, "Okay, Habib, I want you to go work for yourself." I suggested that I wanted to go back to Lebanon. But my father had written me a letter saying that the latest war between the Palestinians and Israelis had not yet ended. The Palestinians were starting to enter South Lebanon and the Israelis were beginning to fight them in the area in which my family lived. My father wrote, "You'd better stay in Nigeria. Things are still bad. When I am confident of peace, I will let you know and you can come back home."

The Lebanese people always tried to stay out of the war, being neither pro-Palestine nor pro-Israel. My father, commenting about the war when I was first leaving the country, explained, "This is not our problem. We are a country of peace. The French army finally left our borders, and we have to pray for God to bring peace between us and the Palestinians, the Israelis, and all of our other neighbors." The Lebanese do not have a history of fighting with anybody. But our country was dragged into the war because the Palestinians, with Arafat leading them in war, hid in southern Lebanon.

Lebanon is a small country, somewhat like Switzerland, and trying to stay neutral. It's a beautiful country with lots of rivers and trees. Our main industry is tourism. Taxis, restaurants, and hotels employ many, many people. Many people have houses with extra rooms that they rent to tourists.

Most young Lebanese immigrate to the United States, to Africa, and to Europe. But everybody still has family in Lebanon. Many people worked in other countries, like me. My father and our family remained in Lebanon. I left to get work. When I first left, if I made $10 by the end of the month, I divided it—$5 for my living expenses and sent $5 to my family. That is how we lived in Lebanon; it was very typical in many families.

There are at least sixteen religions represented in Lebanon. Every religion has to be recognized by the government, and each wants its own church. The religions are very exclusive; everyone tends to stay within their own. I believe that all religions can be good—religion is religion—and it doesn't matter which one you belong to. You can pray to anybody you want, just as long as you are a good person and nice to people. Don't kill anybody. Don't lie. Don't do bad things. Just keep your religion for yourself. But be nice.

Myself, I teach my children to respect ourselves and to respect good people. We don't care whether you are Christian, Jewish, or a member of any other religion. Once we know you are good, you are our friend. If someone is not good, even if he were my brother, I would not like him, and I would not talk with him. I wouldn't do business with him. But when I meet a good person, I don't care what his religious beliefs are. I would like to do business with him. I would like to be friends with him and call him my brother. I would love him because he is a nice man. He is my brother or my sister, because we are humanity. I don't care what religion a person is. We are all children of Adam and Eve. I was born in Lebanon. People I know are from other countries. That is God's plan, I didn't have any control over it, but we are all the children of God.

Because of the political problems in my country, I knew I had to stay in Nigeria for the time being, so I accepted my cousin's offer to help get me started in the transport business. He sold me two Dodge trucks to start my transport business. He sent me loads of goods to transport. I would drive the loads to their destinations and he would pay me. That was my income, but from the profits I had to make payments to him for the trucks. I was disappointed that Hassan didn't give me the two trucks to start my business, in recognition of the good job I had done overseeing his businesses while he was gone.

Maybe his wife influenced him, as she did not like me, and would never allow him to give me anything. I tried to be friendly with her. I didn't want to be trouble, because I know that most men do what their wives tell them to do!!! I have made sure that my kids understand that too! Oh, yes! I tell them they should do everything that their wives tell them. If I tell one of my sons, "This is a glass," but his wife says, "No, this is a paper cup," they believe their wife! They say, "No, Papa, this is paper cup." My kids are very sensible. I love them. I used to listen to my wife. I laugh as I think: sometimes I listened to her; sometimes … noooo. But I always tried to let her *think* I was listening to her!!

Along with the job, Hassan said, "I'm going to rent a house for you." The house he found was not far from his house. He probably did this because his wife may not have wanted me to stay with them any longer. I stayed there until the rainy season. The rainy season lasts only two or three months, sometimes even less than that. The summer is almost nine or ten months, all hot, and everybody stays outdoors. During those two rainy months I would go eat with my cousin, but when I finished, I would go back to my house, to visit my friends, or to help my cousin outside with the transport—with the people—whatever he needed. He called me one time and said, "Come this evening and stay. Where are you spending your nights?" I said, "I spend them at home." He said, "Do you have a girlfriend?" I laughed and responded, "I wish! Can you find me one?"

The trucks that my cousin sold me started with good tires and good engines. They were in very good condition. I arranged for the trucks to be driven to Maiduguri. I rented the same house I had stayed in before. I worked all the summer season with those two trucks, transporting goods to Fort Lamy in the French territory.

One day I was coming back from the trip to Fort Lamy. There were little villages along the road. I stopped near one of them so that the drivers could buy some onions, tomatoes and fruit. I saw that the people of the village were crying. I asked the driver, "What's wrong? Why are they crying?" He said, "There are two bush bulls, one male and one female, and they have come rampaging inside the village. They are destroying the villagers' houses because they are made of mud and grass. Sometimes they kick the children or old people, injuring them." I asked, "Where are they now?" And the village people pointed, "In that bush, over there." They stood outside in the road, and pointed to two *big* bulls, very far away, maybe about a mile—you could easily see a mile or two because it was very flat; there were not a lot of trees. Maybe every hundred feet you would see one dry tree trunk and a few dead branches.

I had an idea. We always had to be prepared for anything in the bush, and usually used the guns for small game to eat while on the transports in the bush. I had a double-barreled shotgun, another gun, and some dum-dum bullets with me. I told my strong Hausa driver, "Let's go hunting!" The big French-made truck had just a wooden bench as the seat for the driver and passenger, and did not have any doors. I got in the back of the truck and I told the driver to steer towards the bush bulls, and then turn slowly so that I could get a shot at them from the back of the truck.

The kids were shouting as we started out. My driver was afraid for me and for himself; since there were no doors, he had no protection from the animals. As we got closer to the bush bulls, the male started following my truck. He got closer and closer, and I steadied the rifle ... and shot! The kick of the rifle unbalanced me, but the shot hit the bull on the forehead, where I had aimed. He rolled forward and then onto his back so that his feet and belly were up in the air. The frightened female started moving off, far away.

The dead bush bull would go bad very quickly in the hot weather. We had a strong rope and had to drag the "mountain to town"—really, just a couple hundred feet to the village. You should have seen the people! They all bowed down at my feet. They thanked me and said, "God give you long life! We are going to eat his skin! We are going to have a feast!" I laugh when I remember how people lined up for the meat and the boys kept cutting and cutting, but the bull did not seem to be getting smaller!

Finally, I told the driver, "Let's go." When I went to the truck, I found five or six bags of onions, two or three cases of tomatoes, some potatoes and pineapples. There were all kinds of fruit, vegetables, chickens, goat meat. I was worried that they were going to bring me their cow! I asked, "Who brought this?" The chief of the town said, "This is for you. God bless you for helping us. This is because you helped us and we were always living in fear. You got the bad one. The female never did anything. The bull was the one that caused all the trouble. Now we can rest. God bless you."

The people started to thank me. They danced in the street and they were so happy. It was like I brought a new life for them. I said, "Thank God. But take your food offerings back. I don't want it all. I will take just a little bit." I told the chief to give back everything to his people, because they were poor. If people were poor, I didn't want to take things unless I paid for them, but I didn't have any money then. I just had a few shillings. I took most of the food out of my truck. I just took one of each item and then I said goodbye. The people and kids ran after me and said goodbye. When I got home, I thought about the incident and felt that I had done a very good job helping the villagers.

Lots of incidents occurred on those African bush roads while I was managing my transports. I remember that one day I was coming back with a load of peanuts and suddenly I came upon one of my cousin's trucks. The driver had just had an accident and the truck had rolled onto the left side of the road. I stopped there and found that the driver had a broken leg, the truck was lying on its side, and half of his load had tumbled onto the ground. So quickly I called my driver, my boys, and some other people that had gathered from around the town. I asked them to help unload the truck. We unloaded the truck and then righted it, but discovered that the bolts for the front wheel were all broken and sheared off. My driver and the other driver offered to sleep there that night to protect the truck and its contents. They thought that the wheel could not be fixed; we would need a front axle and they could go to town to get it the next day. I said, "No. Let's take one bolt off of each of the other wheels. So then each wheel will have an equal number of bolts. So we fixed the wheel that way. We could manage to get to the town, about 150 miles away.

Then we needed to figure out who was going to drive. I had never driven a truck before, only a small Jeep. I told my driver, "Never mind. I will drive my truck. You drive this man's truck." The driver said, "No, sir. You drive the other one and I will drive my own truck because I cannot guarantee the wheels on the other." I said, "Okay. I will drive it, but you have to drive behind me. In case anything happens to me, you are behind me. If you were to go in front of me and anything happened to me you would not see the problem. I would be stuck on the road and you would get home safely without knowing I had broken down." The driver agreed to stay behind me.<masha>

We were on our way, with me driving the injured driver's truck. It was carrying about five tons in the truck bed and another four tons in a two-wheel trailer towed behind it – a nine-ton load. We had a very high hill to climb. I was about nineteen years old, and had hot blood. I was sure I could do anything! I asked two boys from my truck and two boys from the other truck to each get a big piece of wood. I asked them to walk behind me, two behind the truck and two behind the trailer. The truck could only climb the hill at two to three miles an hour. In case I had trouble getting up the hill or the engine died, I asked them to put the wood behind the wheels to stop the truck from sliding backward. It was only 200 or 300 yards but very steep. I shifted into gear and started driving.

Before I reached the top I looked suddenly to my right just to the edge of the road and saw a lion! He was standing right on the edge of the road, only about 20 feet away. He wanted to cross the road in front of me and he wasn't far away. I thought, "What shall I do?" I was still on the hill and I couldn't take my foot from the accelerator.

The truck would slide back down the hill, and it was a long way down. Oh, I had to stay there but keep moving. I was scared that the lion would come and take me or the boys because there was no door. I was so skinny and I thought the lion thought I might look like a good dinner! I looked in the mirror behind me and I saw all the boys jumping into the truck on top of the peanuts. I couldn't do anything. My foot started to dance on the accelerator, shaking because I was so scared. I didn't know what to do. I wanted to pray. I didn't know what to pray!

Then suddenly all of my blood was in my head. I saw the lion look at me and he slowly continued to come down toward me in front of the truck. I was still going up the hill and he just kept padding closer to me. He looked at me and kept padding on. He crossed the road. He looked back at me and finally continued on his way. To myself, I said, "Thank God!" I was still shaking like a leaf. I kept going, and going, and going. I couldn't stop! I finally crested the hill and went about half a mile down. I reached a town.

There was a little village. In front of the village there were huge mangrove trees. I stopped the truck and took the key out of the ignition. Then I *threw* myself out of the truck--literally. I didn't walk. I had no feet; I could not feel my feet. I called the driver and the other boys out of the truck. My driver shouted, "Oh, Zaki! God save your head and God give you a long life. You saved our lives!" They called me Zaki—in the native language it means lion, but this did not have to do directly with the lion incident. At the time, the natives called every white man Zaki, because the lion is a symbol of strength, and they felt that the white man was strong because Europeans governed their countries at the time.

I said, "Just give me the water." We had a four-gallon container of water. I said, "Throw it *all* on me." They washed me with water until I calmed down. All the people in the town came and were looking at me. The boys on top of the peanuts were able to describe the lion and its color to the townspeople. They said, "You got rid of that lion? That lion never let any human see him unless he was being tracked in the evening." Other people said they would have run away. The driver who was following behind me in my truck did not realize what had happened. When he pulled off the road people told him. They told all of us stories about the lion. He said, "There was a lion there! Thank God I didn't see it." When we got home the drivers and boys told my cousin what happened, and they all said, "You are a very strong man."

Another time when we were working, we had tire problems. We could not continue unless we had a spare tire or inner tube. We jacked the truck up and removed the tire. I had an idea: I told the boys to go to the bush and cut as much green grass as they could. They needed to bring big bunches of grass. I then instructed two strong, young boys, "Now I want you to stuff the wheel with the grass—as much as you can." So they started to stuff the wheel and pack it in tight by hitting it with the tire iron. Then we put the jack down and ... it worked! We fixed it. It worked very well. The boys shouted, "Oh, very good, Master!"

On the same trip I had a problem with the gas tank. The tank was located on the outside of the truck between the front and back wheels. Now they design gas tanks inside, to protect them. That day we had been on a rough road and a very large stone must have penetrated the tank, leaving a hole. We were going along the road and I started to smell gas. I said, "Wait, wait, stop!" to the driver. I got out of the truck and looked at the tank, and saw a stream coming out—just like the little kids when they pee. I said, "Come on quick, get me a can." We used the four-gallon water container to catch the leaking gas.

What should we do now? I thought. We needed to solder the tank—otherwise we would not be able to continue. I had the boys start to take the tank off. Then I realized that we always carried a blanket and pillow for those trips. I remembered my mother had many uses for the cotton that pillows were stuffed with. I asked the driver if he had any soap. I cut the soap into pieces and I took some cotton. I mixed it all together with water. I mixed it like you would mix cement. I cleaned the hole in the tank, and around the outside. Then I carefully put a plug of the wet cotton mixture in the hole. I waited one or two hours until it dried. Then I said, "Driver, go bring the gas." They put a little bit of gas in and we watched for a leak. No leak! "Put a little more in." Still no leak! I asked them to put more in, but I could not see any leaking gas and it stayed dry. It worked! When we got home the driver asked if they should take it to be soldered. I asked if it was leaking. He said no. So I said, "Well, then we will leave it."

These incidents with the transporters show how important it was for me to *think* when I was in the bush. You had to think! You had to engineer solutions on the fly. We could not expect anything to be available in the bush. It was isolated. God gave human beings a brain. He gave it to us to use and to construct anything possible to help ourselves. If we were hungry in the bush what were we going to do? We would need to find grass and a bird or a snake or whatever we could find to kill and eat. We always had to think of logical solutions to stay alive.

The problem was that you didn't always have others to depend on in the bush. You had to depend on yourself. That is what I did many, many times. Something unusual always seemed to be happening. Sometimes I would drive a very old car whose floor was rusted out on bad, rough roads. One time, when I got home I parked the car as usual. The next time I went to start the car it didn't start. What was wrong? I got out and immediately checked the battery. There was no battery! That battery was somewhere out deep in the bush. It had fallen out of the car sometime while I was driving and I didn't notice. Luckily, I had not stopped the car during the trip, or it would not have started!

One night I rode in a truck with the driver. I was sitting on the passenger side. I had been leaning my head on my hand and was sleeping. The driver didn't see a big hole on the right side, and suddenly—*whompf!* The truck fell into the hole. I woke up and my chin was out of place; crooked on my face. The impact had dislocated my jaw. I got out of the truck and started spitting blood. The driver said, "Master, what is wrong with you?" I couldn't talk so I just made noises. I put my hand to the side of my face, and without thinking, I just hit myself really hard.

Believe me, when I hit myself, it felt like my chin went to the other side of my face. I tried to feel it. I asked the driver, "How do I look?" And he said, "Oh, Master, are you okay?" We were 50 miles away from the hospital, and the doctor was an American doctor. I knew him and he was my friend. I told the driver to take me to the hospital. The bleeding had stopped by the time we reached it. I looked at my face. It looked normal, but I felt bad. I talked to the doctor, and he said, "Why did you come, Habib? You cured yourself. That was a good idea that you did that." He said it would heal. It hurt when I ate and swallowed. It took almost one year to get over. My jaw made a "crack, crack, crack" noise whenever I ate.

At breakfast, my cousin and his wife asked, "What's wrong?" They could hear my jaw cracking! When I explained the story to them, my cousin's wife said I was lying. "How could you hit your-self?" I said, "Well, I just hit myself. You can ask the driver." Hassan assured me, "No, I believe you," but I insisted that they call the driver. So I called the driver and asked him to tell the story for my cousin's wife. He said, "Mrs., it is true. When he fell down I could see that his lower jaw was on this side. And then he hit himself. I was scared when he did that! Mr. Habib made magic, Mama. Believe me."

I had a French friend, Francois, who worked for a French com-pany. He got supplies for me for free, because we were friends. I often visited with him and we talked. We went to clubs and drank beer together. We played football. He said, "Habib, I am going to hunt for tigers tonight. Do you want to come with me?" I said, "Yes, I will go with you." I thought he was joking. He said, "Do you like to hunt?" I responded, "Yes, I like to hunt." I told him about the lion story and he said that I had better come with him because I had a strong heart. I asked him if he was serious, and he was.

Francois explained that we would go to the water reservoir because that is where the tigers congregated. We would take a leg of lamb and hang it in a tree. And then we would hide and wait for tigers to appear. He brought his gun and I borrowed one. We would shoot them when they came.

The Citroen car had an open front windshield. Francois put music on and was smoking. I didn't smoke. We waited there for a long time—from 7 p.m. until 2 a.m. I got *bored*. I told him I was going down near the reservoir. He told me not to go because of all of the tigers in the area. He told me to not open the car door. Just then, we saw something coming toward us. It was a tiger. We hoped it would go to the lamb. The lamb was high in a tree to make the tiger have to reach up to get the meat. That made the tiger more vulnerable and gave us a clearer shot to his head.

Right when the tiger reached to bite off a hunk of lamb, Francois put the car lights on and *boom!* He shot the tiger in the head with a dum-dum bullet, and the big cat collapsed. I shouted, "Hey, you got him!" Francois cautioned, "Yes, but stay in the car. We won't be able to get the tiger until daybreak. Maybe his brother, his uncle, his cousins are at the reservoir. Do you want to die here? I don't want to die." I said, "Okay, you're right." We stayed there until six in the morning—daybreak.

We finally opened the door and approached the tiger. We lifted the tiger onto the front, or bonnet, of the car. The Citroen hood is very long. We tied him on the car, roping his paws to the front light mountings. When we got into town, we honked the horn; *beep-beep-beep!* We wanted everybody to see the tiger. We were so proud! It was *so* nice. Everybody told us stories of when they had shot tigers. My cousin asked Francois, "Is it true that Habib shot the tiger?" Francois said, "Yes, of course. Habib is the one who shot the tiger." He told everybody that I shot the tiger. He asked me if we were going to go again next week, and I exclaimed, "Not on my life! Maybe there is some white hair on my head now." We spent a good time with all our friends, and lots of funny things happened.

When I returned to Jos at the end of the summer, the trucks were worn out. The heat of the African bush and the bad roads were very hard on their motors and tires. The relationship with my cousin, Hassan, remained difficult, because he was caught between trying to please my father in watching over me, and his wife, who didn't want me around. I was on one side and his wife was on the other. He didn't want to upset his wife, and he wanted to be nice to me. He rented the house for me. He originally helped me by selling me the two trucks and supplying transport loads for me. Now I had to have money to overhaul the trucks.

Hassan offered to overhaul the two trucks. Then he would take one back from me and give me the other one for free. He said, "You take one and I take one. I will do this for free. I don't want anything from you." So now I was back down to one truck. My cousin was going to help me because I did all of this work for him, working the transports all summer. He had promised to rebuild my truck because of the job I did for him—but he didn't do it, because his wife got involved. He wanted to do it. The first time, he told me that he was going to rebuild it for me because of the good job I did for him. We were sitting and talking and his wife called him inside the house. A few minutes later he came out and said, "Okay, I will rebuild them, but I take one for my money, and you take one." I said, "Okay, whatever you said first, never mind."

I tried working with the single truck, but I didn't succeed, because I could not do enough business for me to pay my expenses, my food, and my driver. Sometimes I got work and sometimes I didn't. I finally just took the truck back to him and left it. I threw the key on the table for him. I returned the truck but it was broken down. The engine needed overhauling again, and the tires were bare.

I told him to take the truck and everything else; just feed me and pay for me. He said, "No, you have to try on your own now." I was ashamed to have to go to other people to give me work. I was thinking that I just wanted to work for somebody long enough to earn money for fare to go back to Lebanon. I knew I could not succeed here, because Hassan's wife was fighting me the whole time. She did not like me. She didn't even like her husband helping me. I didn't understand why.

I came from a nice, good, clean family. I came from a Muslim family, and in our custom, women don't wear short or revealing clothing, and they wear head scarves and shawls. In Nigeria, whenever I saw my cousin's wife, she was wearing clothes more revealing than Europeans—miniskirts, sleeveless blouses. I used to suggest that she should be ashamed of herself, that she had daughters who were growing up, and people visiting from outside the family.

"You should be wearing those clothes only for your husband," I told her. "That is our tradition."

"What!" she yelled. "Are you my husband? My husband doesn't tell me what to do. You want to tell me what to do? This is not your life. You don't have to be mixed up with my business. I wear what I like. If you like it, you look. If you don't like it, don't look."

I really believed that what she was doing was wrong. I felt like she was like my sister. She was like my family. I felt I had a responsibility to show her what to do, to respect herself. She should have dressed like others. She should have been modest at least half the time. She could have been half Islamic and half Christian. Mix them together and combine them. That would have been a nice compromise at least!

I stayed with my cousin for almost two years. During the two years things got progressively more difficult between my cousin and me, because his wife didn't like me. She didn't like it when I came back to town for the rainy season; she wouldn't even see me. They wanted me to stay in the bush, but during the rainy season you cannot stay there. There was too much rain. During the rainy season, the road was always blocked between the towns. It was 350 miles between cities. Even inside the town there was no road during the rainy season—just white sand between the houses.

One year, I was working with three of my friends, all about my age. We were stuck down there with our loads. We needed to take the supplies to the French Territory, but the rain wouldn't allow us to go. The authorities would not let us go until it had stopped raining for two days. Forty-four gallons of wine were included in the truckload. We got hungry, and there were no more vegetables or much else to eat because of the supply problems. We had guns and we had vans. I said, "Hey guys, let's go hunting for some meat." They said, "Where? We cannot go outside of the town." I said, "Yes, we can sneak outside town and find guinea fowl, or other birds, or whatever. We can make a barbeque and we have lots of wine here." They thought it was a good idea.

We took our guns. One of my friends drove the van, and the rest of us got in the front and back so that we had another shot if someone missed. I got in back. We drove to the bush and suddenly we saw a gazelle—a nice, good, big one. I said, "Hey, driver, look there!"

"Don't shoot it from this angle," said one of my friends, who was afraid that I would get shot. I said, "No, don't worry." After one hour of chasing the gazelle, we got it; my friend and I shot it. He hit the gazelle on its foot and I hit it on its side so it fell down. We brought it to where the truck was. We made a fire and skinned the gazelle and cleaned its belly. We broke a long branch off a tree and we put it through the gazelle from back to front. We broke two sticks, crossed each of them and put them on either side of the fire that we built. We didn't have any vinegar to marinate the meat. I suggested using the wine, so we added salt, pepper and spices to the wine. We had some big tubs made of aluminum. We wanted to drink wine with the gazelle meat. The wine company reimbursed shippers for bottles of wine broken during transport if the bottoms were broken out and the seal on the cap was still intact. So I told my friend to bring me a hammer and we broke the wine bottle on the bottom and poured it into the tub. But one bottle did not even show up on the bottom! One was not enough! Bring another one! They brought another one, and another one, and another ... I broke them open and poured them in the tub.

Everybody had a hammock, and we hung them in the trees around us. We started to drink wine throughout the evening. We didn't remember anything! In the morning all of the wine was gone and only gazelle bones were scattered all around the fire. A lion or tiger could have come and eaten us easily!

The season for transporting was finished, and I had to stay around the town of Jos. I met a good friend of mine—Kamel Buthros, an Egyptian bachelor in his forties. He was a mechanic, and had a garage with people working for him. He made his big house available for other single people. He had everything he needed. He was a good businessman. God gave him money. He liked to help people get situated in the town and in their jobs. He was a very friendly person and he became a good friend of mine. He always instructed his cook to make a lot of food for all of his friends. Sometimes he would invite me for lunch, or I would stay there for the weekend, visiting with other friends at his house. Occasionally, we would all go to the night-club in town. Sometimes I would tell him about my life and what was going on with me. I would talk to him about how my cousin's wife didn't like me. He always advised me, "Habib, take it easy; he is your cousin. If you have any problems, or need help or money you can always come to me. My house is always open to you. Don't be so sad. If you don't want to go to your cousin's, don't go there. I have four or five rooms. You can sleep in one of them." He had a cousin who was in his twenties, whose name was Ayad. Both of them were Protestant Christians. They were very good people and good friends of mine.

One time Kamel asked me to help arrange a marriage for him. But the story began in Lebanon, where some villages were separated by religion. One village would be Muslim and the next village might be Christian. A Christian girl harvesting vegetables in her family's field met a Muslim man who was out hunting. They made love in the field. The girl's family found out about this and claimed that they wanted to kill the Muslim man unless he married her. That was done in the villages in those days. At one time the villages were friendly with one another, but some incident in the past between a woman and a man caused the villages to be unfriendly to each other ever since.

The girl's family insisted that the man had to change his religion and turn to Christianity if he were to marry her. The man's family did not agree that he needed to change his religion. He secretly went to the girl's family, told them that he would marry her, change his religion, and run away to Africa where a cousin could help him get established. The girl's family agreed. They went to the church, changed religions, got married, and the man and his new wife came to Jos. That is where I met them and learned of their story. After many years, they had two boys and two girls. One of the girls was named Alise. She was very beautiful, and about five feet tall. Kamel, whose house I stayed in, fell in love with Alise. But he was about 40 years old and she was only 18 years old. He was very dark, as he was Egyptian; Alise was very white, with black hair. Kamel was very rich;

Alise's father, Mishell, did not have much money. He built an oven and made pita bread to sell to the community for his income.

Kamel tried many times to tell Mishell that he was in love with Alise, but he just couldn't. Since I knew the family, he asked me to go to Mishell, and ask for Alise's hand. But he wanted me to ask Alise first.

I went to the house. It had two floors. They lived on the first floor where the pita oven was, and they ate there. They slept on the second floor, and had a little sitting room. The people liked me and trusted me. They treated me like a brother. The sons were about my age, and the two girls were a little younger. I came in and asked the mother where Alise was. She said Alise was upstairs. Her sister was downstairs and the boys were away at their work.

When I got to her room, Alise was sitting alone, knitting. She was a very beautiful girl. She was skinny and short and took good care of herself. I said, "Alise, I have a message for you." She said, "What is it? Come sit here." We talked and joked together like brother and sister. I said, "Alise, I found a husband for you. I know someone who wants to marry you." She smiled and said, "Who's that? I don't mind at all."

"You don't mind?" I replied. "You like that man?"

"Which man are you talking about? You aren't talking about you? Look, Habib, don't go left and right. If you want me, I will marry you. Don't worry about my father or my family. You are a Muslim, and I am a Christian. I would change to Muslim, or you could change to Christian. We would repeat the same history as my mother and father."

"No, no, no. Take it easy. It's not me. I am not ready to marry, yet. I haven't earned enough money."

"Who is it then?"

"Kamel Buthros. He loves you, and he asked me to ask you to marry him."

"What?" She put her knitting down and looked at me. "It would be more that he should marry my mother (because of his age). I couldn't marry that man. Are you serious, Habib?"

"Yes," I said. "Kamel asked me to come and ask you. Was that bad?"

"No, but you shouldn't have let him take advantage of your friendship that way."

I could see that she was upset. I responded, "Don't be upset. Don't do anything. It was just a question. Most girls in this world will have boys that like them and ask them to get married. If you want the marriage, fine. If you don't want the marriage, then you say no. Nobody will force you. I am on your side and on his side because both of you are my friends. If you like him, tell me. If you don't like him, don't worry, I can tell Kamel to find another girl to marry."

"Please, Habib, tell him that I can't marry him. I am looking for a good, nice boy like you."

I responded, "I agree, but this man was serious. He has money and you could ask him to buy you a nice car."

"No, no, no. A car and all that money wouldn't make me happy. I want a nice husband—I want to love him and have him love me, even if he has nothing, and we have to eat only bread morning, noon, and night. I want a young man like you."

So I went back to Kamel. I didn't tell him about our discussion. I only said that Alise felt that she was not ready to get married. I told him to forget about her, that Lebanese people were different from Egyptian people, and she was not his type.

One day I was on my way to my cousin's as usual, but I saw that my cousin and his wife were fighting. I found out that they were quarreling about me. She didn't want me at their home. Hassan told her that he couldn't get rid of me because the war was too intense in Lebanon. She kept insisting that he arrange for me to go back to Lebanon. But Hassan told her that he couldn't, because my father had given him instructions "not to send Habib home because all the young people had to join the Palestinian or Israeli armies. The school is spoiled for the young people." Everything was in shambles after the war.

Still, Hassan loved his wife and children, and he wanted to get rid of me to satisfy his wife.

When I experience something that is not right, I cannot shut up. It is in my blood! If I see something wrong, I want to change it. It doesn't matter whether it is for me or for others. I don't like to mince words. I do not even do it politely—I get angry. My son, Said, is like that too. When I am right, I am right! If I am wrong, I will admit it. Our Muslim religion says that everyone should be nice, be good, wear proper clothes, talk to people respectfully, behave, marry and have children. Our religion teaches that if you want to dress up and be beautiful, do that for your husband, not for other people. God made Eve to be nice, gentle and delicate. A woman should be sensitive.

So I told my cousin's wife that. I said, "Look, you are beautiful—a married woman who has children, a husband and friends. You should be proud of yourself. Your husband is young and rich. You have too much money! Why do you look the way you do? The news will become known to your family, and your father strictly follows the religion. You are from a good family."

Oh, when I talked that way to her, it was just like fire; just like I shot her! She exploded in anger.

She wanted me to leave her alone. Her husband was brought up in a good family with my father and my aunt. I don't know how his values changed. Maybe it happened when he got money and mixed with wealthy people, Americans or Lebanese. When I saw them quarreling, I told them not to quarrel about me. I told them I would leave, and returned the house key to them. I didn't want the apartment. I also returned the key to the truck. The truck needed too many repairs, and I couldn't afford to fix it. There seemed to be nothing I could do to improve my situation, so I returned the truck and asked for no compensation in return.

I had worked two years for my cousin, labored like a jackass for him, but I decided it was best to make a clean break. I told them, "I am going to leave this house, and I am not coming back. You leave me alone. Even if you see me in prison, please do not contact me or help me. Remember that you had a cousin in this country—thank you."

They just looked surprised. They wondered where I was going to stay. They asked why I was doing this. They asked if something was wrong. They wanted to know if I had won the lottery. They wanted to know if I had gotten a wife or something. I just left.

I walked to Kamel's house and stayed there. We drank coffee. "Habib," he said, "you look upset. What's wrong?" I told him that I had just fought with my cousin, and suggested that I needed something to cheer me up. He called for his boy to make tea and didn't say anything more until the tea was served. He asked if I was okay and I said, "Now I am okay." He asked me to tell him what was going on. This man was like a brother to me. He was *so* nice.

I said, "I am going to tell you what happened, but can you keep it secret between you and me?" He agreed. I told him that I had just fought with my cousin at his house. "I saw Hassan quarreling with his wife about me, and I got fed up with it." I explained that I had turned their house upside down since my arrival. His wife was upset because she didn't want me there. My cousin felt sorry about the situation, but he was caught in the middle. He was trying to be nice, because he didn't want me to go back to Lebanon, since my father had told him not to send me back.

My cousin was responsible for my immigration status. He paid $1,000 when I arrived in Nigeria. This payment was required so that if the government determined that the visitor should leave, money is on deposit to put the immigrant on a plane, returning them to their original country. My friend reminded me that I had to treat Hassan and his wife well, or they could ship me back to Lebanon. I told my friend, "That would be fine with me! I want to be shipped out of this country so I can live with my dignity and with my self-respect, rather than staying here and bringing trouble to my cousin. Since I have come to this country, my cousin's wife has not liked me. She doesn't want me. I got tired of her getting mad at me when she was mad at her husband. She said I caused trouble." Kamel told me to take it easy. He told me that his house was my house. He told me I could stay there.

He told his boys to make up a room for me. He said that I was his little brother and that he wanted me to stay there. He said that my cousin was a very nice man. I retorted, "If you are helping me for my cousin, I don't want your help." He said, "No, no, forget about your cousin." I told him I needed some time to think. He told me I could stay at his house for the rest of my life. I stayed a few days with him and then I started to go around the town to find work.

I knew all of the Lebanese people in the community, and their businesses. All the clothing stores were grouped on one long street. One of the stores was going out of business. I was curious why. I knew the owners of the businesses on both sides of the store. The one on the left side was the owner of the building. The store on the right side was run by the cousin of the building owner. The owner was an old man, and he had his two sons helping him. One was my age, and the other one was older. They were from the Khoury family. Khoury in Arabic means Christian preacher, or Christian priest. (Arabic names usually have some meaning.)

I went inside and greeted the storekeeper, saying, "*Salaam*" ("Peace be with you"). They greeted me in return, and I sat down. It is the Arabic custom to always quickly call for coffee or tea when people visit. Since it is appropriate to call an old man "Uncle" as a sign of respect, I started the conversation, "Ah, Uncle—why is the store next to you closed?" He said, "Habib, an African man rented this store, working as a tailor, sewing clothes. He had to pay a monthly rent of £15. He left, and we are closing it. We are looking for him to come back and pay that £15!"

I thought quickly. I used my brain just like a computer! I said, "'How about if I myself rent this store, and I'll pay you the £15. Is it possible?"

He said, "Son, the store is yours, whether you pay or not." He offered this deal because he knew that my cousin was a rich and important man in the community. So what could I say? At that time, I didn't even have a penny in my pocket! Sometimes, I just don't know how such good things happen to me; maybe it's the power of my mind. I have very powerful luck. I spoke with authority, like I was a rich man, but I was exactly penniless!

I agreed to take the store, and he said, "Okay, here is the key." He gave me the key. "The house is yours. The store is yours. What you going to open with?" Then the man commented that he thought that I was joking. I said, "I'm not joking. I want to try my luck because

I tried the transport, and it's too much work for what I can earn. I would like this kind of work with cloth. It is nice, easier and not as much trouble as I encountered on the transport runs. They were dangerous. I saw a lion. I saw monkeys. I saw tigers. I was scared! My father wrote to me advising to find steady work." My father wrote to my cousin, too, telling him, "Do not let Habib have a problem with his work. Just give him a job in your businesses."

My father and I always wrote letters back and forth. The letters took two to five weeks to arrive. I scared my family to death—my father told me that my mother cried when I described my encounters with the lion and tigers, and all the other dangers in the bush. When my father read my letters, he spoke to his sister, my aunt, who was Hassan's mother. My mother told her, "Your son wants to kill my son. We sent him to Africa so that Hassan could return to visit you. Before Habib went to Nigeria, there was no one to whom Hassan could depend on in his absence."

There were family discussions. My mother thought I should come back to Lebanon, but she wanted my aunt to guarantee that I would not "join those people to go to fight Israel." The decision was that I should stay in Nigeria. But I could not do anything with my cousin. I was in a position, like it or not, that I had to find some kind of work for myself. I could not go back to my country. I couldn't stay with my cousin. It was obvious that I had to do whatever I could, just to live, to make a living. It was important to me to please my parents and stay away from any trouble with my cousin and his wife.

As a result of all of this, I accepted the key to the cloth shop from the store owner. I thanked him and said, "Okay, I'll see you later to make payment." He responded, "Any time, Habib. Don't worry, don't worry." I left to make arrangements to take over the store. I knew a young Hausa boy, Audu, who did work with me and for my cousin. I took care of him. He was not doing much at the time, just small jobs for my cousin and hanging around the transport drivers. He lived in a house in town with his parents. Luckily, I found him and called him. I said, "Come, and bring brooms and a big pot for cleaning. Then meet me down here. I want you to clean my new shop for me."

Audu quickly ran to his home, and returned with another young boy. I opened the door of the store and saw lots of junk, and old, dirty things. I told him to clean the store with his helper, and then to find me visiting my friend, Kamel, in his garage. They cleaned the whole place—the floor, the tables, and all the shelves where I planned to display the cloth. He then brought the key back to me. I said, "Audu, I have no money. When I have money I will pay you." Audu answered, "That is not bad, Master. I understand everything. *"Bahko me, sanjo mi"* (Hausa for "Don't worry, I will see you later").

Then I told the story to Kamel. He asked, "You rented the store? What are you going to do with it? Do you have capital?" I assured him, "Just wait, Kamel—I have no capital, but I have a way to fill it up with cloth. Look. Just wait. You will be surprised about what I am going to do. I'm not going to lose anything. I already lost. I have nothing. I want to try. Either it is going to work, or it isn't going to work. Nobody is going to take me to jail. If I lose money is anybody going to take me to jail?"

Kamel responded, "Of course not."

I explained, "I don't want to cheat people. I'm not going to lie. I'm not going to do anything dishonest." He again said, "Then what do you want to do with this store? You take it empty, with nothing in it, and it is going to cost you £15." That kind of money was quite a bit in those days.

The next day I went to the traders. I knew all of them, as they were friends of my cousin. The first one I visited imported goods. *"Salaam Alaykum! Salaam Alaykum!"* I said, "I have rented a shop. I want your help because I will be getting some loads coming in from Lagos. I need a few things because I want to open the store within two or three weeks." The townspeople started hearing that I was opening the store. Some looked at me doubtfully. Some of them had no doubts. They wondered why my cousin wouldn't give me any money, but they were too embarrassed to ask me about this.

The traders agreed to my requests and asked how much in goods I wanted. I said, "Twenty pounds, £30, £40—whatever you can do. I don't want too much. Don't bother yourself. But give me something that moves well. I don't know anything about this, but make it good, because if does not sell, I'm going to bring it back to you!" The first trader gave me £20 of goods. I am sure he told himself, "If Habib loses this, let him eat it." The traders were rich people, you see. They weren't going to be concerned over £20.

Audu was with me. I told Audu to take the key and carry the prints back to the store, then to come find me where I would be talking with other traders. He put the pieces of cloth on his shoulder, and started toward the store. He opened the shop, dropped the cloth off and came back looking for me. I trusted that boy! He was a good boy! Meanwhile, I went to the other traders—four or five, one after the other. These were rich people; not the people who bought locally, but who ordered imported goods. In total, I bought about 100 or 115 pounds of cloth for the store. We went to the store and closed the door. I explained to Audu, "You spread them out around the whole shop. Take one kind, and put those two or three pieces together, and keep doing that with all the fabrics." He said, "Yes, Master."

Then I had an idea. I went to Kamel. "Kamel, I need your help. I want to borrow some money from you." He said, "Okay, Habib. How much do you want?" I responded, "I want ticket money—£10, £15, £25." He offered, "Here's £50." I said, "I want £25!" He said, "Here's £50, only £50. If you don't need it, you can bring it back to me. You know where I am. When you get some money, you pay me back. It's just a loan. I am not giving it to you. I'm working hard for this money." He wanted me to take that money, so I took the £50 from him. I went to the railway station and bought a ticket down to Lagos. I knew two families there, very close friends. They imported from Japan and London.

They were excited when they saw me. They all bowed to me, said hello and greeted me. At this time, because of the wars, telephone communication was cut off throughout the country. I explained to them that my father had written me a letter wanting my cousin to help me open my own store because my father was very afraid to continue allowing me to travel in the African bush for the transport business. Also, we worked in the summer, but there was nothing to do during the rainy season. I told the importer friends that I had rented a store, and that I was running it myself; that my cousin had nothing to do with it. I asked them to help me by giving me some goods to fill the store. Then I would continue business with them, refilling my inventory with their imports. They thought that was a good idea.

The first importer made two big bundles of about 500 pounds of cloth each. Then I went to the other man and told him the first importer was going to make four bundles for me. He said, "Look, I'm going to give you only two bundles until you know which one sells and which one is no good." The second man was the brother-in-law of my cousin. He had a big store in Lagos. I got six bundles in total. I told them, "I don't know anything. I want you to send it by railway with my name on it. You pay everything. Put all the costs on the bills. Don't worry—I'm going to pay everything back. Then ship it to me." They agreed, and the deal was complete.

Within a few weeks, the load arrived, and I had about 1,000 pounds from Lagos, and 100 pounds from the local traders. I started to sell 20 or 30 pounds. When I sold 20 pounds, I went to the first trader, paid him the £20, and asked if I could get another stock of cloth. He gave me 30 or 40 pounds. To another man, I returned to pay him his £40, and asked him for more. He gave me another 40 or 50 pounds of stock. I was creating capital from being penniless!

I was so honest with all the people that they grew to like and respect me. There were three or four Indian stores from Bombay. They had many kinds of cloth, very beautiful prints, velvets, and silks made in India. They also sold other things. I told my friend Kamel that I was going to visit the Indian manager to see if he would sell me some of his goods. Kamel said, "How are you going to do that?" I said, "I think I'm going to be able to do it. Here is your £50." He opened his eyes wide in amazement and said, "No, you keep it. I just wonder how you are going to last. How long are you going to keep the shop open?" I retorted, "Don't worry. If you talk like that, I'm going to leave you and stay in the hotel here. I will just rent a place."

He joked, "Oh, now that you have money you want to leave me. If you leave me, I'm going to kill you!" I stayed with him.

I did make the visit to the manager of the Indian store, Shalaram, who knew me. I was hoping he would give me 50 or 60 pounds of cloth. My store was too big, and I needed to fill it. Thousands of pounds of cloth were needed to fill up my store! I asked the Indian workers in the store, "Where is the manager?" and they told me that he was in the basement where the inventory was stored. I went into the basement and saw Shalaram there. He greeted me, "Hello! How are you? How's business?" These people know everything! I asked him, "What are you doing down here?" He said, "Well, Habib, we have some stuff we have to send back to Lagos. It's not moving. This is a big store." I asked him to show me, and he did. (This story will make you realize that if God wants to give something to a person, He will. No one can get in the way; it is God's choice. He helps people He wants to help.)

Shalaram showed me 50 bales of domestic cotton from which bed sheets could be made, about 50 bales of a very delicate fabric, other bales of very, very strong cloth, and about 50 cases of head ties. The head ties were not red—the color women loved for head ties. Instead they were white, yellow and other colors. The whole amount was worth about £3,000 wholesale. I told him, "Look, I have an idea. If you give me all of this for half price for 90 days, I will try to sell it in my store." He said, "Do you really think you can do it?" I said, "Of course!"

He believed me because my cousin was rich—one of the richest people in the town. I had to take advantage of that name, you see, especially because he never paid me for all my work. Even when I was leaving and threw the key on his table, Hassan didn't say, "Cousin, here's £10, £20. Put it in your pocket, you may need something."

Shalaram asked again, "Are you serious, Habib?" I said, "I am serious." He said, "Give me a minute. I need to call the boss." While he was gone, I started talking to myself, "Why did I offer to take the stock? Maybe the owner will agree to the deal! Then what shall I do with this load? Why am I afraid? I will just put the goods in my store. It will show that my store is very big. In 90 days, if they don't sell, let Shalaram come to take his load back. I'm not going to lose anything. So why am I afraid? I am not tricking the man."

Shalaram returned while I was talking to myself, going between yes and no. He said he was happy to congratulate me. "The owner agreed that he would give you the goods for 90 days." I said, "Okay. Start to send the stock to my store. Call your people to help." He called the workers and they started moving bale after bale. They kept looking over at me, thinking, "Why does this foolish man want to buy all this junk?" They started to laugh at me. I said, "I am buying it for a good price." They agreed that I bought the cloth at a good price, but thought that it would not sell. The African people didn't like the color of the head ties. I still insisted that the stock be transferred to my store. This purchase finally filled up the store!

After the bales were in my store, I started to open a box; it was sealed and closed with wire, so it took a few minutes to get it open. It was *full* of red head ties—just what the women loved! The Indian store sold them to me assuming they were white and yellow! White and yellow head ties would sell for £1 or £2 for a dozen, but red head ties sold for £5 per dozen. Even if I charged £2, I made a profit of £1. Oh, I was so lucky, thanks to Allah! When Shalaram had first received his shipment of 100 cases, he had opened about 10 of them, and they were all white and yellow. He assumed the rest of the boxes would contain white and yellow ties, and he could not open more, because he had no place to store them.

I waited impatiently for the end of the day, when I could close the store. I told Audu to open the second case—red. Another case—red. Another case—red! I said, "Do you know what we are going to do, Audu? We are going to open every set of 12 red head ties and take three of them out. We will exchange three of the other colors and give each set of 12, three red ties. When the customers come the next day and ask for all red, we will say, 'There are three red ones in the dozen head ties. Never mind that, I will give you a better price. Instead of £5, I will give them to you for £4.'" That would still give me a profit of £3 on each, and the customers would be happy.

After I'd been in the store one or two weeks, a big storm moved through the country. There was only one bridge connecting Lagos and the outlying areas, including Jos in the south. The bridge was damaged in the storm. Food and goods always came from Lagos by train. It was about 800 to 900 miles through the African bush. Because of the damaged bridge, no more supplies could be delivered to Jos, and the Indian man, Shalaram, came and asked me to return his load. He said, "Can we get our load back? We will give you a small profit." I said, "Get out of here! Don't talk to me until after three months." What I had bought from him, which cost me £1, I sometimes sold for up to £10. Before the 90 days were up, I had made between £6,000 and £8,000 on the £3,000 I spent. I made *good* money! When God wants to open the door for people, and help them, He does!

The store was big now, with lots of merchandise. I was still living with Kamel, but I needed to move, because his relatives were coming to visit. I rented a room with a bed and breakfast for £1 a day, in a hotel run by Lebanese people. The Lebanese wife of the owner of the hotel was very nice. Whatever she cooked for her family that day, she would send to me also. She took very good care of me! Each morning I would open the store and send my boy, Audu, to the hotel to bring me the eggs, potatoes, and Lebanese coffee they fixed for me.

One day in the early evening, about 5:00 p.m., when I was about to close the store and go to visit my friend, an African gentleman came in. He said, "I want to see a piece of print." He was looking at a nice wool print. At that time it cost £2, as it was good cloth. He decided he wanted that piece. I took it out and gave it to him. He asked me how much it would cost. I told him that it was £2. He said okay, and he put his hand in his pocket but only took out £1. I started to wrap the cloth for him and he said, "Can you keep it here for me? Tomorrow, I will bring you the other pound and take the cloth." I asked, "Are you buying it for someone?" He answered, "Yes, my wife. We are celebrating a marriage day. (A marriage day is a wedding.) And my wife wants this to wrap around herself." The style of dress is called a *lappa*.

I could see that the man was anxious to buy the cloth for his wife. I suggested, "Why don't you take it, and tomorrow if you get the £1, you can bring it to pay me back." He asked, "Are you serious?" I said,

"Yes, I am serious." He said, "Do you know me?" I said, "No, I don't know you, but you look like a gentleman, and you are anxious to have this cloth. Maybe the wedding is tonight or something like that. If you were to buy it tomorrow, there would be no use for it. So you can have it, and tomorrow you bring me the £1, okay? If you don't bring the £1, no problem."

He said, "God go with you. Are you sure you don't know me?"

"I have never seen your face before," I replied. "And why do you ask me these questions? I am just being friendly. I like you. You look like a handsome man, a gentleman. Because I tell you to take the cloth now, you ask me too many questions. Just take it, my friend, and go. I want to close. My friend is waiting for me."

"Who's your friend?"

"Why do you want to know?"

"Because I am from Jos. Is your friend Kamel Buthros, the garage man?"

"Yes, how do you know?"

"I used to see you there," he said.

"Well, he is waiting for me."

"Okay Habib—Mr. Habib."

"Oh, oh, you know my name!"

"Yes, I know your name. Friends of mine told me about you. They suggested that I come to your store for the cloth."

I thought, *Maybe it is okay and this man has heard of me.* So I said, "All right, have a nice day. Goodbye." Then the man took his cloth and left.

The next day at about 10:00 a.m., I was sitting, having my breakfast with coffee. I watched a big sergeant come toward my store. He lifted his arm with its three stripes and saluted me. I looked at him closely. It was the man who took the piece of print the day before!

I said, "Hello, is that you?" He asked, "Do you know me?" I said, "I can't forget a face. You are a sergeant, and you didn't tell me. Sergeant of what?" He said, "Sergeant of Immigration." Oh, wow!!!

"So you are a big man," I said. "I didn't know." He assured me, "Habib, I believed you when you said that you didn't know me. You had not been to my office before I came here. Here is your £1." I told him that I did not want the £1 for the cloth. I said, "I am not taking this £1 from you, not because you tell me you are a sergeant or with the immigration office, but because it is a present from me to your wife."

Then he asked if I knew his wife! I reiterated, "I don't know you. I don't know your wife. I feel happy today, and did well in business today because I sold a lot. Is there any problem if I give you something?" He told me, "Habib, I like you, and I know you are talking from your heart. Everything you told me yesterday, I believed, and I came here to tell you I will help you for nothing." I didn't understand what he was saying, and I asked, "What do you want to help me for? What did I do? I didn't kill, I'm not a thief, I haven't done anything bad."

He said, "Yes, you have."

Startled, I replied, "What?"

I believe his name was Sergeant Armadul. He explained, "Your cousin, who was your sponsor, sent us a letter that he wants his deposit money from the Immigration Office returned to him. We got the letter to start the process. We have to deport you from this country."

I asked, "Are you serious?"

And he responded, "I am serious, Habib, and this is the letter." He showed it to me. "Your cousin wrote to the bank, asking for his money back and saying that he did not want to be responsible for you. Now, we have to write you a letter stating that you have to pay £3,000 for yourself."

I asked, "What shall I do? Can you take the money in installments?" He explained that the Immigration Office never took installment payments. But he added, "Don't worry Habib, I'm going to help you."

I said, "Will you come inside now so that we talk better? I have coffee here. Do you drink coffee?" He said, "Yes, I like coffee."

He sat down. I poured Arabic coffee in the little cups for him. He asked to see my passport. I always had it with me in a small table with a drawer, so I gave it to him. I used to put the money that I made every day in there, and then I would either hide the money and passport in the closet, or take them with me. I did not have a safe.

The next day I would take the money to the bank or send Audu to make the deposit.

Sergeant Armadul explained that he would write a letter for me. When it was ready, he would have me meet with a British officer about my immigration status. He said he would be able to change my status from needing a sponsor to being an independent businessman. I said, "Can you do that? How much will it cost?" He said, "Nothing." I agreed to the process and he called me in couple days to arrange the meeting.

He sent a soldier to take me to the Immigration Office. I had to call one of my neighbors to watch the store for me while I was gone. I met Sergeant Armadul sitting at a table in his outside office. He instructed me, "Habib, the white man is inside." He was referring to the British officer. "Go inside. Don't talk or say anything. Just give him this letter. And then whatever he says to you, respond by saying, 'Yes, sir. Yes, sir.' And then he will call me, and I will do the rest." The British ran Nigeria at the time, so my immigration had to go through the British Embassy there. The local police had responsibility for much of the immigration activities.

I sat and waited for Sergeant Armadul to tell the British officer my story. Then the officer called me in. He was a very young man. I had seen him visiting with my cousin many times, at the store and in the club. He said, "I recognize you! Aren't you Hassan's cousin? Why do you want to leave your cousin?" The officer did not know about my problem, because the Sergeant kept the letter from my cousin, and did not pass it on to him. Remembering what Sergeant Armadul told me to do, I just replied, "Yes, sir. Anything you say, sir."

He then called for the sergeant and said that he knew my cousin. The sergeant assured the officer that he had checked me out, and that I was managing a good business, and that my cousin had allowed me to open the store because he didn't want me to continue in the transport business, as I was young and afraid when traveling in the bush. Sergeant Armadul kept explaining why I would be successful. He defended my cousin and me. He expounded on the fact that my cousin was very rich and a good businessman.

The British officer asked, "So, then, do you think he's okay?" When the sergeant said yes, the officer took my passport and stamped it inside. He said, "Now, Habib, you are okay. You do not need a deposit with the bank anymore. You have a permit to stay in this country and no longer need a sponsor." He told the sergeant to write the letter to the bank to say that there was no need to have a sponsor. He instructed me to tell my cousin to withdraw his deposit with the bank.

The sergeant and I went back outside. He said, "Congratulations," and signed the papers, giving me copies. Sergeant Armadul told me I had to pay £10 as a registration fee. I paid the £10 and asked him if I could pay more—I was so happy and relieved. Sergeant Armadul chuckled and said, "Habib, just go!" I said, "Okay. God bless you." He responded, "No, God bless *you*. You are a nice man and you deserve this. We need many more people like you in this country."

I became very good friends with the sergeant after that. He always came to the store to visit, and I tried to occasionally give him gifts that I thought he would like.

Although Hassan, my cousin, knew most of what was going on in the town, he hadn't known that the police had come to close my store and send me back to Lebanon. He didn't know this because his wife had instigated it. She had someone write a letter to the bank about my status, and it was passed on to the Immigration Office.

I never said anything about this to my cousin. But one day my sergeant friend said he was going to tell Hassan what had happened to me. He wrote the letter as the British officer had requested of him, telling my cousin that he could withdraw his deposit money from the bank. He explained that I didn't need his sponsorship in the future because I had become an entrepreneur and had a permit to stay in the country.

Hassan was so surprised to get that letter! He told his wife, "You know, Fahimah, Habib did it! He is established. He has a good job with his own business." She said, "Just wait to see what is going to happen to him."

"Ah!" he replied. "*You* are the person who wrote that letter to the bank!"

She replied, "Yes, I did write it."

"Well, no matter now—calm down. I got the letter from Immigration saying that Habib can be here in his own name and have his own business. He got himself a permit. He doesn't care about what you have tried to do to him. Immigration sent me letter authorizing me to withdraw my money from the bank and not to interfere with Habib. Are you happy now?" (I learned of this conversation many years later, while talking to Hassan's son after his mother had died.)

My cousin was a friend of the man from whom I rented the store. One day, Hassan stopped by in his new car to visit his friends. I remember that it was a blue or green Hudson. At that time, cars were rationed, so you couldn't just go out and buy one. You had to apply to the government. They were American cars—Cadillac, Pontiac, Hudson—and whatever car came when you were next on the list, was what you had to buy.

Hassan came to the front of my store while I was arranging head ties and doing other work. He saw me and said, "Hello, Cousin." I said, "Hello, Cousin. Welcome." This was the first time after many months that we talked together. He said, "Are you okay?" I responded, "I am okay, with your blessing, Cousin." He said, "God bless you. You are a man. I know that God helps you."

He was so happy. We start seeing each other again. I met him someplace in the town anytime we wanted to visit. But I never again went to his house. I never ate at his house or spoke with his wife.

Business started going very well for me. I needed to find a more permanent place to live. My father had written to me, asking if he could send my second brother, Hassan, to me in Nigeria. He wanted to get my brother out of Lebanon because of the war.

I called on Sergeant Armadul, and he helped me to get Hassan a visa. I needed to rent a villa, house, or apartment. I went to a neighbor living opposite my store. They had built a very nice house for their daughters for when they got married, but the daughters were still young, and not ready to be married. They were willing to rent it to me because they knew me, and knew I would be responsible with their property. After that, I arranged for a visa for my little brother, Mohammed. He was only 12 years old when he came to live with me in Nigeria. This was in 1949. I was just 21 years old, and responsible for two of my brothers, and ownership of my fabric store.

I became good friends with the Shidiak family. They had a store opposite me, and they had a young cousin, Maroun, just about my age. He told his cousin that he wanted my store; he was jealous because I was making money. Their store was huge and they ordered special merchandise from other countries, including head ties. They ordered from Japan, India and other Eastern countries. The shipping was too expensive to order from the United States, or even London. I got very lucky with them! You wouldn't believe how much luck—and with head ties again! The African people liked brightly colored scarves that they used to tie their hair. They bought them in sets of a dozen. They didn't like white, because white head ties got dirty and they couldn't wash them, since they were made of silk.

Maroun had ordered 100 cases of silk head ties from Japan. When the shipment arrived he opened a case. It was all white! He opened another case. White, again! Maroun opened a third case and it was white, too. No one would buy them! Maroun knew I had some boxes with red ties. He called me, "Habib, would you like to buy some cases of head ties?" He didn't tell me that he opened some to discover that they were white. You see, he wanted to block, or undermine me.

Not knowing this, I said I was interested, and we agreed on a price. I said, "Okay, send me one case." He said, "No, how about buying two cases?" The accepted way of doing business was to receive, from the ship, purchased cases that were unopened, to guarantee that the goods were still intact. Maroun wanted to be present in my store when I opened the cases he sold me.

When I was ready to have Audu open a case, we called Maroun over so that he could watch. What was inside? All the head ties were red! (Remember that Maroun opened three of his cases and they were all white.) Maroun wondered, "Are you sure that this is my case?" I said, "It is your case. Look at the number, the name." After he verified it, he asked, "Can you open the other case?" The other case was on the other side of the walk. I told Audu to open it for him to see. We opened it. The head ties were all red! Maroun got *so* upset. He went back to his store to tell his father. He said, "Habib opened two cases, two cases were red." His father said to him, "Well, Habib has a clean house. Whatever he touches is good, because he is a peacemaker and a good boy. Not like you, because you have a different mind. Leave Habib alone."

Maroun said, "No, I want to open one more case." He brought one more case of his own to open. The head ties were all white. His father suggested to him, "My son, you know what you can do. Go ask Habib if he will buy all the 95 cases from you, and give him a good price or give them to him at your cost." Maroun asked, "How? I want to make money." The father said, "But if you open them, you are going to lose. Maybe Habib will buy them all."

Maroun came back to me and explained, "My father said I should sell you all 95 cases. Will you buy them?" I said, "If you give me a good price, I'll buy them." He said, "How much do you want to pay?" I said, "Half price." He said, "No, Habib. You want me to lose money!"

The cases used to cost about 100 *naira*, and each *naira* was equivalent to about one dollar. This currency is still used in Nigeria. I offered 50 *naira* for each case, and told Maroun that I would pay him in three months, after I had a chance to sell the merchandise. He wasn't satisfied, and started to argue with me, so I said, "Let's go talk to your father."

His father was an old man, sitting in his office. I explained, "Look, Papa, your son wants to sell me 95 cases, and I am telling him that I will pay half-price."

He turned to his son and said, "My son, Habib is offering you an acceptable price for the cases." He said to me, "My son has made a mistake. It is his first mistake in the trade business. He has to pay for it. Pay us as much as you feel is fair. I am not forcing you to make the purchase, and I don't want to hear tomorrow that we forced the sale."

I agreed to pay half-price and accept that it was my risk if they did not sell. I told him that I did not want his son to come and bother me. Maroun said, "No! I will agree to give you that price, but I want you to call me so that I can be there each time you open a case." I asked, "Why? When you see what is inside, it might make you sick? Do you want to go to the hospital?" (He would be very disgusted if, when I opened the cases, the colors were other than white.)

I did buy all of them. About one-third were white and two-thirds were all red. I had an idea: In the evening, when we were less busy, I called Audu, my houseboy, and asked him to open all the cases. He was very smart, and a good worker. He opened one dozen white head ties and about 10 dozen red. Just as before, in each set Audu replaced one or two red ties with one or two white ones. When the customers came to look, they saw only one or two white ties among the sets of red, so they didn't mind purchasing the set. I was able to sell them all, and I made money. I did not lose money on that deal!

I ran that store for three or four years. Business was very good. I was on a straight arrow path. There were no problems; I wasn't gambling, dancing, drinking, or with women. I was content to work hard and make myself a successful person. All during that time I was taking care of my two brothers and sending money to my parents. I would either send it with someone who was traveling to Lebanon or by cashier's check from the bank. My family was always very happy to receive the much-needed funds. Often they called to ask me to come home for a visit. But it was very difficult, because I couldn't leave the store.

On the street opposite the store, there was a family from the same town—Miziara, Lebanon—as the people from whom I rented my living quarters. This family had a store, and a little house with two bedrooms, a salon (living room), kitchen, and so forth. The father had two daughters and one son. The son went to Lebanon to school, and the two daughters stayed in Nigeria. Elizabeth was 18 and Victoria was 20 years old. I often used to visit them after closing my store in the evenings. The father, Mr. Shidiak, bought goods from the United Square Company, USC, headquartered in Jos. They imported fabrics, based on the local business people's wholesale orders. Good businessmen would order a quantity of cases of a variety of cloth every month. Because it was wholesale, only the store that made the order got that design, thus you could price it any way you wished. You could make good money with these special wholesale orders. Sometimes I would buy 50 to 80 pieces from Mr. Shidiak. He would give me a good price. That man and other townspeople liked me. They observed that I was alone, and that I was working hard and making a good name for myself. It was no longer so important that I had my rich cousin, Hassan.

I wanted to keep growing my business. By this time, two of my brothers were with me in Jos. I needed to go to Lagos to purchase goods from distributors who could provide me more varied goods for my store. I bought a Mercedes 180 so that I could make the trip each month. I always looked for Lebanese people to accompany me, because it was a long journey. I wouldn't let anyone drive my car. But I wanted the company and one, two, or three people to visit with during the trip. I used to take my gun and bullet cartridge to defend myself, since this was driving through the dangerous African bush again.

I had a friend whose son, Ahmad, was 16 years old. My friend wanted me to take his son to visit friends in Lagos. I told everyone that was going with me to be ready at 4:00 a.m. There were two other passengers, men in their 30s and 40s. One of them was a close friend; he sat in the front passenger seat. Ahmad and the other man sat in back. Ahmad had brought his double-barreled hunting gun that used birdshot. I asked why he wanted to bring his gun. I told him not to put any ammunition in it, and to put it on the floor of the car.

We drove, stopped to rest, drove some more, and stopped again. The road was unpaved gravel; it was dusty and had lots of holes. We piled out of the car, and all went into the bush to go to the bathroom. Suddenly, I heard, *Booommmm!!!*" I looked behind me. Ahmad had taken his gun, loaded it, and shot at a rhinoceros—with birdshot!!! The rhinoceros was only about 100 feet away. I looked at that young boy and yelled a common saying, "Everybody who loves Mohammed, run to the car!!" I took that boy and *threw* him into the car.

The rhinoceros was coming toward us, charging the car. We drove a little distance, and everyone started to calm down. I took a deep breath and asked Ahmad, "Why did you do that? Do you want to be spanked with your belt?"

One of the other men said that if I hadn't been there, he would have done more than that to Ahmad. He said, "Ahmad ruined my pants!" I said, "Never mind, it is only water." But he responded, "It is not only water!" We drove a little while longer and found a nice place to stop. Everyone had his suitcase with him. I told everyone who wanted to change his pants, to do so. We all went behind trees and changed our clothes. To the man who had been so scared that he had the accident, I asked, "What did you do with your pants?" He said, "I threw them away! I am going to make you pay for new pants!"

We finally got to Lagos and I met with the distributors. When we made arrangements to go back early the next day, I left Ahmad there. I told him to tell his father to send him an airline ticket so that he could get back home that way.

Once my two brothers were with me, my father asked me if I was planning to get married. But my intention was to make money, to help my brothers, and provide money for my family. I was enjoying myself, and did not want to think of women, getting married, or other responsibilities beyond what I already had. There was a European club in the town that allowed only European and Lebanese people membership. We used to go there to play golf, tennis, soccer, and to visit. We had very nice parties there, especially at Christmas and New Year's. We all paid membership fees to maintain the club.

Elizabeth was the younger of Mr. Shidiak's two girls. They lived across the street from my store, and I saw Elizabeth often in the house. We visited for dinner with their family, and played Monopoly with them in the evenings. Maroun fell in love with Elizabeth. Elizabeth didn't want him. Mrs. Shidiak asked her daughter, "Why don't you want to marry him? He is from our town. He is a businessman." Elizabeth told her mother that she didn't love Maroun. Her mother asked, "Who are you going to love? There are no young people here that are good for marriage; you would have to go back to Lebanon." Elizabeth said, "How about Habib?" Elizabeth's mother asked, "Oh, you love Habib?" Elizabeth responded, "Yes, I love Habib." But Mrs.

Shidiak said, "But Habib is Muslim, and we are Christian. It will not work." The Catholic Christians were very strict. They were Maronite Christians with very rigid beliefs.

I thought that Elizabeth was very beautiful, and a very nice girl. But I was meeting a lot of girls. When I would travel to Lagos, many times I would be invited to dinner with the man's family with whom I had just completed business. The families usually included two or three girls. People started to invite me because I was a bachelor who was successful in business. *[And he was handsome!—interjected by the author.]*

In Jos there were two or three girls whose families were interested in me. One family was Irish. The father was an engineer who worked with iron ore. They lived about 15 miles away in a small village, and came into town to visit friends of mine. One of the Irish daughters was also named Elizabeth, and she was about 18 years old. One day the Irish Elizabeth asked me to take her to the cinema. I said, "How can I take you to the cinema? I have to ask your parents." She said, "I already asked them if they would let me go to the cinema with you, and they said yes." This girl was very beautiful, too! And there was another girl, Mariam, whose father was the tradesperson who helped me get started in my store by selling me the first 20 pounds of cloth. He owned about 10 to15 stores. He was a rich man! Ahmad, who shot the rhinoceros with birdshot, was her brother.

By then I had too many girlfriends. I had about three girls interested in me in the Jos area, and another three in Lagos. I didn't know what to do—I was confused! One of the girls in Lagos was blonde, with blue eyes—very beautiful! Her father always invited me to stay at their house rather than in a hotel when I was in Lagos. It was getting so that everyone wanted me to stay at their houses. No more hotels!

I liked one of the Lagos girls. She was *very* beautiful and her father was *very* rich. I accepted invitations to stay overnight with them. One early morning, she knocked on my bedroom door while I was asleep. She opened the door, and was wearing a nightgown. I could smell the delicious Arabic coffee she had brought with her. When I opened my eyes, I could see her beautiful body. To myself, I said, "Oh, my God.

I'm scared! I don't know what to do!" It was hot in the town and I was sleeping in my underwear, not pajamas.

I didn't know what to do; I couldn't get up. She said, "Get up, let's drink the coffee together." I exclaimed, "What! Together? No, no, no—not together. You leave it here and I will put on my clothes." She said, "Never mind, never mind. We are going to be such close friends. We are going to be so, so." That meant that she was ready to be married. I thought, "Oh, my God!" I said, "No, please. Leave the tray on the table, and go away."

I could tell from her expression that she was crushed. I put my clothes on and ran away! I was about 24 years old, but I was shy. I was very naïve; most 18 or 19 years old boys knew much more than me. I was always working, and so focused on helping my parents that I didn't really go through the normal teenage years. I felt like I was being attacked by too many women. When I complained to my brothers, they laughed and said, "Marry them all!"

Elizabeth's mother came to me and said that I could have her daughter. She offered me the house and the store. That dowry sounded good to me. I thought I could ask to have her buy me a car also. I think I was more "in business" than I was "in love!" She said I only had to do one thing. I said, "What? Do you want my Citroen?" Elizabeth's mother said "No, I want you to become a Christian."

I explained, "I am a Christian; I believe in Jesus Christ. I believe in Moses; I am Jewish, and I believe in Mohammed; I am Muslim. I believe in all three. What do you want me to do?" She said that I had to go to the priest and be baptized and change my name. I told her I wanted to keep my name, so she agreed to that. I said, "Look, Mrs. Shidiak. I don't care about what religion your daughter is. I love her and I love your community."

I loved her mother and I respected her. She was a wonderful woman. They were like family to me. I helped them because her husband was not well. He was in his 60s and Mrs. Shidiak was in her 40s. They used to ask Maroun to help them, but they had forgotten him, and turned to me.

I told her, "I don't care whether your daughter wants to stay

Christian, or become Jewish or Muslim. I don't care. The religion is about God. The men who came after God are only messengers—Jesus Christ, Moses and Mohammed. God gave people brains to understand that there is a God. All religions are one. We are all human beings. We love each other, we help each other, we must be nice to each other. I don't care whether your daughter goes to church on Sunday to pray, and I go to the mosque on Friday to pray. Or we can make our church and mosque in the house and worship God every day. But to change myself, to make myself a Christian would not work for my family. How could I go to my hometown and face my father, mother, sister, cousin, and family? The whole town is Muslim. They would say, 'Because of a woman, he changed his religion, left his family and left his tradition!' I could not do that to my parents."

Even though I thought Elizabeth's mother was going to give me a car, I really wasn't so interested in that. I used to buy cars myself. I would buy all American cars in Lagos—Chryslers, Oldsmobiles, Studebakers. I would wait until the employees at the American Embassy wanted to sell their cars when they were about to move back home. I tipped the guard so that he would call me when he knew someone was leaving. I would fly to Lagos, buy the car, and drive back home. I would use it a few months, and then make good money by selling it. The Hausa men loved big cars. They had several wives and many children, and they were proud to drive big, American cars carrying their big families.

At one time, I owned a green Oldsmobile '89 Rocket. The British Queen was coming to Nigeria to give the country its independence. The chief of the town, who the citizens referred to as "King," came to me and asked to buy my car. He wanted to have that car in which to meet the Queen. I said, "It is going to be too much money for you, Mr. King." He asked how much I would sell it for. I think I bought the car for about £750; it would have been about $1,500. But I told him, "I bought this car for £3,000. It is too expensive for you." He said, "Habib, it is not too expensive. You can't tell the King that £3,000 is too much for him!" He called to his son, who was wearing a gun and gun belt with all English paper (money) in it. The boy gave the belt to his father, and the King counted £3,000, then £500. He gave me the £3,500 and said, "£3,000 and another £500 profit for you." I said, "Okay, I will accept it. If you were not the King, I would charge you £1,000 profit!" Ha, that was quite a profit!

Another time I bought a 1950 Mercury for £950. Another local king came to ask to purchase that car. I did the same thing, and said, "I bought it for £3,000 and I want £3,500 for it." He agreed and took the car. My brother exclaimed, "How could you tell them that you bought it for £3,000? You swear to them, and they believe you." I retorted, "Well, this is business! Sit down and stay out of it."

One day, about six weeks after discussing marriage with Elizabeth's mother, the mailman came to the store and said, "Mr. Fakih, you have a telegram from Lebanon." That scared my brothers and me, as telegrams usually meant someone had died or there was some other big problem. One of my brothers was near the door of the store, so I told him to take the telegram and sign for it. I took it and started reading. Then I laughed.

My brothers were surprised and waiting for hear the news. "Why are you laughing, and what is going on?" I had written to my father about all my problems with my girlfriends. In the telegram, my father told me that I had a wife already, and I was to expect her within a few weeks! My brothers exclaimed, "What!!" I said, "Yes, our father found a girl for me, and he asked for her hand in marriage for me."

The custom in our religion is that the father can do anything for his sons and daughters. For example, if my daughter wants to get married, and I like the boy and his family, I shake hands and we all agree. In our family the children respect the father, and don't say no to him. Some other families do not agree with this method. But because I loved and respected my father, I accepted that he could do anything for me, and make decisions on my behalf.

My father asked many of his friends to help find the right wife for me. He told them that he needed to find a wife for me because I had too many girls interested in me, and he was scared that it wouldn't be a good decision. He found a girl that was very close to his work, from the same town, same religion, and the daughter of a good friend. He discussed this girl with my mother, my aunt, and the whole family. They all thought that she was a good choice.

My father understood me, and would try to make a good decision for me. I always gave him my full respect, exactly like how Said treats me. I never shouted, got upset, or said no to him in my whole life. Maybe it was because I lived away from him so much of the time. When I came to visit from Palestine or Nigeria, we treated each other more like close friends. I treated him like a god. I respected him when he spoke, when he wanted to do activities. When he wanted to smoke his hubbly-bubbly, I always offered to help him—but he said he liked to do it. When I was in my pajamas and my mother needed something from the store, I offered to get dressed and go get the supplies. But my father said, "No, I will get it." He was quicker to get dressed than me!

There were few telephones at the time, and it had taken almost a week to get the wire, so, from the telegram, it sounded like my wife would be coming very soon. My brothers said, "How can our father do this?" I told them that he could do anything he wanted, and that I trusted him. But I did insist that my brothers not tell anyone about it. Not friends, other people we worked with, my cousin—and especially not our neighbors, the Shidiaks. I didn't want them to take my house away, and they were still cooking food for us. I didn't want that to stop, until I was sure that this marriage was going to occur. I was happy because of what my father had arranged. But I was scared and confused about what I should do regarding all the families in Nigeria who were hoping for their daughters' marriage to me.

In planning for the marriage, I realized that this woman that I would be marrying would probably be coming by plane to Kano. It was 350 miles away, and the only other international airport in Nigeria, other than Lagos, was 800 miles away. I needed to buy a car, because I had just sold my Citroen. I hadn't had a car for a couple weeks. I mentioned to my brother, "We have a problem. Suppose it is true that my bride is really going to come in a few weeks and I don't have a car." I decided that I had to get ready to buy a car. I could not borrow my friend's car, because I would need it for one week—350 miles going and 350 miles returning.

I was lucky once again. I went to the hotel that my friends owned, and sat with the son, Shoui, at the bar. Shoui took over for his father as the barman sometimes. I ordered a beer and chatted with him. He asked me, "Habib, do you have a car?" I said, "No, I am looking for one. Do you have one?" He continued, "No, but there is an American army major who wants to sell his car before he leaves the country." I asked, "Where is it?" and he pointed me outside.

I went outside and saw that it was a 1950 or 1951 Chevrolet, painted army olive green. It had a stick shift on the steering column. It was in good condition. I said, "Where is the man, Shoui?" He said, "He is over there, speaking with friends." I said, "Did he tell you how much he wants for it?" Shoui said that he wanted £500.

I went up to the man and greeted him. I asked, "Can I talk to you, sir?" He said yes and got up from the table, and we sat down at another table.

"Shoui told me that you want to sell your car. How much do you want for it?"

The man said, "£500."

I asked if he would accept any less, or if the car needed any repairs. He said, "Look, I am not going to accept less for it. If you want it, you buy it and do what you want with it. It is running in good condition. It belongs to the army—it is not my personal car. The army instructed me to sell it because it would cost too much money to transport it across the country and then ship it back to America. If you are ready to buy, I will sell it to you. If you are not ready, I will sell it to someone else here."

I said, "I am ready."

I took my checkbook and wrote the check. He asked, "Do I know you?" I said, "No, you don't know me, but will you believe Shoui, the barman?" He said, "Yes, of course, he is my friend." I said, "Then ask him." The man was holding my check and he shouted, "Shoui, is this check good?" Shoui responded, "It is guaranteed to be good, Habib is a responsible person." The man said, "Okay, here is the key."

I said, "Hey, wait a minute. Give me a paper or something! Do you want the army to take me to jail?" He said, "Okay." He gave me a paper and a small note that had his name—something like Colonel Jones—on it, and he started to write that he sold the car to me. He said, "What's your name?" I said, "Habib Fakih." He said, "What is it?" I repeated, loudly, "Fakih." He said, "Don't you have another name?" I said, "No, that's my name." He asked, "Is that a respected name?" I said, "Oh yes. In my country it is very good—like a king in your country." He said, "Oh, okay. How do you write it?"

I got the ownership papers for the car and directly took it down the road to the French garage, ESCOA. I knew the manager, mechanic and the painter there. We were friends, and sometimes met in the club, and occasionally played tennis and football together. I wanted to change the color of the car. They teased, "Oh, we thought you were a general in the army now!"

We went into their office and I looked through the sample books. I selected a maroon color for the roof, and a cream color for the body. They thought that combination would look nice. I asked how long it would take, and they said, "One week." I said, "Can you make it earlier?" They said, "Why are you so much in a rush?" I told them that my bride was expected very shortly. "Please keep it a secret," I added. "I don't know yet ..."

They said, "Don't worry, if it is not ready we will lend you our car." I asked what kind of car it was, and the owner showed me his pickup. I exclaimed, "Do you want me to go get my new wife with this thing!" We all laughed. I left them and went back to work. I told Hassan and Mohammed that I bought a car. They asked, "If you bought a car, why is it in the garage?" I explained that I had taken it there only for a paint job; the car was army green.

We started to make some money. I was very busy teaching my brothers all the aspects of the business. That month was the longest month since I had been in Africa! We hadn't received another telegram, or any other communication from my family. We were all waiting to meet my bride. This was in April of 1954. Even though it cost more money to send a lengthy telegram, I finally got the information explaining my new wife's arrival plans in the early morning, 6:00 a.m., at the Kano airport in less than a week. Even though it cost my family more money because the telegram was long, my bride was worth it!!

After the telegram arrived, I did get a letter from my father with my bride's picture. He explained who her family was. When I read that, I remembered that I did know who she was. When I was very young, about ten years old, my father would ask me to go get some water for his hubbly-bubbly. I had to walk by an alley on the way to the store, very close to her house. The commercial water was much farther away, but behind a gate at her house was her family's water tank. Her father was a friend of my father, and let us use the water tank. But she and her older sister used to follow me with a stick and shout at me. I would start to go after them, and they would run away. She was just a little kid, probably about four or five years old at the time. I found out later that she did not remember me. She only knew my younger brothers because they all grew up in the same area.

I picked up the newly painted car from the garage. It was very beautiful—a good car. My cousin, Hassan, was jealous of me. Hassan was very rich, and liked to spend money on cars and women. My two brothers would visit him occasionally. One time they came back saying that Hassan had said, "Ask your brother if he wants to sell the car. I will pay him £1,000." He still didn't know that I was getting married. We were all still keeping it a secret. With the cost of painting, I had about £600 into the car. My brothers told Hassan that they didn't know how much the car cost me, and didn't know if I would be willing to sell it. I had taught my brothers to not talk about our business with anyone. When I drove that car around town, people remarked, "How did Habib get that fancy car? It is a very beautiful car." They assumed it cost a lot of money because it was an American car and they knew it had to be transported through Russia at that time.

Elizabeth—the girl I liked, was part of the family who owned the house I was renting, admired the car. She talked to me about it. I was uncomfortable because I was talking with her, even though I had received the letter about my new bride. But I didn't know my new bride, how she acted, how tall she was, whether we would get along. I was anxious and worried. There were so many questions and unknown things. Normally in Lebanon, the family and mother help her son get ready for a new bride. But my brothers and I had to do it alone. People in the town were curious about why I was buying furniture and pictures for the house, and why my brothers and I were cleaning it so well. We had to do this because my new bride did not have experience away from her house, and our parents were not there to help. In Lebanon, in those days, the girls stayed close to home and took care of the house and family. They did not even go to the cities very often.

My bride had completed elementary school. Usually only girls of rich families could go to school. This was a problem in our country. Schooling for girls was not prohibited, but the additional cost of books, clothes, and supplies were too much for most middle-class and poor families. They could only afford for the boys to attend school. The girls would also have to be taken and brought back every day by one of their older brothers, or the men in the family—whereas the boys could come and go without an escort. The boys had government-paid schooling, and only had to pay for books and clothing.

Then it was time to prepare for the 350-mile trip to the Kano airport. I put spare gas and oil in the car and some food. I took Audu, the boy who worked in my store, with me—in case something happened to the car.

We had driven quite a ways on our trip, when suddenly I saw some water covering the road that I could not avoid. I started through it, but my car fell into a large hole that I couldn't see. I heard something crack. I stopped by the side of the road and discovered that the car was listing to one side. A spring had broken and was missing somewhere in the water. I was telling Audu about the spring, and a truck pulled up on the side of the road next to me. The driver asked what was going on, and I told him about the spring. He jacked the car up. I said to him, "Do you have a machete?" He said yes, and I told Audu to go cut a piece of strong, green wood. We connected the spring and the wood, and then tied the spring back onto the car with pieces of rope that the truck driver offered. We took the car down off the jack, and it worked fine!

Audu said, "Oh, Master, you have lots of sense! You are 'Zaki! Zaki,' you did very well." ("Zaki" is "lion" in the Hausa language. The Hausas referred to every white man as zaki, because white men had the political power in Nigeria at that time.) I gave a few pounds to the truck driver for helping, and we drove the rest of the way to our hotel. I unpacked and then went back down to look at the car. It was just as we had repaired it, with no problems. Audu said, "Master, it is good to drive back with." But I told him, "No, we are going to take it to the garage tomorrow to fix it. I can't trust it with my new bride."

There was a lot of time between when we arrived and 6:00 a.m. the next morning, when my new bride was to arrive. I was very nervous. I thought to myself, "What should I do? I have lots of friends in the town." I hadn't called them ahead of time because it was too expensive, and I didn't really want to talk to them, because I didn't want to tell anyone yet about my new bride.

I gave some money to Audu so he could go see some of his relatives in the town, but told him to come back to the hotel in the morning. I went to the hotel restaurant for dinner. I told the hotel manager to wake me up by 4:00 a.m. That night was the longest night of my life. I couldn't sleep! I got up and sat down. I saw the Koran and a Bible on the table, and read a little. Maybe I napped a little. Then the telephone rang, and the manager said, "It's 4:00 a.m., sir." I said, "Okay, thank you. Please make me a cup of coffee." Then I took a cold bath to wake me up.

I went to the restaurant and had my coffee. I left the hotel at 5:00 a.m. to go to the airport. I went into the area where the people wait to meet the passengers. I saw a sergeant at the gate. We could not go past the gate to the customs area. We had to wait behind the gate until the passengers went through customs. I gave him £2 and said, "Look, Sergeant. Today I should have the right to go in any area of the airport." He said, "Why?" I explained, "Because my new wife is coming on that plane, and believe it or not, I don't know her and she doesn't know me! All I have is this photo." I showed him the photo. He laughed and said, "Okay. What is your name?" I told him, and he said, "Okay, Habib. Ten or fifteen minutes before the plane comes, I will take you so that you can watch for your wife. You sit down right here for now." I said, "Thank you."

A little later, the sergeant came to me and told me that the plane was close. "Come with me now, let's go," he said. He took me even as far as the open veranda area! He said, "Enjoy yourself. When you see her, let me know so that I can say hello and good luck." He told his policemen, "Leave that man alone. He is a VIP—a very important man." I laugh when I remember that.

I was waiting for the plane to land. Believe it or not, the pilot was from my town in Lebanon, and I knew him through my cousins, but I didn't know he would be flying the plane. Also, there was a woman from my town on the plane. She lived in Lagos at the time, and she knew me. She used to invite me to lunch, and I visited with her family many times when I was in Lagos. My father knew her family also, and when she was in Lebanon, my father said to her, "I want to trust you with my son's bride. Do you know Habib?" She said, "Of course I know Habib. Habib is our friend." My father explained, "Well, he does not know his new wife. He only knows to expect her; that she is coming. Please, when you arrive, introduce his new wife to him. Please help them to meet each other." She exclaimed, "What a wonderful time this is going to be!"

The propeller jet plane landed about 50 yards away in the bright, early morning sunshine. The people started deplaning. I kept looking at them: *This one? No, not that one. This one? No, not that one. This one? No, not that one.* I saw one red-haired woman—good-looking, tall, with a nice figure. A short woman with black hair was with her. I thought, *Maybe that one? But no, she must be European.* I kept talking to myself. *What is a European doing in Lebanon then coming to Kano?* I looked past them, continuing to look at the people coming off the airplane, and still thinking, *She? Not her. She? Not her.*

Suddenly I heard someone say, "Hello, Habib." I turned and saw the lady I knew from Lagos, and the red-haired woman. They had come up behind me! I said, "Hello. How are you? Who is this lady with you?" She said, "This is your new wife, Siham!" I exclaimed, "Oh, that's my wife? Oh, thank you, Allah!!"

I said to my new wife, "Come on, wife." The lady said, "Where are you going?" I responded, "I am taking my wife. What do you want me for? Thank you for your help." She said, "No, no, no. You have to find me transport to go to my husband in Lagos. We have to find out what time the local plane leaves Kano for Lagos." I said, "Okay." I went over to the sergeant and he said, "Did you get your wife?" I said, "Yes, and this is another tip for you." When he asked what it was for, I asked him to take care of the other woman and get her on a plane to Lagos. He said, "Don't worry. You take your new wife and go." We went to get her luggage. She had a big suitcase and a smaller one.

We went back to the airport hotel. We got to the room and I called room service to bring breakfast—a big tray of tea, fried eggs, potatoes, cheese, and toasted bread. But this was not Lebanese food. My wife looked at it, and said, "What is that?" I said, "This is breakfast." She said, "No, no, no. I don't eat other people's food. I brought my food with me." I said, "Really? But this is breakfast." She asked, "Do you eat this kind of breakfast?" I responded, "Yes, this is the only kind of food I have been eating for a long time." She said, "No way!" and went to the small suitcase. She pulled out half a dozen boiled eggs, boiled potatoes, fried snapper fish, onions and Lebanese bread. (Siham disagrees with me, but I remember well!!) So she ate her food and I ate the food from the hotel!

I called the garage to have the spring fixed. The mechanic came to the hotel, picked up the car keys, and drove my car to the garage for the repair. It was ready in a few hours. Siham and I walked around the town, starting to get to know each other. She had been on the plane during the night and looked tired. We slept one night in the hotel. The next day I said, "How about if we stay here for a few more days?" Siham replied, "No, no. Let's go to the house. I don't like to stay in hotels. I don't enjoy it." I said, "But we have to have a honeymoon!" She responded, "We can have the honeymoon down there. What kind of honeymoon? I don't eat honey! I don't like honey!"

We prepared to go home. I paid the hotel and we started the long trip to Jos. We left in the morning and arrived in Jos in the afternoon. Hassan and Mohammed had closed the store and were sitting on the veranda drinking coffee. When they saw my car and Siham, they were surprised. They knew Siham from Nabatieh because they were closer to her age, and I left the town when she was so young. We all caught up on the news of our families and friends. The other people in the town were surprised. Elizabeth asked, "Who is this?" Hassan explained, "I am sorry to tell you, but our father found a wife for Habib, and sent her to him. He picked her up at the Kano airport."

Elizabeth said, "Just like that? You didn't tell anybody?"

Hassan said, "Daddy did not tell us. He sent a telegram and told Habib to go to the airport to meet someone. Habib called us from the airport to tell us, but we had no time to tell anyone." Then the news spread throughout the town. They said, "Oh, Habib got a very nice wife. Blonde-red hair, tall—very beautiful." Everybody came to meet Siham, and she was the talk of the town!

There were a few hundred families in the town—mostly Lebanese, Christian and Muslim. We were all like brothers, or very good friends. If someone got married, everybody came to the celebration. If someone died, everyone went to extend their sympathies. If anything happened, everyone participated. You can imagine that when they heard, "Habib has a wife," they all had to come say hello and meet her. My brothers got all kinds of drinks and chocolate for the guests. Siham had also brought sweets from Lebanon. That was our celebration. We didn't have a wedding ceremony in Nigeria.

Back in my hometown, my family had a celebration that lasted six days, but without Siham and me. It was traditional for the wedding celebration to last six nights, with lots of food, coffee, tea, dancing and visiting. People would come and go all the time. In Jos, everyone came to congratulate us —except my cousin, Hassan. His wife would not let him come. This was especially surprising, as Hassan's wife was related to my wife. Her grandmother was the wife of Siham's grandfather, because he had had two wives.

Time passed easily for us. I had to watch my step. I was embarrassed to visit Elizabeth's family. When I would go to Lagos to shop,

I stayed away from the people who had expected me to marry their daughters. By this time, Siham was pregnant with Elham, our first child. I started to make some good money and did things on the weekends with my Egyptian friend, Kamel. I got to know many of the rich people, making connections for the business.

Kamel and his friend Isaac liked to gamble. One day I was visiting them, and an Italian, the last person for a poker foursome they had arranged, did not show up. He had called, saying that he had to take his wife out to dance, and that he would be late. (They went out together on Saturday, European-style). Kamel did not want to wait for him, so they suggested that I take his chair. I said, "I don't know how to play." They said, "Okay, we will give you capital to start playing. Everyone will give you £10 and that way we can complete the foursome." I said, "Okay, if everyone is going to give me their money, I will play."

I was so happy during that time. My first child was a daughter, Elham, even though I was expecting a boy. It is a tradition in our country that we hope for a first-born boy, but my daughter was so smart, just like my future granddaughter Summer. Elham was just a few months old, and I would say to her, "Ha, ha!" My daughter would smile and respond, "Ha, ha." I would play with her.

My brothers were happy in Jos; we were beginning to make money. We started doing some wholesale business. Small traders came to us, just like I had started in the business. They would buy £100 of merchandise from me, then £200, and work up to £500. Some Lebanese ordered £1000 on credit, each week paying £200 or £300. Many African people were very trustworthy in their business dealings with me. They came 100 miles from the bush, and picked up £100 or £200 in cloth. After four or five times, I extended them credit too, for two weeks to a month.

I thought it was time for Hassan, my youngest brother, to open his own business in Maiduguri. I was familiar with Maiduguri, and knew that the people needed the goods that I had, because it was where I stayed when I was in the transport business hauling goods to eastern Nigeria. I went to Maiduguri and rented a shop and house for Hassan. I supplied him with the goods, and this extended my business. My younger brother, Mo (Mohammed) stayed with me in the store in Jos.

By the time my second girl, Lila, was born, I was a little bored, looking for other interests. I had some money because of the store's success. I was always meeting with the traders and my other connections in the store. Traders and other business people gathered on Sundays when the businesses were closed. Men would slaughter a sheep, make lots of food, and open their houses for their friends to visit. For example, there was an old man who did this and invited me to join them. I started to gamble with his rich friends. It was not good. I left my wife working at the store. She had learned the business and she was able to speak the local languages. We had an African nanny who came each morning for the kids. We also hired a cook and an African boy who did the cleaning and washed the clothes. I hired a driver to take Mama around to visit her friends. We had to live like other people with whom we were doing business. It was not good to be higher or lower in social status than they were.

One day my brother arrived back from Maiduguri with the goods that I had sent with him to open his store. He had arranged the cloth on the shelves, tried to sell the stock, and then packed it up and brought it back after only a month! I asked, "Why did you do that?" "Because," he said, "There are no sales. I am alone and I am fed up, so I brought all your goods back." We were a little short. He had put the African boys that were helping him in the back of the truck with the goods. Only God knows what they did with that cloth!

So we lost a little bit of money, but I said, "It's okay, that is not a problem." We found another location for Hassan in the town of Jos so that he could have his own business.

By now we had our third girl, Olla. This was about 1957. Things were getting bad because of my gambling. A Syrian customer, Fakri started coming into the store. He was a small man, married to a native woman who was very large. She was at least three times bigger than him! He started buying cloth from me, first for £1,000 that he paid. The next time, he took £1,500 worth and paid £1,000, came back for

£2,000 worth, paying £1,500. He kept growing, buying cloth valued at £3,000, paying me £2,000, and so on. One day he reached the £5,000 level. When the imported goods arrived in Nigeria, I would go to Lagos and spend £10,000 to £20,000 on cloth. The people knew me and would give me credit for a month. I had the goods shipped by railway to Jos. My own capital was about £7,000 or £8,000; that is how much I owned outright. The rest was on credit—money of other businesspeople who trusted me.

After a few months, Fakri's account had reached about £14,000. Then he broke his leg in a car accident and was in the hospital. I was so scared when I found out about that. His wife was taking care of the business. He was a good and honest man—but she was very strong, and there was a rumor that when they fought, she would beat him up. I went to visit him in the hospital. He had a cast on his leg. He assured me that he was going to be fine, and that I shouldn't worry about the business.

Two or three days later, my brother came to tell me, "Bad news, Brother. The wife of your friend, Fakri, cleaned out their store and ran away with the goods. She took a truck to the store in the middle of the night and loaded it with all the cloth." She fled to the north of Nigeria—almost 1,000 miles away. It was very easy to hide there, as it was big, undeveloped, and isolated. For myself, I put my hand on my head and thought, "Oh, all my profit and what I owe other people!"

I went to see Fakri. He was crying, and said, "Don't worry, Habib, I will go find her, bring her back, and bring the money." I asked, "Do you have any money in the bank?" He said, "No, I have nothing in the bank. I had money hidden in the house, but she took it all, as well as the children, and everything else. Oh, I'm not going to see my children."

I shouted, "Never mind your children! What about my money?"

He said, "Habib, don't be afraid." Within one week he had called the police. But she was like salt put in water. It would be impossible to find her. She was gone! I liked Fakri so much. He was a nice, good man. But I could not have imagined what actually happened, and that his wife would take off with the goods. Normally, a wife would sit near her husband and take care of him if he was injured or sick.

Lebanon. I planned to send Siham and the three girls to Nabatieh with him, because business was bad, and I needed to work with the trucks.

I also had fought with the people with whom I was gambling. We were always borrowing money from each other to stay in the game. One day I had only £50 and we went two or three rounds. We had been drinking whiskey and eating, so we didn't know what we were doing. I asked a rich transporter, Hassan, who was about 10 or 15 years older than me, and was playing with us, to lend me some money. I had loaned him money many times. He responded, "Oh, Habib, if you are coming to gamble, why don't you bring enough money with you?"

I had never criticized Hassan when he needed loans in the past. I was wearing new shoes, and they were a little tight, so I had taken them off under the table. I looked at him. I took one of my new shoes and put it on the table on top of the cards, and shouted, "All of you: You always borrow from that shoe. Now, when I ask you to lend me money, you tell me I have to bring more money! You stupid people!" And then I said a *bad word*! I took the shoe off of the table, put my foot back in it, and got up from the table.

They yelled, "Habib, don't be upset. We are just joking with you." I lifted the edge of the table and flipped it over. They started to talk nicely to me. I started to forgive them and forget; to warm up to them again. They wanted me because they wanted to get all my money. They didn't want to lose me. The rest of the men started to yell at Hassan, "Why did you tell him that?" Then the situation became big in my mind. I said, "Get out, all of you, from my sight." We were sitting on the second floor of the house. I started to go down the stairs, and they followed me. They yelled after me, "Take anything you want!" They started to take money from their pockets. I yelled back, "I will never come back to this house, and I will never gamble again!" And from that day forward, I have never gambled, and that was 1959!

We had moved to another house, very close to the building that housed the local cinema. I was managing the transport business with just two trucks, shipping goods to Fort Lamy. It was a very small business. In comparison, Hassan, my cousin, had about 20 trucks. The French manager of ESCOA was so kind to me. He said, "Habib, you send the trucks and whatever they make, we will give you half in cash." Each month we would earn £1,000 or £2,000, and they would take half and give me half. Each time they gave me the money, I would pay down some debts, and just keep enough for expenses.

My cousin never tried to help me. He was so happy to see me in this position. He knew about my gambling. He gambled too; he was the one that taught me. There were people that were good, and did not gamble or party. But Hassan is the one who showed me to "enjoy life." I learned it from him. He used to go out, gambling and partying. I tried to be like Hassan—better than Hassan. I wanted to show him that I could make more money than him, and be more independently successful than him. I would have succeeded if Fakri had not broken his leg and caused me to lose the £14,000.

I used to keep my money with me in the house, not in the bank. I gave Siham £2,000 or £3,000 to keep in a locked cupboard for emergencies. She also had jewelry in the house, worth about £4,000— which was a lot at the time. By now, the mother of my cousin, Hassan, was dead, and we were friendly with him again. But I never again did business with him. One day, Siham returned from visiting them, and discovered that the cupboard had been broken into. The money and jewelry were gone! I told my wife, "Don't worry, we make the money; the money doesn't make us."

Hassan, my cousin, was preparing for a visit to Lebanon. His mother, my aunt, had died, and he wanted to check on the family affairs. I had asked if I could send Siham and the children back with him. Things were not so good with us at the time. I was too tired of worrying about the family and maintaining my status in the community. I started questioning myself, "Why did I do that? Why did this happen? Why did the man get a broken leg and myself have a big problem? Why does this always happen to me?" I started drinking too much beer, whiskey or brandy—but not enough to lose my mind. I was so discouraged after Siham left. I said to myself, *This is not going to happen*. After a few months, I started worrying about Siham and the kids. I got a visa and made plans to go back to Lebanon. I left my two brothers, Mohammed and Hassan, to take care of the business. It was slow during that time, because it was the rainy season.

My family was so surprised and happy when I arrived home in Lebanon. My whole family was living with my parents in a three-bedroom house with a kitchen, sitting room and bathroom. It had a veranda and small garden on the side. Suad was born there, in Lebanon. I stayed one month after her birth, then I left for Sierra Leone, and I let God take care of my family. When I returned almost a year later, Suad was walking when I greeted my family at the airport.

While visiting the family, I learned that Hesniyeh, my youngest sister, and the sixth of my parents' seven children, had married a man from a nearby town. He was over 50 years old—very old for her—and sick. She was young—18 or 19 years old. He bluffed my family, telling them that Sierra Leone was very close to Nigeria. "It is a few hours by car." It is not—it is a few hours by plane!

Hesniyeh wanted to marry him, because she thought she would be happy only being a few hours from her three brothers living in Nigeria. She had been gone almost a year, and my mother was crying as she explained to me that she had not ever heard from her daughter during that time. There were no telephone calls, no letters, no communication. I was going to spend another month in Lebanon, but changed my plans to go to Sierra Leone to find Hesniyeh on my way back to Nigeria. I went to the British Embassy to get a visa to be able to enter Sierra Leone and visit for a couple months. There was no problem—they gave me a visa for a three-month visit.

As soon as I arrived, I discovered that my wife's sister and her husband, Zahed, who I did not previously know, lived in the same town as my sister! They wanted me to stay and visit them. I agreed that I would stay with my sister for a few days, and then stay with them.

When I first saw Hesniyeh, I realized that my family had done something very stupid for my sister. She was very young and beautiful—a nice, good, handsome girl. Her husband was very old—a little bit ugly—and was controlled by his older sister. I asked her, "Why did you marry him? For the money—because he is rich?"

She responded, "No, my brother. I married him because he said he was living in Sierra Leone, and I wanted to live near you."

I said, "Do you know how many hours by plane? If you come by sea, it takes two or three days." She said, "Well, okay. But that is how it happened." After I had been there two or three days, I told Hesniyeh, "I am not going to let you stay here. I don't like the looks of that man." I went back to my brother-in-law's home. Zahed ran a pharmacy that sold medicine. He and my sister-in-law were so nice. They told me more about Hesniyeh's husband. He had been married twice before. One girl was a virgin, but he could not consummate the marriage; he had been living in Africa and had relations with African women resulting in various diseases.

I was so upset. I had gone to Sierra Leone because I was worried. Then more problems became apparent in the situation with my sister. I forgot my family and myself. I needed to take care of my sister. I equated her to a candle; she was beaten down and was going to melt. After one week, I went to her husband. I said, "Look, you have to divorce my sister. My sister is not suited to you, and you do not fit with her." Especially at that time, divorce was not common. In a divorce the original marriage dowry stays with the wife, if the man initiates the divorce. But if the woman wants the divorce, she leaves with nothing. Marriage is just like a contract.

The dowry was 1,000 Lebanese dollars in advance, and was to be 5,000 Lebanese dollars later. He also gave her some jewelry. But he didn't buy the jewelry—it was originally given to his first wife, then his second wife, and now my sister, his third wife. I continued, "Look, we don't want anything, just the divorce. And I will pay you for her transport back home to Lebanon."

He did not agree to the arrangement. I went back and discussed the problem with my brother-in-law. He said, "I can show you one way. It is the only way that you can guarantee that he will divorce your sister." I exclaimed, "For God's sake, tell me! What is it?" He said, "I don't know if you can do it." I replied, "I can do it – I will do anything!" Zahed explained, "Hesniyeh's husband loves his older sister, and she controls him. If she tells him to divorce, he will do it. If she tells him not to do anything, he will not divorce your sister."

I asked, "So what shall I do about his sister—go beat her up?" He said, "No, no, no, no, no. Their houses are right next to each other and the windows face each other on one side. They can hear each other talking in the houses. Go to Hesniyeh and talk to her about the controlling sister, so that she will overhear the conversation. Don't say anything about sex, but say things that would hurt the sister's feelings."

I went back to Hesniyeh's house and discovered her crying. I said, "What is wrong? Why are you crying?" She answered, "My husband is accusing me of keeping his money from his onion sales and giving it to you." Her husband was in the produce business, selling onions, potatoes, and other vegetables. I said, "You sell bags of onions for £5 or £6—what is that amount of money going to do for me? That is so cheap—so cheap, like his sister! Don't blame him. He is so cheap like his sister. His sister married a rich man and he died and left her a house and money. They are afraid to be poor and have to beg people for food. That's why they act like that. Don't mind them. They are poor people. They have less quality—they are low and cheap. They are not rich, and had not had money before. Now they get some money and they want to hold on tight to it. You come from a good family. You remember how much money I sent to you from Africa— how many good dresses you bought? All the money those people have cannot buy one dress of your wardrobe. Why are you worried, my sister? Don't listen to them. They are like slaves to you."

Hesniyeh whispered to me, "Shhh, they will hear you."

I whispered back, "I want them to hear me—go along with it." I continued out loud, "Sister, are you happy with these people? How do you manage to be happy? How do you have an appetite to eat their bread and food, looking at their faces? I nearly vomited the first time I saw your husband's sister!" And then I left the house.

The next day, the controlling sister sent someone to where I was staying, telling me to come and take my sister. It took only one time for our plan to work!

The following day, I went to the priest of the mosque, to discuss the divorce. The priest tried to discourage us from pursuing the divorce, reminding us that, although it is allowed, God does not want people to divorce. I explained that my sister was very young and from a good family, and her husband was very old and greedy. The priest asked, "Is there no other way to resolve this?" I responded that there was no other way. Her husband agreed, "I don't want her again, I don't want her again!"

The priest finalized the divorce and said, "Your sister is now divorced from this man. She can go with you." Her husband said, "I don't want to give her anything. She just has to go." I said, "Okay." The priest said, "This is no good. The gold, the clothing belongs to her. You stayed with her long enough that those things belong to her. You slept with her. That is what she is due." I interrupted and said to the priest, "I don't want anything from him, not even a little gold symbol of the Koran that I gave her." I said to Hesniyeh, "Leave it to him. We don't want it."

We got the divorce papers and the priest said, "Do you want to say anything, Habib?" I replied, "Yes. I thank God because we were in a hole of shit and now we can get out and clean ourselves!" The priest was startled and said, "Habib, you didn't say that!" I reiterated, "No, I did say that. I am so happy! My sister—we are free from the shit!" Then I went to Hesniyeh, sitting in one area with the women, and said, "Congratulations!" I took her to the airport, bought a ticket for her trip to Lebanon, and saw her off. This was in about 1959.

While I was in Sierra Leone, Mohammed and Hassan continued to live in the house in Nigeria. Hassan had developed a successful fabric business. Mo had met some Americans in the supermarket business in Port Harcourt, and was working with them. He was trying to find a way to go to the United States, and eventually immigrated to Chicago. Meanwhile, there was a man who had been in love with Hesniyeh before her marriage to the old man, but he did not have much money. My parents had given Hesniyeh to the silly, old, rich man instead. The first man was still in love with her, and as soon as she arrived back in Lebanon, he asked to marry her. I told my parents that I liked this man and thought she should marry him, and they agreed. She has been happy ever since, and they had two boys and two girls over the years. She lives in Beirut City. I visit her each year when I visit Lebanon. I finally rested, once my sister was settled and happy with a new husband.

I wanted to get back to Nigeria and my businesses. But I didn't have any money. I had spent three to four months in Sierra Leone. I was being reported to the Immigration Office, because my visa had just run out. A friend of mine from my hometown in Lebanon was good friends with the Immigration official, so I met him and discussed the problem. Also, his wife was the same age as Siham, and they knew each other when living in Lebanon. In fact, they were from the same family. Siham's sister was a very good friend of this woman.

I asked my brother-in-law, Zahed, if he could lend me about £100 or £200 so that I could take a ship to Nigeria, or take the plane that went once a week. But Zahed told me that he had to buy a small truck to transport supplies for his business. He had a store that was like a pharmacy, but sold native medicines, herbal remedies, and "over the counter" drugs that did not require doctors' prescriptions. I told him that I had worked with trucks in my transport jobs, and described my fabric store businesses to him. Zahed told me that he had bought a 1950s model truck because he had a long-time African servant whose brother was a driver and knew all the cities and villages in the area. The African was working for Zahed as a transporter for supplies and construction materials that the outlying towns needed, in addition to pharmaceuticals.

He said that I could earn the money by using his truck to do the transporting for a couple months. We would split everything 50:50. If I still wanted to go back to Nigeria after that, then I could go. Siham's sister wanted me to stay in Sierra Leone because if I stayed she knew Siham would join me with the children, and she would be close to her sister. So I decided to study the area in Sierra Leone and see if I could make a business there. Also, I really didn't want to go back to Nigeria where everyone had known me as a successful businessperson, then watched me as I lost all my businesses. I didn't want to go visit all my friends to whom I had been equal before I lost the money. I had left my brothers to work in their businesses, and

I didn't want them taking care of me, because I had been used to taking care of them. It felt to me like a person who is swimming and gets tired. He wants to hold onto something to rest. If he sees a bit of dry grass, he wants to hold it in his hand just to get rest, even though it might not make him last longer.

I agreed to do the job for Zahed and started the next day. I took his truck with the driver, we loaded, and took a road outside of town that I was not familiar with. I was sitting next to the driver in the passenger seat, and he started to complain about the procedure for the loading operations. I told him to leave and give me the money that he had for trip expenses. He said, "No, this money is mine." I replied, "Okay, it is yours." I didn't want to fight the man, as I was under his direction and only he knew the area. I didn't know what he knew. I tried to be so nice to him for the rest of the trip.

When we came back, I told my brother-in-law that he was taking money, £5 or £10, enough to pay for the motor oil for each trip. Zahed called the man in but he denied my story. He said, "There was very little money." I said to my brother-in-law, "I will tell you a secret. He might do something to me on the road now that I accused him of cheating you. I don't know. I am not going with him anymore." Zahed said, "No, you take the truck. I will send the African away because he was cheating me all this time." The driver's sister (the family servant) begged my in-laws to take him back and promised that he would do whatever they requested, and give them all the money due. I agreed to work with him again and said, "Okay, never mind. If you want to bring him back, bring him. I will not be afraid of him. I will watch him." We worked for one month, and made some good money.

One day we loaded the truck and were driving to an area that was about 200 miles away on rough roads. We heard some noise coming from the engine. We stopped at a village, opened the hood and found that there was no oil, the pistons were worn, and the engine was smoking.

"What is that, Master? What do we have to do?" asked the driver. I said, "The engine is spoiled. We have to fix the engine." You see, I had experience from my other transport jobs in the bush. Experience is good, even if you don't make money. But if you have experience

That is why they say to never marry outside your own people. It causes problems. Your family and your own people will always take better care of you than people from the outside.

The rest of the traders were smaller, but I always tried to get all my money from them. One time one of the Africans who had a £2,000 account did not show up at the store when I thought he should. I decided to get my money, so I made the long trip to his village, which was about 500 miles away. That area was very hot and dry. The ground was cracked, with ants crawling out of the cracks. The people there were all very short, with charcoal-black skin. They lived in grass houses that had "basements" dug out of the ground underneath, so they could stay cool. When I found the man, he invited me into his house. It was over 100 degrees outside, but it was very cold in his underground room.

I said, "What's wrong? Why haven't you come to pay me and get more cloth?" He replied, "Master, did you think I was running away? I couldn't come because I was so sick." He immediately got up and brought me the money that he owed me. Then he fried a chicken and brought it to me. I ate the chicken. He offered water, but I had water and beer in the car. I left for the long journey back to Jos. It took about 10 hours driving, each way, just to collect that money. I never lost a penny doing business with the Africans.

Because of Fakri's accident, there went my future. What should I do? The people wanted their money. They would not sell me any more goods, because I couldn't pay what I already owed. I was not going to be able to get more credit. I was so ashamed. On top of all that, Elizabeth's family—who originally liked me so well—kicked me out of the store. The friendship had been strained anyway, since I had married. They were not speaking to me, and I always had one of my brothers delivering the rent money.

I needed to have a business, so I went to the ESCOA transport garage, where I was friendly with the owner. He told me, "Habib, we have some trucks for sale. I can trust you with two or three trucks. We will give you a load to Fort Lamy." I agreed. Siham was pregnant with Suad, the fourth girl, and it was 1959. Hassan was going home to you can save yourself from many, many troubles. We took the top of the engine and the plate off, and found that the bearings and pistons were stuck because the oil had leaked out. I lost everything. It took us until evening to check the engine.

I told the driver to go back to his master (my brother-in-law) to find used engine parts from one of the Lebanese mechanics in the area. I needed pistons, a crankshaft, bearings, etc. The driver told Zahed how he was fixing the truck. My brother-in-law clarified, "Are *you* doing all of that?" The driver said, "Yes, I am doing it and your brother-in-law is helping a little. But maybe when he comes back tomorrow, he will tell you that *he* did all the work and I didn't do anything. Anyhow, I did it for God because you are my master."

Zahed took him to a garage and the mechanic said that he had only one old engine. The driver took all the pistons and other parts that he needed. I had told him not to forget to bring new oil—the most important thing. He brought all the parts and the oil and we fixed the engine the next day. The engine started and ran real well!

I slept at the home of an African family in the village that night. They were so nice. They said they would watch the truck. Their house was only about 10 feet by 12 feet, made from mud. The roof was palm tree fronds and grass. It was so hot, with lots of mosquitoes. There was a creek nearby and the frogs were very loud all night— *squawk, squawk, squawk!* So I didn't get much sleep; I just rested my body a little bit.

In the morning, at about ten o'clock, the boy arrived and we left. We were about 30 or 40 miles from Freetown. We drove and unloaded our goods, and then purchased peanuts and other supplies for the trip back. When we arrived back home, I told Zahed, "This engine needs to be replaced. We can't keep using it. We managed, but we had to put in three or four gallons of oil on the way back." I tried to make him understand business. I showed him that we would spend all the profits from the business on oil, repair of the engine, and time lost for repairs if the engine was not replaced. He said, "What shall we do?" I said, "I don't know. I can't travel with this truck."

When I was in Freetown, I had gotten my passport and paperwork in preparation for traveling to Nigeria. I gave the documents to Zahed to keep in his safe. I said, "Zahed, I can't go with the truck. I don't need any money from you." We had earned about £1,000 and had agreed to split it evenly. My whole intention was to work enough so that I could go back to Nigeria or have my own business. I did not want to keep staying with other people. I needed to build a business of my own. I didn't want to keep doing the same work that my drivers and boys had done for me when my business in Nigeria was successful. But the whole time, I did not lose hope in myself. I was always thinking and strong. I was anxious to find some good job, an opportunity for my own business.

I left my in-laws after staying there for a few months, and went to some distant relatives who came from my hometown of Nabatieh, Lebanon. One of the men, Said Hejazze, was about my father's age. They had gone to school together, and were good friends. I greeted him with, "*Salaam Alaykum*." He was a rich man. He owned stores and lived in the same building. He had two sons, and a brother-in-law, who was about my age. The brother-in-law owned an ice cream factory. They made the ice cream and the cones. I visited his brother-in-law, and he showed me the manufacturing operations. He showed me how they made the ice cream in kettles, and then transferred it to the freezer. He hired African people to make the cones and bake them in his ovens. He had boys putting kettles of the ice cream on wheeled carts, surrounded by ice. They set the cones, a spoon, water and towels on the side of the cart. They would pay the man for the products and then go out into the streets to sell the ice cream. When the kettle was empty, they would wash it, and bring it back the next day. He had 20 or 30 boys selling ice cream this way every day.

I thought that this was a good business. He asked me how the transport business was. I told him it was not good. I explained that I liked Zahed, but that we had a little quarrel because he did not want to buy a new engine for the truck, and that I let Zahed keep all the money from the business. He said, "Okay, I have a job for you." I said, "What kind of job? I don't want a job. I want to go back to my brothers to do the work I know. I don't think I can make any money or succeed in this country." He said, "No, let's go see the Capos." That means "big man" and was Said Hejazze, my father's friend. Said suggested, "How about if we send Habib to Kenema?" I said, "What! Kenema? What would you want me to do there?"

I knew Kenema from the transport business. He said, "Sit down," and they brought a chair and asked that Lebanese coffee be served to us. Mr. Hejazze explained, "We have a machine to make ice cream. A friend had a son in Kenema and wanted to find a job for his son. We bought a second hand machine, sold it to the man, and went to Kenema to install it for the son. The man paid for it, but now tells us that his son does not want to do the work anymore. He has asked that we come pick it up. It is a big machine, very long, and all iron, with the engine on one side."

He said, "Look, Habib, you can come with us. You have explained that you were in the transport business. Do you know anything about electrical work?" I answered, "Yes, I know electrical work. Not enough to build a house and do the electrical wiring. But I know some of the repair. Maybe I can figure out the wiring and repairs, maybe not. I can't promise." He said, "Okay. You come with us, we will go look at that machine. If you repair it for us and come back, we will give you— how much do you want? £50? £100? I am going to give you money to buy a ticket to get home by plane—plus pocket money. I want you to go and see what is wrong with this machine—if you can repair it, or not. You will go with us and come back with us. That's all we want, and we will provide all expenses—eating, sleeping, everything. The people are Lebanese, and they are nice. They will put us up in their home, and feed us. We don't need to go to a hotel. It will be fun."

I agreed to go. The next day we got in his car. Kenema was about 210 miles, but the road was awful, and it took us seven or eight hours to get there. The car was a four-door red Ford that had bad suspension over the ruts—it swayed this way and that, the whole trip. But we managed to get there in the late evening, after the stores were closed. We went to the place where the machinery was, and where the family lived. They made a nice dinner for us and provided two rooms for us to sleep. They built the ice cream machine in the store attached to their house. But the next morning, they took us to an African store that they rented. It was an old mud house that had two small bedrooms. The store was in the front and there was a backyard with bushes and mango trees. Just outside the back door was a pipe for water for washing.

I thought to myself, *Habib, do you remember when you were playing golf for £50 or £100, buying new shoes, buying a new house, going to the city to shop for presents for your wife and kids—always the expensive ones?* I chuckled ruefully when I thought of the changes in my life. I thought, "God, okay. If you want to teach me something, I will agree. Do what you want with me." This little mud house was at 13 Kombema Road, and it is where my first son, Said, was born a little later. The address changed to 21 Kombema Road while we were living there.

In the morning we had breakfast and said thank you to the people. The house was at the end of the town. The major street was Hangar Road, only one mile long. We crossed the main street, and went to the house. It was low and wide, and it had a little veranda with a cement wall that we could sit on. It was made with wood and dirt.

We went inside the store, then to the storeroom where the machinery was kept. I saw a long machine, about 10 feet in length. The engine was on one side. There was salt water all around it, and the meter box with the fuses and wiring was on the wall near it. We wanted to try the machine, so we turned it on. It worked. But when Said Hejazze put his hand on the electrical box, he got a big shock!

They explained that that was the problem. "Can you do something about it, Habib?" I looked, and said, "Yes, go get me some wire, screwdrivers, gloves. I need tools; I can't do this with my hands." So they took me to a Lebanese man who had a building material supply store near the mosque. I got 200 or 300 yards of coiled electric wire, plastic handled pliers, an electrical tester, Phillips and regular screwdrivers. The asked me, "Okay, Habib, is there anything more that you want?"

I said, "Yes, go get me a half dozen cold beers. If I get electrocuted while trying to fix the machinery, at least I would die happy!" Said laughed and asked what kind of beer I wanted. I asked for Heineken, and they went to get a six-pack of bottles of beer at an Indian store.

I liked Heineken or Beck's beer. That is what I drank at home when I was earning good money. They brought the beer back and told me they had work to do in the adjoining house. When they asked me if I wanted anything to eat, I said, "No, no, no. Just leave me alone. You guys can close the door behind you and let me work here."

After they left, I opened the first beer and sat on a box on the floor. I started to drink and make a plan for the work. I finished one bottle and took the wire cutting pliers. I attached the meter to the wall. Then I took all the fuses out and put them to the side. I went wire by wire, tracing each one from the meter box to the motor. They were all red, so I used yellow to distinguish. I started to replace each wire, wire by wire. When I thought I had finished, I started the motor. It worked!

By then, I was on my third bottle of beer. I brought my screwdriver and put the tester on the wall. Then I went inside the store and found the big pot that held the salt water used in the process of making ice cream. The temperature gauge needed to show that the salt water was about five or ten degrees below zero. To get it to the proper temperature, I again traced the wires, wire by wire. After checking it all and making adjustments, I started the motor up again. I touched the screwdriver to the tester and, *Whompf!* Something shocked me, and threw me against the wall.

Luckily, I was sitting on a wooden bench. I hadn't put it there on purpose; I am lucky that it wasn't metal. I sat down again and took beer number four. I drank it and went back to the fuse box. I had been working on this five or six hours by then. I was looking here, there, and everywhere. I found a wire that was completely naked and in the back, lying against the metal of the box. Where did this come from? I used to watch my uncle and others, and knew that the electricity needed to be grounded. In their homes, they used to make sure that every piece of electrical equipment was grounded, in case of lightning storms. Some used to put a thin pole on their roofs with a wire going into the ground. I thought, "Oh my God! Thank you, God!" I pulled the wire off and threw it away. I started the motor back up and it worked fine.

I finished my fifth bottle of beer, waiting to see if the machine would get cold. In about half an hour, I saw that the needle on the meter was going below zero. I was so happy! I started dancing around. This meant that I would earn my money to go back to Nigeria. I looked around the room and saw a big can that said "Made in Holland." I opened it and saw that it was three-quarters full. This was the ice cream mix. I thought, "How about if I make some ice cream! But how do I do it?" I found the directions on the side of the can. I thought, "Ah ha! Now I am going to make some good ice cream!"

I found the paddles and put them in the can. The directions said something about adding five pounds of the mix to a certain amount of milk, but I didn't see anything with which to measure; there was no scale. So I said to myself, *Come on, Habib. Try to do it. If I add too much, it will be nice, if not enough, I will add more milk later.* I went outside with a kettle and washed it, then put clean water in it. I put the mix inside the mixer and stirred to blend it with the milk. I remembered how to make ice cream because my cousin's wife in Nigeria used a little ice cream maker. While waiting for the ice cream to freeze, I took the sixth bottle of beer and said to myself, *You are the last one. I am going to enjoy this!* I was so happy that I did the job well. Later on I taped all the wires and made the work look nice. I laughed to myself, "Now I am an electrician! When I go back to Nigeria, I can claim that I was in Europe learning to be an electrician."

By now it was about noon. The men had said they would come back for me at about ten o'clock. They didn't show up. I heard something—bump-bump, bump-bump, bump-bump. The ice cream was beginning to flow over and push the lid off of the can. I lifted the lid further and put my finger in the ice cream to scoop it up. Oh, it was good! I looked around through the boxes. Most were empty, but I found one that was half full of cones. "Oh, God!" I said. "You make things easy for me." I was eating ice cream and laughing and dancing around the room. With six beers I was *so* happy!

Said and the other man finally came back and said, "Hey, Habib. What are you doing?" I invited them in. "Enjoy yourselves," I said. They exclaimed, "You did it?" I said, "Yes, you can touch the machine." They commented on how good the ice cream was. When they asked how much mix I used, I told them I had never made ice cream in my life.

Then I said, "Where is the money?" Said said, "Wait a minute, Habib. Before we came here, we said that if you could fix the machine, we would offer you a deal." I looked at them, and said, "I have had six bottles of beer. I am so happy right now. Don't let me decide anything right now." Said offered, "Habib, this shop is a nice store. There is also a bedroom, shower, water, freezers, and a store behind, with a counter to do your business. How about if you stay here and run the store, and we supply you with everything? We will supply general goods for the store and all the ingredients for the ice cream. We would split the profits evenly. We would provide the capital, and you provide the work. You could try it for one or two years. You have told us that you have to start from zero in Nigeria. Why don't you start here from zero—but we would help you? You stay here. We will give you money to buy a bed and some food and make this house your house. Let's go introduce you to the Lebanese people around here."

They introduced me around the town. I met a good Lebanese man, Abdullah, who had grown up close to my town in Lebanon. He had returned from Lebanon just a few months earlier, after getting married. He had a huge store, selling clothing wholesale and retail. He was in his 30's, close to my age, and his bride was just 18 or 19.

They invited us to drink coffee. Said said, "Take care of Habib. We are going to be partners with him in the little general store. We took possession of the ice cream machine from the man who had bought it for his son to have a business. He didn't want any money back so we can give the equipment to Habib. I would like to help him." Said explained to Abdullah that his father and my father were neighbors back in Lebanon, and had gone to school together. "I want to help Habib—because of his father, and because he is clever. He made the machine work after we were going to throw it away. Now it is working and he is smart. He has had good and bad times in Nigeria." He explained my whole story to Abdullah.

SIERRA LEONE

THIS WAS IN ABOUT 1959. I NEEDED TO WORK TO MAKE MONEY TO SEND back to Lebanon to support my wife and four girls. My father was still doing a little saddlery work. He was working on commission for another man. This was a better way to work, and he made a little more profit. My father was still young. I was only about 16 years younger, as my parents had married very young. So my father was like my older brother. When he talked to me, I gave him all my respect. I was always afraid to make him upset, or do something he didn't like. We used to walk outside the town together, to the area where we lived in the summer and during one of the wars. We would sit under a tree and discuss things; I would tell him everything that was happening with me, and I would get his advice. He was so nice to my family and my children.

I decided to stay in Sierra Leone for a while and see whether I could develop a business there, so that my family could rejoin me from Lebanon. I told Abdullah that Said had given me money to buy a bed and some supplies before he left the town. But Abdullah said, "No, Habib. Now you can come and sleep here. We have a spare room. You can sleep here for a few days. We will then go buy you a bed and supplies. We will find you a cook, or, if necessary, you can come here to eat. There are only two of us. Whatever we cook is always enough for four. Why don't you do that until you have your own house?"

I replied, "Okay, I will do that. No problem. You save me trouble, you save me from cooking, you save me from many problems. But do you promise to help me get things for my own house?" We agreed, and I stayed with them for a few weeks. He was so nice and his wife was so good. We listened to music and enjoyed our evenings together.

Abdullah did not have many friends in the area, so he needed me, and I needed him.

The next morning I went to the store to start cleaning, and I hired a boy to clean the house and take care of it. I started to run the refrigerator and make the ice cream. I still had about a thousand cones left in the case that I had found earlier. Meanwhile, I was waiting for Said to send me a load of goods. Once the ice cream was ready, I started to offer it to the neighbors as they passed by the front of the store. I called out to them, "Hey, Daddy [or big man, or young boy]—do you want some ice cream?" I offered them ice cream for free.

These people had never had ice cream before, and did not know what it was! Some people licked the ice cream and threw away the biscuit, or cone; others ate the cone and threw away the ice cream. So I took a little one for myself and showed them how to eat it. They exclaimed, "Oh, oh, oh. This is magic!" One man with a big mouth took the whole thing and put it in his mouth. It was too cold all at once! Some of them bought more. I charged a nickel. One man ate the free cone and asked for another, but I told him, "This time you have to pay a nickel."

So I started to teach the people how to eat ice cream. I sold two pounds a day, sometimes five pounds. When people saw me around town, they would say, "Hello, Mr. Kagome." *Kagome* in their African language means "something to lick." They didn't have a word for ice cream, so I became "Mr. Licker Man." That name stayed with me until we left Sierra Leone many years later. When people would refer to my store, they would say, "Go to Kagome." The name stuck even after I had my store with food supplies beyond just ice cream. It followed me to Freetown. One time when I was down there arranging transport, I said to the man, "Do you know the ice cream store?" And he responded, "Yes, Kagome. I know Kagome."

In a couple days, a truck arrived in front of my store with the supplies from Said. He sent some cans of ice cream mix, a few cases of soda and 20 cases of soap. That area had diamond mines. You had to sell items that the people needed to take back to the bush country. They were all Muslim, and they needed grass mats for praying, and they also used them for picnics. Originally, they were made mostly in India, and were called *Indiamatta*. The load also included a big case of tobacco, shovels and sifting pans for the ore.

The driver asked for £40. I said, "Hey, I don't have money here." I gave him a little note to take to Abdullah asking for the money. Then I started unpacking the load with the boy I had hired. I started putting all the items on the floor. Said had sent me a list of the cost of the items and how much I should sell them for. But when I saw Abdullah the next day, he told me that all the prices Said had charged me were what the customer would pay on the street, not the wholesale price! I would have been selling the merchandise and sending Said the total amount of money I earned! "How can I sell something costing me £2.5," I asked Abdullah, "if it's selling on the street for £2.5? That means no profit for me!"

I was selling a few staples, making a few pennies here, a few pennies there. The ice cream sales were increasing. I could buy a little bread and food for the evening. With the little money I earned, I bought a bed, mattress and pillow. I continued to have dinner with Abdullah and his wife but I told him not to send food to me in the evenings. I stayed in the store late because people passed by the store as they left the town after work to return to their villages. They asked for certain items. People asked for the wine, Santa Maria. Even at that time, it was being imported from Mexico.

I had an idea to make a little profit. I sold the merchandise that Said sent me for the retail price of, for example, £2.5, which was also my wholesale cost. Before I paid him, I would go to an Indian man who had a large store and distribution operation, and I would pay from those proceeds to buy other supplies at wholesale. Then I would turn around and sell those at retail. Before I sent Said his money, I would use it as capital and that way, I was able to make a little profit. I told Abdullah my idea and he responded, "That's a good idea, Habib!"

I started doing business with the Indian man. He was very young, and so nice. He said, "I want to help you, Habib." He had visited my store and said, "I will help you fill your store. Take what you want.

Fill your store. I will give you £1,000 of merchandise and then you can pay me little by little, £100, £200." I said, "Okay, but you have to give me a good price." He replied, "No, I am going to give you a better price than wholesale. I want to help you, Habib." He gave me cigarettes, candy, cosmetics, sugar, milk—everything to help me develop my business into a general store.

Meanwhile I asked Said to send me cones and shovels, and other items needed in the town. He wrote me a letter asking where the money was. He told me to open a bank account in both of our names so that he could draw on it. I continued to sell his merchandise at cost or below cost. Then I took his money and went shopping at the wholesale stores. This process went on for about a year. I opened my store at about eight o'clock in the morning. I had a boy who made breakfast and lunch for me. I stayed open until ten o'clock in the evening. Sometimes I got together with Abdullah and his wife for a late dinner.

When I had been in Sierra Leone for a while, Hassan, the oldest of my younger brothers, was considering moving from Nigeria to Sierra Leone. He left his wife and children in Nigeria and came to stay with me for a few days to decide where to move. We had a cousin in Monrovia, Liberia, and he was considering there, also, and discussing it with me. Liberia was only a few hundred miles from Kenema. I could drive him to the border. From the border, Hassan could hire a car to take him to the city, where he had the address of our cousin. When we got to the border, it was in the early evening, and the police said that he would need to stay there overnight and take a bus into the city in the morning. The bus was called "kuda-kuda" and went from village to village, stopping at each along its route.

I asked Hassan, "What do you want to do, my brother? Do you want me to stay with you? Can you stay here by yourself so that I can get back to my wife and family?" He replied, "No problem." So I left him there. I took a different, longer route back to Kenema, because I was curious and wanted to see the area. It was a diamond area. It was about 10:00 p.m. by the time I got home, and Siham had lots of food set up. I asked, "What is all this food for?" She replied, "Somebody is waiting for you in the house."

"Who is that?" I asked.

She said, "It's a surprise. Go, see."

Guess who I saw! My brother, Hassan! I asked, "What are you doing here?" He said, "I was so scared. I didn't like the area." Someone was passing by him, and asked, "What are you doing here, white man?" Hassan explained that he was waiting for the kuda-kuda the next morning. The man asked where Hassan came from, and Hassan explained, "From my brother, Habib, the one who makes ice cream. I was staying with him." Many Africans knew me because of the ice cream, and so the man said, "Oh, Habib, ice cream. Habib is my good friend. Wait a minute—you are going to Monrovia?" My brother changed his mind and said, "Take me with you, back to Kenema!"

He stayed with me a few more weeks and then went to Freetown to visit people he knew there. After a few days, Joe, my other brother, came to Kenema from Nigeria. He was handsome, young, in his early twenties, a little foolish, and not yet married. When Hassan and Mo came to Nigeria to stay with me, Joe also wanted to come, but our father said that he was too young, and should stay in Lebanon and finish his education. Our father promised that Joe could join his brothers in Africa after he graduated. But when he graduated, our father told Joe that he could not go—that he had to stay with his parents.

Joe was very upset. He had always had a desire to go to Africa to show that he could do this by himself, especially since our parents initially refused to let him go. He worked in Lebanon as a waiter for a while, and finally got an offer to work for someone he knew in Nigeria. He worked there for less than a year, but didn't really like it. That's when he came to visit me.

I needed someone to work with me, so I started teaching Joe all about the business. At the time, we had the store, the cold room, and a newspaper, and there was a lot to do.

One day Joe, Siham, and I were sitting at the house, talking about the business. We talked about having Joe stay in Kenema to take care of the store, so that Siham and I could take the kids and move to Freetown, where there were much better schools. Since I would be in Freetown, I could go to the big auctions held as the food supplies passed through customs. I would be able to get much better prices for the merchandise we needed for the store. We all agreed on this idea. I went to Freetown to find a store there. A man was moving his store to a bigger space. He was nice enough to rent it to me just for what he was paying. I leased a large upstairs apartment for the family. I was so lucky; I think my parents prayed very much for me. The house was new, and was owned by a man from my town. So in one week, I rented the store and the house. I didn't have to pay anything yet. They just gave me the keys. I drove back to Kenema. I told Joe to take care of the store, and split the furniture, put ads in the newspaper for some of it, and got everything arranged to move to Freetown.

We started living in Freetown, enrolling the children in school there. I opened the store, and was able to buy fruit and vegetables very cheaply at the auctions. My business started doing well. There was a store run by an Indian nearby, but he only accepted cash, and I would let people owe me money. So the people liked me and they came to my business. I started to load up the van each week with produce and supplies I bought at the auction, to transport to Joe in Kenema. We divided everything between us. The van was going back and forth.

After about a month, I thought I should go to Kenema to check on how Joe was doing. I didn't tell him that I was coming—I just drove up there. When I arrived, I didn't see the Coca-Cola refrigerator in the Kenema store! I asked, "Joe, did you sell the Coca-Cola fridge?" He said, "Oh, no. My friend had a party, and I lent it to him." I looked for the van, and I didn't see it. I asked Joe, "Where is the van?" He replied, "I lent it to my friend." I thought, *Oh, my God!*

I closed the door and we started to talk. We were chatting, and the telephone rang. Joe was in the kitchen, and the telephone was close to me, so I answered it. The lady on the telephone said, "Joe, how are you? Oh, I am sorry, I am keeping the books. I can't sell the books today for you. Did you get new ones?" I asked, "Who is speaking, please?" She gave her name. I knew that she was a married woman, who had an old husband and a baby. I could tell by the way she was speaking that there was some connection between her and Joe. So I said, "For your information, lady, I am not Joe. I am his brother, Habib. Do you want me to tell him that?"

She hung up on me. Joe came back in the room and asked, "Who was that?" I said, "Your sweetheart. And she said she could not send you the books today; she would send them tomorrow, because her husband would not be there."

The next day we got up in the morning and went to the store. The customers started coming in. A lady came and said, "Joe, do you have cabbage?" Joe said, "No, we didn't get cabbage." I said, "Joe, did you sell the whole bag in two or three days?" He replied, "No, I don't know. I don't remember. Did you send me cabbage?" I asked, "Oh, you didn't check in the goods when the driver came with the delivery?" He said, "No, when the driver came, I told him to put the things in the cold room and on the outside." I said, "Wait a minute, ma'am."

I went into the cold room and discovered lots of produce laying on the floor in the bags I had sent in the van. I opened the bag of cabbage, but the first head I pulled out was starting to rot. The lady wanted two heads of cabbage, but I had to clean several heads of cabbage, removing the rot, to give her the amount that she wanted.

Then I said, "Brother. It has only been a month or two and you have lent out half of the store and you don't care about the other half. What is left in the store that you haven't lent out, my brother?" Joe mumbled, "Well, I don't know. Everything." Then I went into the office that was on the side of the store. I opened a drawer and saw a letter not yet finished. I opened it and read. Joe was writing to a friend in Lebanon saying that he regretted his move to Sierra Leone. He explained that I had set him up in a store to sell food, whiskey, and brandy, but he regretted it. He added that every hour that he spent with the friend in Lebanon was better that a good ten-karat diamond. Joe's life dream as a young man was to go to Africa, but it didn't turn out to be as much fun as he expected. He didn't know as many people, and it wasn't as social for him.

So, I spent a few days with Joe, and realized that he was not good at business. I said to myself, *Boy, you'd better change this before you lose the store.* I called on my experience. I helped Joe clean up the cold room and the rest of the store. I helped him get the loaned equipment back from his friends. Two nice, beautiful girls came in the store and said, "Joe, Joe, thank you very much for the nice evening. We had such good fun. Shall we do it again?" They had had a party, and Joe had loaned them the fridge, the van, some of the chairs from the house—lots of things. There was a photograph of a friend of Joe's and his two sisters. Anytime Joe had free time, he stayed with his friend so that he could spend time with the two sisters. Oh, Joe knew how to live! In all my life, I had never danced with one girl—but Joe made up for it. He enjoyed his life when he was young!

I drove back to Freetown. When I went inside the house, my wife asked, "What's wrong?" I told her what I had found on my trip to Kenema. I asked, "Do you prefer to go back to Kenema?" She exclaimed, "What! I am making friends here. The business is good here."

"Either we go close Kenema and stay here," I said, "or we close Freetown and go home. The best thing is that we know Freetown has good future business because of the diamond dealers. Business is never slow. And our business is food. People have to eat. Whether they get money or not, they still eat. We have the ice cream factory in Kenema. We cannot compete with the people in Freetown for ice cream. There are already two or three ice cream companies." Siham responded, "Okay, whatever you decide."

We started to load the furniture and transport it back to Kenema. I told the owner of the store and paid him for two months. He asked why, and I explained that my brother was not happy. He wanted to go back to Lebanon, so I had to go back to Kenema to operate the business. I asked, "How much do I owe you?" He said, "Nothing." He was so nice. So we returned to Kenema and started getting the store back in shape. Joe told me he was leaving. I wished him good luck. "Have a nice trip," I said. "Go and have fun." He was very good with people. He had fun, and was a playboy before he married.

When Joe returned to Lebanon, he worked in restaurants again and as a barman. One of our sisters took the money that he had saved from his time in Nigeria and saved it for him so that he wouldn't spend it all. The family was trying to keep Joe from spending money. They decided that they needed to find him a wife so that he could settle down. Except for one, each of my sisters had a girl in mind to become Joe's wife. The sister that had not identified a potential wife remembered that one of her friend's friends was very nice and beautiful, but she was already engaged. My sister liked her right away when she met her. After some time, my sister asked about the beautiful friend again and found that the engagement had not worked out and that she was free.

My sister took Joe to see the girl. He had been introduced to so many girls and had turned them all down and wasn't interested. But that changed with Zena. They planned the marriage. Zena was driven by my sister and her husband to Joe's house. My sister's husband, Hassan, said that they were going to "shoot the hyena"—that is a saying for describing the first night of marriage. But Zena's mother didn't know the saying and said, "How come, in Beirut is there a hyena?" She didn't know that it was just a saying; she didn't know they were joking. My sister told her, "Sometimes the hyena comes from the bushes."

After Joe and Zena married, there was a long period of time that Joe worked and there was more war in Lebanon. Zena had Lena and other children. They didn't move to Nigeria again until Lena was about 17 years old. The war was very bad, and Joe was broke, so he managed to get a contract to work in Nigeria. It was only supposed to be for three months, but it lasted much longer.

I remember when I went to Lebanon and visited them. Lena, my niece, was just about to turn one year old. She was crawling, but had not yet started walking. I bought her a device that surrounds a baby so that she can stand and practice walking (a *marche bebe*). I announced, "This is my first payment for Said!" I sort of joked that this was the first item in a dowry for Said, my first-born son, and Lena, my brother's first-born daughter, to someday marry. I asked Lena, "Have you learned to walk?" Then she walked to me. It was on her first birthday.

I didn't see Lena again until she was about 14 years old. Her family knew that her uncles, my brothers, were coming to visit, but it was a surprise that I was also coming. When we arrived, all the relatives greeted us and everyone was so happy. But Lena wasn't among the greeters. She remained upstairs cleaning and getting ready for us, the visitors. She later told me that she didn't think I would remember her. But I did. I kept asking for her, and her brother went upstairs to find her. Lena thought he was joking that I wanted to see her, so she didn't come downstairs. Finally her mother yelled upstairs for her to come down to greet us. Lena ran down the stairs and said hello to everyone. She hugged me, but she was very quiet and shy.

Important people like police officers, the judge and other town managers used to come to my store in Sierra Leone. Since they were congregating at my store, I took the wooden crates that the Santa Maria came in, put them on the veranda, near the door of my store, and we used them as chairs. It was cheaper to buy wine from me than go to the hotel or a bar. Then more and more people were coming to visit. They bought crackers, cigarettes, and everything else that they needed. I put lights outside, so that people could sit down and talk and enjoy the evenings. If you wanted to find the manager of the town, everyone knew they could find him at my store in the evenings!

One rainy day, I was sitting inside my store wearing knickers and a shirt. All the flies were coming inside because of the weather, and I was spraying them with Sheltox. I looked out and saw Said and the people who brought me to the store had arrived and were getting out of the car. I greeted them, and said, "Hello! Why didn't you tell me you were coming, so I could have prepared for you?" They came into the store, very serious. They looked at me, they looked around the store. By now I had big bags of rice and other supplies stacked up all around—lots of inventory. In the middle was a counter, and shelves on the three sides. It was so crowded with merchandise that only a few people could come inside.

Said asked, "How much do you owe people for all these goods?" I said, "I don't owe any people money. I sell the items that you sent me at cost or below cost. Then I go to the Indian company, the English company, the French company, or any place else that I see goods that the customers want, and I buy those goods with the money I earned. Abdullah, the friend that you introduced me to, also sells me merchandise at a good price. You sent me £2,000 and these goods are worth £4,000. So £1,000 extra for you, and £1,000 for me."

Said responded, "What happened?" I assured him, "Nothing happened." He asked, "Are you sure you don't owe anybody money?" I reassured him that I didn't, and he finally accepted that. I laugh now, when I think how shocked he was. He had heard bad news about me, but when he came to the store, he realized he had assumed a bad conclusion. Then he turned to the side and whispered to the young man with him. I believe it was his cousin, or his wife's cousin, Amir. Said then turned back to me and said, "Habib, congratulations. We didn't expect this from you. You made money from nothing. We are sorry. We came here quickly because we had other business in town and decided to visit you also. We can't stay here long because the roads are bad." I asked if they were going to stay the night. He said, "Yes. We are going to stay with our friend, Abdullah."

They left, and I thought to myself, "I'd better close early." It was eight or nine o'clock, and I usually closed around ten. I walked to Abdullah's house and asked, "Where are your friends?" Abdullah said, "What friends? They came here and had coffee and then left." I was surprised and asked, "Why?"

Abdullah laughed heartily. "Ha, ha, ha, ha! Ha, ha, ha, ha! Come sit down," he said. "I'll tell you what happened."

I was *so* scared. He said, "You know your father's friend, Said?" I said, "Of course I know him." He said, "Your brother-in-law told Said that you sold everything and you used the money to return to Nigeria. You sold everything of theirs without letting them know or giving them any money." I asked, "Did they believe him?" He said, "Yes. They believed him. That's why they came here. When they found you still here, they were shocked. They came to my home to visit, but they didn't want to see you again because they felt guilty. With that rotten car that they are driving, I don't know if they will reach home safely on that road. I tried to talk them into staying, but they refused."

I said, "So, Said believed my brother-in-law. And they think I am cheating them, taking their money and running away. Okay. When are you going down to Freetown?" He said, "Tomorrow, I am going down to Freetown." In the winter, it took five to six hours to get there, but in the summer, just a couple hours.

The next day, I told Abdullah that I wanted to go with him to Freetown. He asked, "What do you want to go to Freetown for?" I explained that I wanted to talk to Said and make an arrangement. I had been managing the store for one year and I wanted to explain the work that I had done. Since my family was in Lebanon, I also wanted to send them some money. He agreed.

In Freetown, I went straight to Said. He was sitting in his office and Amir was working with the ice cream. Said said, "Hello, Habib." He got up and hugged me. We sat down and he made coffee. I said, "Look here, Mr. Said. You tell me you are my friend, my father's friend, and you help me because of my father. And, after all that, you didn't trust me. How can you be a friend of my father? I don't like a friend like you to be a friend of my father. For you to have a bad idea or to think one day I am a thief or I am a bad man."

He replied, "No, no, Habib. You know...I hear that." I was so upset. I asked, "Why didn't you call? There is a telephone here, a telephone to Abdullah—many telephones!" He said, "You are right, but maybe ... ah ... nobody will give me the true idea. So I have to rest my mind. I went there ... ah ... frankly, to see. When I saw you there, I was shocked, and I came back. I couldn't go back to you and talk to you, and I am ashamed. Will you forgive me for this?"

At that time in Africa, businessmen used to import workers under a quota system. They were responsible for up to five workers. Said had five quotas. He would import the workers, and when they finished the projects, they would return to their own countries. He offered me one of the quotas to allow me to stay in Sierra Leone and have me work under him.

I told him, "No. This is the key to the house and the store. This is the statement showing the inventory of goods of over £4,000. This is your invoice for the £2,000 of goods you sent to me. So we have about £2,500, or £3,000 of profit. We have made good money. Also, if I eat bread and food from the store, I write it down here to keep track of my personal expenses."

He interrupted, "Oh, forget about that. It should be on the store."

I said, "Now I want to split from you. I want you to take your store back and give me my money so that I can go back to my brothers in Nigeria. I don't want to continue to do business with a person who thinks of me as a thief." Said said, "Habib, I don't want to hear this from you. You take the key and go back to your store."

By that time, Amir came in and asked, "What is happening?" Said said, "Habib wants to leave the store, and he brought the key. He wants us to send somebody to pick up his money. He wants to go back to Nigeria." Amir said, "Let me talk to him." He talked to me … talk, talk, talk. He wanted me to go back to the store. I said, "Never! When someone thinks of you as a thief, you can't work for him anymore. I started working with you because you people acted like you trusted me. I worked from my heart. I saved every penny, which was your money and my money. I did not spend it any other way. If I knew that store was mine, I could spend anything I wanted, but because I have a partner, and you trusted me, I did only the necessary things. I didn't buy a shirt. I didn't replace pants. I didn't buy shoes. I didn't buy anything for myself. All of what we had in the store, we still have. Because I have a partner, I don't want you to, one day, accuse me of using your money buy something for myself. I did not even spend the whole amount of money you gave me to buy a bed and other things. I put the rest of the money in the store."

After listening to me, Amir asked, "What do you want to do now?" I said, "Take your store back, and give me the money you owe me. I don't want to work with you guys at all." He said, "Okay." He went back to Said and explained, "Habib said he wants you to take the store back and give him his money so that he can get away." But Amir returned and suggested, "How about if *you* take the store and pay us our money?"

I thought about that, and said, "Okay. I'll go along with this agreement, but I don't have any money. I'll have to make payments."

Amir said, "Let's go talk to Said." Amir told Said, "Habib agreed to buy the store himself. He wants to break the partnership. What do you think?" Said responded, "That would be okay for Habib, but how can he pay me my money? Habib, are you able to pay the money owed to me?" Frustrated, I replied, "Here we go again! Where can I get your money? There is no money in my hand; I'll make payments, if you agree. If you don't agree, thank you, just give me my money. That's all I want. I'll wait one day, two days, three days, one week, two weeks, until you get me my money, or give me half my money, just so that I can get back to Nigeria. The other half—if you want to send it to me, send it. You don't want to send it for me, I worked for you, but I don't care." This was only a little money to me when I was successful in Nigeria. It was just pocket money. When I would leave to gamble, I would put that amount of money in my pocket!

Said looked at me and said, "Habib, you are strong like your father. I know him to be exactly like you are." I said, "Well, I don't take a bribe, I don't take this, I don't take that." Said agreed, "Okay, now we will arrange the sale on payment terms, but we need some-body to be a witness to guarantee payment. Do you have someone who will guarantee payment?" I asked, "Do you want a person to stand in for me?" Said said, "Yes." He wanted to make me upset because I made him very upset. I said, "Okay. I don't like that word. I will just leave. I'll come back later."

I walked along the street—thinking, thinking, thinking. Suddenly I heard somebody behind me blow a horn: *beep-beep-beep-beep-beep-beep!* They forced me to the side of the road—to the deep gutter, where water flowed. I was afraid I was going to be pushed into the gutter, and I got nervous. I yelled, "You stupid man! You are going to push me into that gutter!"

But when I looked, I saw that it was my friend, Abdulla! He said, "What's wrong with you? I was honking the horn from very far away behind you!" I said, "Oh, I am sorry. I was thinking." He asked, "Thinking what? What did you say to Said? Come home with me and come inside."

I explained what I had said. He thought, "Okay, you should go back to Said. Let's go. Do you want to speak with him further? Let me help. You don't want me to help?" I responded, "No, I do want you to help." So we went back to Said and Abdullah started, "Said, have you agreed to sell the store to Habib, and he would make payments?"

Said replied, "Yes. I want to sell Habib the store and for him to make payments, but I need a person to guarantee his payments." Abdullah asked, "Would you accept my guarantee?" Said said, "Yes." Abdullah asked, "We will write checks to you; how much do you want each month?" He said, "Three hundred pounds every month."

I said, "I can't pay you that much." He said, "How much can you pay?" I replied, "I will pay £100 per month." Said countered, "No, too small." Abdullah offered, "How about £150 a month?" Finally, Said agreed. But I interjected, "Wait! The deal is not done. The quota documents are in your name. I want you to assign me that quota. I want you to go to the Immigration Office and tell them that you don't need that quota, and to cut it from you to give to me, so that I am independent in this country." This way, I would not be under him. It would protect me. Without my independence from Said, he could decide he didn't want me, and the police could come, put me on a plane, and send me back.

Abdullah asked if Said wanted to sell the quota documents to me. But Said said, "No, I'll give them to him free, because we made him upset—so they are free." I said, "Okay. Call your clerk. Let him prepare the documents right away. Send them to the Immigration Office before you change your mind." We laughed, and he said, "Habib, I like you."

Said called his clerk to prepare the papers. I had my passport and other important papers right with me. Said said, "Give me your passport." I said, "I'm not giving you my passport. We're going to the Immigration Office." Abdullah took us to the Immigration Office and Abdullah tipped the people – I gave them £5 or £10 for the police there. They were so quick in making the documents; they stamped my passport, and gave me identification papers confirming that I was a free businessman. Every two years they would need to be renewed.

Abdullah asked, "Are you happy now?" Then Said asked Abdullah,

"Can you make me a check for the amount of the inventory and the monthly payment?" We worked out the amount for the check, and Abdullah wrote it and gave it to Said. Said completed another document stating that he sold all his inventory and interest in the Kenema business to me; that I, alone, was responsible for the business, and the payment terms.

Then I exclaimed, "Oh God, thank you! Now you are doing good for me." I drove back to Kenema with Abdullah. The next day, I went shopping. I went around, seeing my friends in the town. I had come back to Kenema as an independent businessman—the owner of a store. I was so excited because I was back on top again after one year. Abdullah asked, "Now, Habib, what is your next step?" I responded, "My next step is to plan for my wife and my children. I have to think of them. I have to do well in my business so I can pay £150 to Said each month—but I will make it."

I told Abdullah that I needed to talk to the Immigration Office and ask them if I could get my wife and children into Sierra Leone to join me. Abdullah asked if I wanted him to accompany me. As I have mentioned, the police officers, the judge, the health officers, all the city managers came to my store to sit on the veranda on crates, have drinks, and visit in the evenings. I didn't have to go to them. So I replied, "To go where? To see the immigration officer? No, Abdullah, don't worry, he comes here every evening. He drinks Santa Maria in my store. So I will talk to him." Abdullah offered, "Okay. If you need any money—anything, Habib, don't worry." I said, "I won't worry, but I will let you know if I need something."

In the evening, the immigration officer, Mr. Bangura, came to my store. His uniform had stripes and a star like a colonel. I said, "Mr. Bangura?" He responded, "Yes, Habib. What's wrong?" I said, "I want to see you in my office." He asked, "Where's your office? What do you want?" I said, "Can I talk to you?" He answered, "Yeah, sure." I offered, "I hope you will accept this Santa Maria. It is for the talk." Mr. Bangura said, "Okay, I'll take it. What's the trouble? Do you have any problem, any trouble?" I said, "I have a big, big problem." He asked, "What kind? Did anybody do something bad?"

I replied, "No, but you are going to do something good for me." He asked, "What can I do?" I explained, "I have my wife, and I have my four daughters in Lebanon. But I think … I don't know if you can get visas to bring them back—all of them, or my wife with the little one, while the other ones just stay with my parents in Lebanon. I want to get them here so that we can be a family like other people. Everybody here has his wife and his children. Me, I am alone."

He said, "No, no, no, Habib! You don't have to have only part of your family here. Tomorrow you come to my office and bring £300 as a deposit to start the immigration process for your wife and children. Then I will complete the visas for you. Do you want to send it by cable to the British Consulate in Beirut, or do you want it in a letter to be sent as soon as possible?" I replied, "No. I want it to go by cable—whatever it costs." He said, "Okay. I'll send the cable for you, and then everything will be okay, Habib. Anyone you want to bring will be okay. You are my friend. Before anybody else, I will do the work for you. Do you want to make me ashamed before my friends here?"

I laughed, and said, "No. That is why I keep you guys, feed you, and make you happy here—for when I need you!" He said, "There you go now. Anything you want!" I said, "Okay," and left. Then I went to Abdullah and asked to borrow £300. He said, "Here's £300, here's the check." I took the check to the bank and gave it to the manager. He was a nice man, an Englishman named Mr. William. I said, "I want to pay the deposit for the immigration of my wife." He replied, "So you want to bring your wife here, Habib?" I said, "Yes, and my daughters, and my little girl who is almost one year old. The officer said I only have to pay the £300 deposit for my wife. It is just a guarantee or something, a deposit. Then after a couple years, I can draw that money back." He said, "Yes." I then instructed him, "And I want to send the cable." He said, "I'll do that for you." He took the information to put in the cable, and who it should go to. He took the £300 and gave me a receipt.

I took it to Mr. Bangura. He said, "It's okay, Habib. I will see you when your wife comes." I said, "How about tonight?" He said,

"Tonight! Is your wife coming tonight?" I laughed, and said, "No." He said, "What do you want from me now?" I said, "Nothing. What do you mean?" He said, "How about some Santa Maria sometime? We'll drink it in your house, in your store. You don't have to think about leaving the country anymore. Anything you want—if anybody gives you trouble or anything, you come here. We want you to stay in the town because we enjoy your place."

I told Abdullah, "Everything is okay, Abdullah. Maybe now I want money to send to buy the tickets." He helped me arrange that. My business was going well. I transferred money to a certain bank in Freetown that had a relationship with a bank in Lebanon so that they could easily wire money back and forth. I met the manager. He was Palestinian, but I think he grew up in Lebanon, and he was well-educated. I said, "I want to send the money for the tickets for my family." They were £100 or £150 at that time.

I waited another couple of weeks, maybe a month, and then I had a letter from my father. *Your wife and youngest daughter, Suad, are coming soon*, it said. *We will send you a cable with the exact date for you to meet them at the international airport.* During that time, I was living in Kenema. I had settled down to run my store and get my name and business established. I would be so happy and comfortable to have my wife and children come. So I had no problems. I knew that the business was improving, and I tried to forget about Nigeria and all the bad things that happened there. I patiently waited while working in the store as I used to. I had lots of customers, and many were high-ranking people. They came to visit and stay with me because my house was at the end of the marketing section of town. The other end of the town was the hospital side.

The people liked me and came to visit. I made friends with them all. My friend, Abdullah's brother-in-law, Hisne, also traveled to Kenema with several Arab Lebanese people. I made good friends with all these people; I wanted my wife to have many friends she could visit when she arrived. These people were all married, and had children, so they would have many things in common with my family, and my wife would enjoy spending time with them. I did not want my wife to be lonely when she came.

Soon, I got the telegram saying that Siham and my daughter would be arriving shortly. I had to meet them at the international airport. Since my business was just starting, I did not have a car at the time. Abdullah had told me that he would lend me his car when I needed to pick up my wife. I borrowed his car and drove down early to Freetown. My brother, Hassan, who was with me in Nigeria, had moved to Freetown, Sierra Leone a couple of months earlier. So I stayed with him and we visited while I was waiting for Siham to arrive. He had left Jos, Nigeria because his business was slow. He had visited me and seen Freetown earlier, and liked it. Hassan knew some people who were willing to sponsor him so that he could get a visa and work permit. He was in the clothing business, in partnership with someone I didn't know, importing clothing from London.

Finally came the day that Siham was to arrive. We went to the airport, but it was very foggy that day, so we had to wait a couple of hours for the flight. Then we heard the sound of the airplane. It was a Lebanese plane and was flying above the fog, looking for a break so it could see to land. The Egyptian man in the control tower said that it was very difficult to direct the plane—not like all the technological systems of today. They know everything today!

The airport managers told the pilot to fly on to Liberia, a couple hours away, because of the fog, and the pilot agreed. A little while went by and we didn't hear the sound of the plane anymore. We assumed that it had flown to Liberia and would come back the following day. When we were turning back from the veranda of the airport, someone yelled, "Look, the plane is on the runway!" We looked back and saw the plane come down. We were all surprised. I saw my wife and little girl come off the plane. My daughter Suad was one year old exactly and took her first steps at the airport!

My brother knew the pilot because he was from our home town. We started talking with him. My brother asked, "How were you able to come down—what happened?" The pilot responded, "We were going on to Monrovia, Liberia, but I saw a little hole ... I saw the airport before me! So I angled into the hole to see where I was in relation to the runway. God help me—I came out right in the middle! I knew I could manage to stop at the end of the runway. I knew if I went a little too far, I would still be okay, because there is only bush, no trees at the end of the airport." So the pilot landed the plane. Everyone was happy. All the people met their families and friends. The plane was full of Lebanese people coming from Beirut.

I drove Siham straight to Kenema. I didn't take her back through Freetown. There was a shortcut from the airport to the outlying areas toward Kenema. Lungi airport is on an island, near the ocean. The city of Freetown is mountainous, so there is no good place for an airport. You had to go about one-half hour by ferry to get to the airport. We arrived in Kenema the same night, but very late. Siham was very happy to get there with our daughter and be with me. We had been waiting a long time to see each other. Our other three daughters stayed in Lebanon with my parents so that they could attend school. It was so nice. Siham joined me in Sierra Leone, Africa in 1960.

I had sold a very old Volkswagen and bought a BSE 350 motorcycle when my wife came to Kenema. One day when Suad was about two years old, she said, "Papa, Papa, I want to go with you." I said, "Okay," and I told Siham I was taking Suad for a ride. I had to go to the bank and to run errands. I put her in front of me. The chief of police knew me. He drank Santa Maria on the veranda of my store on many evenings. I drove very slowly, 15 or 20 miles an hour. We rode to the end of the gravel road, beyond where the town ended. We came to a narrow road. I was close to a truck, loaded with iron rods, and I saw another car coming. What should I do? If I braked, I was going to skid on the gravel. If I continued, the car might hit me. Suddenly, I had to jump the gutter on the side of the road. It was wide, I guided my motorcycle along, inside the gutter and finally into the grass and bushes. I held onto my daughter and let the motorcycle go. It continued down the gutter, still running, tick-tick-ticking. I was holding my daughter so tight and hard that she didn't hit the ground at all. I fell onto my arm and leg.

She asked, "Are you okay, Daddy?" I said, "Yes, I am okay. You stand here." I ran down the road and got the motorcycle. I put Suad on my lap, just in front of me, and we drove home going only about 10 miles an hour the whole way. The minute we arrived home, Suad started yelling, "Mama, Mama! Papa, Papa! Daddy took me on the motorcycle!" Then Siham asked me, "Is it true what she is saying?" I replied, "Yes." Siham started yelling at me. "Don't I tell you not to take that girl with you ... @!#% ... This time is okay, but not anymore! I am not going to stay in this house if you keep that motorcycle!"

The next day, I took it to the company where I had purchased it. I told the man, "Me and my wife fight. I ride the motorcycle and she doesn't ride anything. She wants me to return the motorcycle to you and buy a car." The manager said, "She is right. Why do you want to ride the motorcycle? Either you have to buy another motorcycle for her ..."

"You are silly," I interrupted. "Have you ever seen a Lebanese woman ride a motorcycle?"

He responded, "No, sir."

I suggested, "Look, I bought it from you for £110. Give me £100 and keep the £10 for yourself. I have only had the motorcycle a few months and didn't use it very much." He agreed to the deal and gave me £100. I went home and told Siham that I sold the motorcycle and only lost £10. She said, "Good. Now take the £100 and go buy a car."

We bought a van, and I had one of the workers use it to deliver people around the town. The first day, he brought me £80, the next day £60, the next day £40, and after five days, £20. I said, "Give me that key. Tomorrow you may bring me nothing. I better keep my van. Maybe tomorrow you will sell it and go away. Get out." I went back to the auto company and this time bought a Volkswagen bug.

To the right of my store, there was some empty land owned by an African. He explained that he was going to build a store with a house on top. I had been renting my house from a wealthy Lebanese man. I paid him about £100 per year. It was a house made of mud and grass—a style called a "cob house." I told him, "If you are going to build a store and a house, I want it myself. Don't rent it to anyone. How much are you going to charge?" We agreed on a price for the rent and negotiated all the other points for the deal. He planned to give it to me when he finished construction. He promised me—and when the African people give you their word, it is better than signed papers. He was very nice.

The owner of the house that I was currently renting had a 20-year-old son who was a very spoiled boy. He caroused with his friends and was irresponsible, so the owner wanted his son to start getting serious about work, and become a man. When the owner found out that the African was building next door to him, he asked if he could rent it so that he could get his son started in business. But the African explained that he had already arranged to rent the building to me. He said, "Go talk to Habib. If he doesn't want it, I will rent it to you."

The owner came to me and explained that he wanted to find a job for his son, and wanted the new location. He said, "I will give you anything you want. I will give you one year free rent." After offering me good deals, I said, "No, no. I can't accept, because I don't want to stay in this place. My business is improving, and I want a bigger store. The store is too small. I am scared to put too many goods out, because people can steal things too easily."

He said, "Habib, how about if I sell you the place?" I said, "I don't have money." He asked, "How much are you going to pay?" The place I wanted next door was big; one acre, planned with a big store and nice house. I repeated, "I don't have the money." He replied, "Never mind. You can pay me £30, £50—whatever you can, every month. How much do you want to pay?" I said, "How much do you want to sell it for?" He answered, "I will give it to you for £2,000." I said, "It is too much." I just wanted to get out of that rental; I didn't like it. The owner said, "Okay, I will give it to you for £1,000; you pay whenever you can. How about that? I cannot give it to you for less than that."

I thought, *Oh, my God! £1,000. That is a good deal. I cannot do better than that.* I told Siham about it. At the time, she was also working in the store.

We discussed that it would be better if I owned the store than if

I rented from someone. If I owned it, I could make improvements to it. I said, "Okay, but I want someone to look at this deal and help me decide if it is a good idea." I knew a wealthy man from Lebanon who had been in Africa for at least 25 years. Mr. Aboud knew business. He had helped me get supplies, and I trusted his advice. When I first had the store and was trying to build my inventory he had offered help. I had asked for money to initially fund my business for a week, but he had insisted on a month. "Habib, take it," he had said. "I know you are a good boy. I don't want to make a profit. I have the money, and you have the ability. I want to help you. When I came to this country, I was like you. So now I want to help you to build your business and be like me." He was *so* nice.

So I went to this man. He was from the same area in Lebanon as my landlord, the owner of the house. He invited me to sit down and he asked for coffee. "Yes, Habib," he began. "What is it?"

I explained the situation and asked for his advice. Since this man knew my landlord, I asked if he was trustworthy and whether I should do this. He asked, "Do you like this place, this idea, Habib?" I responded, "Well, my wife and I are interested, because for £1,000 we would get our own house. In the future, if I get more money, we can build on to it." He said, "That is a good idea, Habib. Very good. And what do you want me to do?" I said, "I am just asking you if that is a good deal—if I can rely on the man. People say he is very strict in business. I am afraid to enter into a deal that is not good for me and my family."

He said, "Yes, you are right. But I will do everything; you don't have to do anything. I will make an appointment with him, and when he comes, I will have him sign the papers. Then I will call you and you can sign. Don't worry about the money. When you have the money, you bring it to me. Don't pay him directly. Bring it to me and I will pay him myself." I was very appreciative and said, "Thank you!" He replied, "You go. The house is yours. Don't worry." I went home and told my wife and she was so happy.

After a few days the wealthy Lebanese man who was helping me had to go to the government to take care of the documents for the property transfer. He called me and sent his car with a driver for me. He said, "Habib, you sign here. I will give you and the man who sold it to you a copy. I will keep one here in my safe. If he changes his mind, or does anything, you just come to me." The seller, my old landlord, exclaimed, "No, no, no. I won't do anything. I like Habib." Mr. Aboud said, "Now, if you have money, you give it to me, and I will pay him. If you don't have money, no one will come after you."

I explained, "I have £100 that I want to make as a down payment. I intend to pay. I don't like debt." He said, "I know you, Habib. When you buy something, you don't sleep unless you pay for it. I know you very well. That is why I like you. I like you better than my towns-people, and the people of my own religion!" You see, he was a Christian. It did not take me more than six months to pay off the house.

The house that I bought was very big, and it was behind our store. We divided the floor space so that two-thirds was the bedroom area, and one-third had the plumbing for the sink. But the toilet was still outside, in the backyard. Siham was pregnant with another baby—our fifth child. I was working one day in December 1961, and at about five or six o'clock in the evening, someone came to get me, and told me that Siham was about to have our baby. I was so happy! I called my two friends who were mechanics. One lived next door, the other was a little farther away. They brought their wives with them to the house, so that the women could help my wife with the delivery, along with other Lebanese friends.

When I got a big shipment in, I had to keep some of the goods in our sitting room. I had cases of 7-Up and Pepsi-Cola stacked to the ceiling. In the store, I had whiskey, brandy, rum, and gin. The Lebanese people did a lot of business with diamonds, and they liked to buy liquor to develop business relationships with the Africans: £100 plus two bottles of whiskey, £20 plus one bottle of gin! The Africans had lots of boys working for them, so when they went back to the mines in the bush, they celebrated with their workers. Our store stayed open until about 10 p.m., and in the late afternoon, the Lebanese people would send their drivers to me, "Go see Habib. Have him give you one bottle, two bottles." Sometimes the drivers came without money, but I gave them the liquor. One or two weeks later the Lebanese people would come into the store and ask how much they owed. I would say, "£15, £20, £25." They would respond, "That's not enough"—and they would hand me £50. They all knew me, and knew that I was just starting out. It was a small town, and they knew my story, and we all helped each other.

While the women were helping my wife with the birth, I brought bottles of whiskey, gin, rum, and brandy for my friends and me to drink. I put the bottles on the table. We had a tape recorder and put on Arabic music. We started to sing and were very happy. I had a big metal bucket outside that we used for cleaning. One of my friends went out and cleaned it real well. He brought it in and we emptied all the bottles together into the bucket. We each had a tin cup, like a camping cup. My friend took the table away and put the bucket in the middle of all of us. We were singing with the tape and dipping the tin cups into the bucket. Singing, singing, singing! Come on! Cheerio! Sing it again!

At about midnight, a blind African singer came by with his accordion. He started to sing for us. The whole neighborhood was drifting over to my house. Since this was close to Christmas, I had been preparing for the holidays. I had lots of fireworks, noisemakers, and sparklers. In Sierra Leone, they display fireworks between Christmas and New Year. Those two holidays are big celebrations over there. We started to use the fireworks, shooting them off outside. We had begun to decorate and light the house for Christmas, so it was bright—very nice, and everybody was happy. We were celebrating our first son, after four girls!

In Nigeria I did not eat well some of the time, and had trouble with the drinking water when I worked in the transport business. Sometimes I didn't feel well. In Lebanon, I was fine, but when I went back to Africa, I started feeling pain again. Then my wife joined me in Sierra Leone, and started to help me in the store. I relaxed a little bit, I went shopping in Freetown, and Siham made good food. But after a couple years, I started having more kidney problems. I went to Dr. Aboud, who was originally from Lebanon and had trained at

Hammersmith Hospital in London, England. He was a relative of Mr. Aboud, my advisor when buying my first house—the house we were living in.

Dr. Aboud was very nice. He gave me medicine to ease the pain, but it came on very quickly and strong sometimes. Siham prepared hot baths for me to sit in when the pain was bad. The doctor finally told me, "Habib, you have to have an operation. The stone is caught between the kidney and the bladder, in the tube called the ureter. The right kidney is working, but the left one is not functioning." This was when Said was just a baby, and Siham was pregnant with Haidar. I couldn't leave her alone to go to another country to have the operation.

I waited until Haidar was born, and then I went to the bank manager and told him that the doctor told me I had to go to London for an operation. I asked for a traveler's check for £2,000, and explained that I was going to go to Freetown to get my travel papers. I had discussed this with my wife, and she said, "Don't worry, I will take care of the store, myself, and the kids." On a Monday, I told Dr. Aboud, "I have decided to go to London. Can you get me the necessary documents, x-rays and chart notes?" He said, "I will prepare everything for you. But now you must go to the British Consulate to get your travel documents." I explained that I had obtained those in Freetown. He said, "Go there and get your visa and tell them you need to go this Friday. Your condition is very, very dangerous. If you stay one or two more weeks, it could explode, and then you are finished!"

I was really scared now! I went straight to the embassy and met the Consul. He said, "I'm sorry. I cannot give you a visa for that. There are lots of doctors here that can treat you." I responded, "But Dr. Aboud sent me to you. He said that I have to go to London because the surgery must be done out of the country, where it is more advanced and safer." The Consul again apologized, but said he could not give me a visa.

I went back to Dr. Aboud and explained what just happened. He exclaimed, "What! You sit down." He immediately telephoned the Consul and told him, "If Habib doesn't have an operation within a week, I am going to hold you responsible—for his life, for his family, for the entire problem! I am going to call the police and tell them that you refused to give this man a visa so that he could have an operation. He is a father of children, he is a businessman, he is not a trouble maker ..."

The doctor started to shout on the telephone. I could hear the Consul on the telephone. He said, "Wait, wait, wait! Send him back. How soon can he come back? Please don't go to the police; don't do anything. I will give him a visa." The doctor turned to me and said, "Go straight back to him." I went back immediately. It was one o'clock in the afternoon, when all the offices usually close, but he was holding his open for me. The policeman was waiting by the door. When I identified myself and told him I was sent by Dr. Aboud, he said, "Come inside. The Consul is waiting for you." When I met with him, he said, "I am sorry. I thought you were just using that as an excuse. You know, some people try to leave the country to smuggle diamonds out. We have been catching many of them." I asked, "Now do you believe me?" The Consul responded, "Yes, I believe what Dr. Aboud explained. I will give you a visa for one month. If you need to extend it, the embassy in London can do it for you."

I returned to Dr. Aboud with my visa. He sent me to Mr. Yazbec, the travel agent. I chuckle when I think about that big family! I asked for a seat to leave on Friday. Mr. Yazbec said that the plane was full but that he would squeeze me in. I promised that I would return on Thursday, after giving my wife some instructions about our business, saying goodbye to her and the children, and picking up the £1,000 cashier's check and £1,000 traveler's checks for which I had previously arranged. I also asked the bank manager to go to my wife to pick up money from the store while I was gone. He said that he would send his wife to help Siham, as we had become good friends. We had gone to the seaside together. The manager gave me a letter that I could present to the British West Africa Bank in London if I needed more money while I was there. He had arranged for a transfer of money to me, in case I needed it.

On Thursday, I drove down to Freetown and met my brother. On

Friday morning he went with me as we took the ferry to the airport. The plane was a direct flight and I arrived in London at about six o'clock in the evening. At the airport, they told me to take the train downtown to Victoria Station. From there I took a taxi to the hotel. Dr. Aboud was so nice. He had lived in that area of London, and had given me directions and addresses for the hospital and the hotel. The owner of the hotel was a Lebanese-Armenian. When I arrived at about nine o'clock at night, I didn't see the owner, but I did see the man who was in charge. He was a nice, handsome Spanish man, John. I explained that Dr. Aboud had sent me.

He exclaimed, "Aboud! I know him! Dr. Aboud. How is he?" I responded that he was okay. John asked, "Is he in Africa?" I said yes, and explained that he had set up an appointment for me to see Dr. Rung at the hospital in London on Monday. Dr. Aboud had called the doctor and explained my situation to him.

The hotel manager gave me a room upstairs and assured me that he would take care of me when I returned from the operation. I told John that I was hungry, and asked for a cup of coffee. He had me sit down, and made me some coffee and sandwiches. I told him that I didn't want any pork, so he apologized and changed the sandwich for me. After I ate, he said, "Habib, you look tired. I will take you to your room now." It was November and very cold. He showed me the thermostat in the room, and explained that the heater would turn on for a few hours every time I put a shilling in the meter. He worked out that I would need to deposit about five shillings to have the heater work through the night.

I slept through the night and went down to the lobby in the morning. John explained that they charged £2 each night for bed and breakfast, but for the Lebanese, it was £1.5. He had forgotten to ask for my passport the night before, so I showed him that I was Lebanese. I told him that Dr. Aboud had assured me that I could trust him. I gave him my traveler's checks, money, and traveling documents. He agreed that he would charge me at the end of my stay, rather than each day, and he put all my documents and money in his safe.

After I had breakfast, I tried to talk to people in the hotel, and watched the television in the corner. But I got bored and went out-side. It was Saturday morning—a beautiful, sunny day, and I started walking. I left the paperwork from Dr. Aboud with the address of the hotel in my room, and I forgot to take a hotel business card with me. It was Queen's Park Hotel, in the Baywater area. (In 2001, my cousin took me to see it again. It is still there; it used to have gardens around it, but now is surrounded by tall buildings.) I noted the name and area, and I saw a double decker bus, Number 13.

As a sightseeing adventure, I thought I would take the bus to the end of its route and then come back. I didn't tell John that I was going on the bus. I rode the bus to Trafalgar Square. I saw Pic-cadilly. I thought, "Oh, I recognize these places from when I played Monopoly!" I traveled to SoHo. It was nice, with lots of people. I got off the bus and walked along the street. Then I saw people put pic-tures of girls on the sidewalk. I thought, "This is not for me. Maybe I can find a movie to go to." So I started to walk … and walk … and walk. I ended up near the Queen's castle. I saw the guards, and saw people gathered near a fountain. I saw people selling cake and other food from carts. I bought a cake and started to walk again. I got to the London Bridge. By then it was about three o'clock in the after-noon; I had left the hotel at about 9:30 in the morning. "Oh my God. I need to leave here!"

I started to look for Bus Number 13. I started to jump from bus to bus. I kept asking where Bus Number 13 was, or whether it went a certain way. People would say, "Oh, I don't think so." I kept transfer-ring from bus to bus. By then it was about five o'clock in the evening and I was on the outside of London. There were nice houses, trees, and flowers that you don't see in the middle of London. The bus that I was riding stopped, and the driver said it was the end of the route and for everyone to get out. I asked, "This is the end?" He said, "Yes, now you have to take a bus in the other direction." During the day, whenever I had asked directions of the drivers or the conductors, they didn't tell me anything. They didn't know, and my English was very broken. I tried using Pidgin English like the Africans use, but it didn't help.

At the end of this route, I saw an inspector. I said, "Sir, I think you can help me." He asked, "How can I help you?" I replied, "I am lost." He said, "How are you lost?" I explained, "Yesterday, I came from Africa. I went to Queen's Park Hotel in Baywater." He said, "Son, what are you doing here? This is the end of London; the end of the bus line." I asked, "Can't you help me? Can you tell me how to get back to my hotel?" He said, "Yes, I'll help you." He asked for a piece of paper from one of the conductors. He wrote several bus numbers on the paper and signed his name. "A bus is leaving in five minutes. You get on it and tell the conductor when he comes to take money from you that you are lost and that you need him to tell you when you need to transfer to this bus next. Do you have a pen? You cross that one out. These are all the buses you have to transfer to before you can get to your hotel. Don't say anything, except that you are lost. Show the conductor this paper. Do you understand, my son?" I said, "Thank you very much. Can I cross now?" He said, "Yes, but watch for the cars!" He was a very old man with grey hair. I am sure he is dead now; God rest his soul, he was very nice to me.

So I went to the other bus, and I sat next to the door. It was completely empty! When the bus started to move the conductor came to me, "Where are you going, sir?" so that he could calculate how much I needed to pay him. I responded, "I am lost. Can you get me to this bus number?" He looked at the paper and said, "Yes, sit down." I asked, "How much?" and he said, "Nothing. Just sit down." Each time the bus stopped, I looked at him. Each time, he said, "Wait."

I finally got to the next bus, and I told that conductor, "I am lost. Can you get me to the next bus?" They were not charging me, and this went on with each bus transfer until I got to the last bus I needed to ride, Number 15. For the entire time that I was lost, I had been looking for a taxi or a policeman. But I didn't see any. Finally, right at the end, I saw a taxi and policeman, both! Then Bus Number 15 stopped. I started to get on, and as usual, explained that I was lost and trying to get to Baywater. The conductor said, "You are taking the wrong one. Do you want to do the same thing all over again? This bus is coming *from* the Baywater area, not going to Baywater." So I had to cross to the other side of the street and wait for the correct bus. By then, it was about seven or eight o'clock in the evening.

When I finally arrived back at the hotel, John, the manager was so worried. He had all of my property and my passport in his safe. "My God! Where have you been?" I explained that I had gotten lost. He asked, "Why didn't you tell me you were going out? I would have given you a card and all the directions that you needed." I said, "I thought you only had one bus, Number 13." He shouted, "We have a *million* buses!" He was so nice. He made me a pot of tea and sandwiches. I ate and told him that I was tired, and was going to go to my room and sleep. The people sitting in the lobby were all watching me. There were all different people—blondes and brunettes, from all different countries—but no one talked to me.

The next day, Sunday, I told John that I was not going to go very far—just to the end of the street. I didn't want to stay around the people in the hotel because they didn't talk with me. He gave me a paper with all the directions and addresses. I walked a little bit, and saw a store that was selling Arabic papers. Even though they were two days old, I bought the Lebanese and Egyptian papers. I wanted to sit down and read the newspaper. All the hotel guests were watching television, but we didn't have television in Africa. I wasn't used to watching television.

John noticed when I returned, and asked, "Are you back already?" He ordered some coffee for me. I put my Arabic papers on the table, and the other guests all looked at me. They asked, "Are you Arabic?" I said, "What the hell! Do you think I am Japanese or Chinese?" This started to open the people up. The men were from Jordan, Iraq, Kuwait, Syria. We shook hands and started talking. But one man still did not join in. He was different. The Arabic people were there for a car show.

At that time, two new guests came in and were trying to talk to John, the manager. But I noticed that he could not understand what they were saying. I understood that they were talking about their passports, and were trying to explain that they wanted to stay one week. I called over, *"Marhaba"*—which means "hello." They responded in Arabic and told me that they did not understand John's

English. They were Jordanian. I offered to translate for them and helped make room arrangements.

A couple hours went by, and I was still reading the newspapers. One of the older men who I had noticed in the lobby the night before was an Armenian. He was very friendly, and he started talking to me and asking me about my kidney problem. He told me that he was there because of medical problems too. He had five children, and wanted something to make him stronger, and able to have more children.

A few minutes later, John called me over. "Habib," he said. "Can you speak Iraqi?" I said yes, so John told me that two brothers were coming to London for college. I was surprised that, since they were going to college, they did not know English. I did the translation for them, and John did not charge me for the sandwich that he made me that day. Later, a Kuwaiti or Syrian came into the hotel, and I again translated for John. We all ended up reading my newspapers and visiting with each other in the hotel lobby. I enjoyed having the people around me, keeping me company.

The next day, Monday morning, I came down from my room with my medical file from Dr. Aboud, ready to go to the hospital. I asked John to call a taxi. John said, "Why do you want a taxi, Habib? It is too expensive. You should go on the train." I responded, "What train? I didn't see any train." He said he would show me where to get on the train, and explained that it ran underground in London. I was worried and said, "How can I take the train? Maybe I will get lost again." He assured me, "No, it is very easy. You go to the end of this road, turn left, and see the big sign and lots of people. You go down the stairs, enter the train, and go one, two, three, four, five stops. At the fifth stop, you get off the train, go back up the stairs, walk a little bit, and the hospital will be just opposite you. You can't miss it at all, and you will only pay about a shilling. Now do you still want to go by taxi – they will charge you £2 or £3? I will save you money. And if you get lost, this is the card to bring you back to my hotel."

John told me to go east on the train, and not to jump across the tracks to go to the other train. John also told me not to push myself onto a crowded train, because the doors closed quickly and could squeeze me. "Just wait until the next one comes," he said. I laugh now, when I remember how John instructed me on how to take the trains, just as if he were my father, advising me. I said, "Good. Thank you very much."

I walked to the end of the street, turned left and saw people going down some stairs. I went down them too, and did just what John told me to do. I sat near the door. I found the correct stop, got out, and walked just a little bit. Then I saw the huge hospital, like a castle, with big trees all around it. I had never been in London before, and had never been to a hospital. There was a small hospital in Africa but I hadn't ever been there either, because I gave the doctors ice cream, so when my family and I needed medical attention, they came to us. They brought the hospital to my wife when she delivered her babies—all for a bottle of whiskey!

I went to the door of the hospital, and spoke first with the guard. He told me to go inside, and they would tell me everything I needed to know. I asked at the desk, "Is Dr. Rung here? I have a message for him." They called someone on the phone, and then turned back to me. "Go down the hall, take the lift up to the fourth floor, walk straight, and then ask a nurse or anyone in uniform to direct you to Dr. Rung's office." I thanked them, and did exactly what they said. It was so nice and clean in his office, and so quiet you could hear a pin drop. The building was very old, probably 100 to 200 years old. There were sculptures of lions, lots of artwork, and thick carpets so plush that half of my shoes disappeared when I walked in them.

I was so intrigued looking around, that I forgot myself. I saw a nurse passing and finally said, "Please, please. Can I talk to you?" The nurse said, "Yes, what can I do for you?" I asked her direct me to Dr. Rung's office, and she told me to follow her. She took me to an office to wait and asked me to sit down, saying that she would find him. After about 10 or 15 minutes, a man came in and asked if I was looking for him. I said, "Are you Dr. Rung?" He said, "Yes," and pointed out his big name patch on his jacket. I told him I had a package for him from Dr. Aboud, and he asked, "Are you Habib?"

He took the package and reviewed the information. Then he said that he wanted to take new x-rays. He said, "I want you to come back in three days. You look fine right now." I chuckled and said, "Yes, I did a lot of walking Saturday because I got lost in London. Before that walk, I had to continually use the restroom, but I was much better after that long walk." I told the doctor that I used to have to go to the bathroom every five or ten minutes. On the plane, the stewardess even had me sit near the restroom for everyone's convenience. Dr. Rung looked at me again and said, "You look okay. Dr. Aboud told me that you were going to die within one week!"

Then he explained that he would set aside some time for me in a few days because he was so very busy, as was the x-ray department. He also explained that he would do a complete examination before deciding what should be done next. He said that I would have to deposit about £300 with the hospital, and asked if I had it. I said, "Yes. I have my traveler's checks." He left to arrange everything, and came back in 15 fifteen minutes to tell me to come back on Wednesday morning at the same time. He said not to eat anything after Tuesday evening, because of all the tests he wanted to run. He asked for my local address and telephone number, and he gave it to his nurse.

I left to pay the deposit. It was £250—big money at that time. I had taken about £2,000 with me. The hospital offered private rooms, or rooms with many other patients in them. I asked for the private room, with the private doctor and surgeon. My room would even include a television. After making those arrangements, I left to take the train back to my hotel. I did everything in reverse, exactly as John had taught me. When I returned to the hotel, he asked me how everything was. I explained that I would be going back on Wednesday morning for all the tests. John wrote everything down—when I could eat, when I had to stop eating for the tests.

Then he told me that he was going to make a sandwich for me, but I told him, "No, I am going to celebrate today. I want to go to a restaurant." I had seen a restaurant at the front of the hotel. John explained that a widowed lady ran the restaurant after her husband died, serving breakfast and lunch. He said that she served very nice steak, mashed potatoes, boiled cauliflower, and apple pie—typical English dishes. I said I was going to have lunch there, and John told me to tell the proprietress that he had sent me to her. When I arrived, I told her that John had sent me. She said, "Oh, John sent you." I relaxed and had some tea after the meal. It cost about two shillings and was so nice.

I told Dr. Rung when I went back to have my tests on Wednesday that it took me much longer to go to the bathroom than normal, and I felt very much better afterwards. I thought maybe it was the food, the tea, the climate, or the exercise from the long walk. I had my tests and then they had me sit in a waiting room. Dr. Rung told the staff to get me something to eat. They asked me what kind of sandwich I wanted, and I told them, "Anything; I am very hungry." They brought me two slices of cheese and a cup of coffee. Dr. Rung called me in again and explained: "Habib, we looked at everything. You look a lot better now. You, yourself, said that you feel much better. You are not going to the restroom every few minutes." I agreed.

He continued, "Habib, I want to tell you something. Because you are drinking this London water, and in this climate, I think you are improving. You say that you come from Lebanon, where the climate is even better than London. But if you have to go back to Africa, you need an operation. There was a kidney stone between the kidney and the bladder. One kidney is almost gone; there is very little left of it. And some of your liver is destroyed. If you want to stay in London or go back to Lebanon, you don't need an operation. You are still young—in your mid-thirties—and your body will heal. You can take medicines and improve. If you drink lots of water in London or Lebanon, the water will dissolve the stone. Since you arrived here and started drinking the London water, a little opening has developed to reduce the blockage. If you want to return to Africa, you will need an operation, and we have to find a new kidney for you. Otherwise, you could get very sick and it is very dangerous to your health."

Dr. Rung told me I had to tell him then whether I was planning on staying in Africa or whether I would be able to move to London or Lebanon. Even if I did not return to Africa, I would need to stay in

London for a few months for treatment to dissolve the kidney stone. I said, "Doctor, my job is there, my business is in Africa. I can't do any work in Lebanon because I have been gone from Lebanon for 15 years. If I were to go back to my country, and trouble or war broke out, then I would need to take my children and leave again. That is why I left my country in the first place."

Dr. Rung responded, "Okay. Then we have to look for a kidney for you, and you have to stay alert and near a telephone so that we can call you at any time. We have lots of accidents and people dying, and they leave their bodies to charity. You need a kidney. You stay here, and every three or four days we will check you and test your blood. It will take a few minutes each time. We will need to do this until we can find a kidney that matches your blood. Then we will call you, do the operation and you can go back home, after one or two months." I commented that my visa was only good for one month. He asked, "Where is your passport?" and I told him it was back in the hotel. Dr. Rung said, "Okay, don't worry about that. I will call the Immigration Office, and they will do the necessary things for you."

I waited about two weeks, and then Dr. Rung called me. He said, "You have to be in the hospital by six o'clock tomorrow night. You will have the operation at eight o'clock in the morning. Tell your hotel manager that you will be having this operation, and that you don't know how long it will be before you come back to your room. If you want to send a letter to your family to explain that you are having the operation, you need to do that now."

In the evening, I packed pajamas, shirts, and pants, as the doctor had asked me to do. I told John, the hotel manager, where I would be staying in the hospital. I had met a businessman from Trinidad, a big man, who was also staying at the hotel. I told him about my upcoming operation. He said, "I will come visit you, Habib. I will make sure to see you after your operation." Then I wrote a letter to my wife, telling her about the operation.

But just then, in London, there was a mail strike for one or two weeks, so the letter did not get out! Siham had been waiting for a letter or cable from me, and was worried. She went to our bank manager in Kenema, who told her about the strike in London.

When I entered the hospital, they asked me if I wanted a private room, and if I wanted a master surgeon. The master surgeon was somewhere near London. They called him and told him he needed to come to the hospital for my surgery, and they would send someone to pick him up. He asked for £200! I said, "Okay, I will pay whatever necessary. But I want a good surgeon, good nurse, good doctor—good everything!!" I had the money; I didn't care.

That night they prepared me for the surgery—they shaved my skin, gave me some very nice soup and a glass of water, and made the room warm. I didn't get to have bread or coffee, and they said I could not eat anything else. I put my pajamas on, and they brought me some Arabic books. They had books in all languages; a big cart with all kinds of books. The staff asked what books I wanted. I chose an old-time Arabic book that I liked. I read it for about an hour. Then I got sleepy and went to bed. I don't know what they put in the food. I wondered – it was only eight o'clock—how could I be so sleepy? I know their tricks!

I slept, and the nurses woke me up at six o'clock in the morning and got me ready for the surgery. Then I waited, since they said they were not ready yet. The person who was donating his kidney had not yet died. He had been in an accident and was still fighting for his life. I would get a very fresh kidney. Finally, at ten o'clock the nurses came and gave me an injection of anesthetic to put me to sleep. I started talking to the nurses; I wasn't getting sleepy and they reported this to the doctor. He asked me, "Habib, when you were in Africa, did you drink alcohol?" I said, "Yes, too much." He asked again, "Like how much, too much?" I replied, "Sometimes one-half bottle of whiskey, or one-half bottle of brandy. If I was enjoying everything, maybe I would finish the bottle."

The surgeon shouted, "What! A *bottle* of whiskey?"

I explained, "Yes, but Doctor, not all at once. It takes time—a few hours. I eat and drink, visit with my friends. We finish one bottle, and then go to the next one." The doctor turned to the nurses and spoke to them. Then they brought in two *big* injections—shoot, shoot. Then the doctor said, "Habib, tell us about Africa." I asked, "What do you want to know? The black women are very nice, very sweet." I started to joke with him, then I couldn't remember anything else. I went to sleep.

It took six hours to do the operation. They cut me from my kidney all the way to my groin. The doctors split my ureter where the stone was, and removed it, and cleaned the area. They got the kidney out and cleaned it. But after inspecting the kidney, they decided not to change it. One-half of it was rotten but the other half was good. I was 33 years old at the time and they thought I was young enough to heal and continue with the partial kidney. They inspected the liver and saw that pieces of it were gone. They cleaned it, put medicine on it and put it back in my abdomen. Then they sewed me back up.

I woke up at four or five o'clock in the evening. I was so thirsty. I was hooked up to IVs for blood and fluids. I opened my eyes and the doctor said, "Are you okay, Habib?" I asked, "When is the operation going to be done?" He replied, "The operation has been completed." I asked, "Do I have a new kidney?" The doctor told me, "Habib, we will explain what we did later. Don't worry." The nurses removed the IVs and left me to rest, because I was so tired.

The next day, I woke up with all my bandages, and attached to bags to collect my urine, because they had to make sure that my system was working again. But nothing was draining into the bags, so they were worried. The doctor came and said, "Habib, you have to start going to the bathroom again." They were feeding me water, beer, any liquids to help me. The young nurses, 17 or 18 years old, would come to put a bedpan under me. I told them, "You guys, I can't go this way. I'm not used to somebody watching me when I have to go to the bathroom." The head nurse came to me in the afternoon and explained, "Habib, the doctor said that, if by tomorrow, you still can't go to the bathroom, we will have to operate again to see where there is a blockage, and to re-open the tube."

I was scared. I told her, "I feel like I could go to the bathroom, but I can't do it with people all around me. I am embarrassed to do it around people. And I have to stand or sit; I can't do it lying in bed." She understood and called two orderlies to help get me out of bed. She said, "This is going to be hard for you, Habib." But I said, "It's okay if it is hard for me. Just help me get on my feet and then everybody go out the door." They tied a rope around me to help me stand and tied the bell to my hand. I was just like a dead man; only my mouth was working. They put the container on the floor, but I said, "Give it to me." She said, "No, you go on the floor, go anyplace you want, but just do it." They all left the room.

I thought, "Oh, God, help me." Then I start counting, "One ... two ... three"—all the way to one hundred. Then, *szszszszsz*. I finally started going; urine and blood from the operation. I don't know if the people were watching me from the little window in the door, but they all came in clapping and congratulating me. During polo season medals were given to the players who accomplished something, so they jokingly said that they were going to call and get a medal for me! I apologized for making a mess, but they said, "Don't worry, we are glad you finally did it. We are happy. You have saved a few hours in surgery because now you don't need an operation." The doctor came and told me again that the operation was a success, and that they did not need to change my kidney. For two years, he said that I had to stay on a diet that he would give me. They would continue my diet while I was in London. When I got ready to go back to Africa, they would write it all out for me.

The businessman from Trinidad, who I met in the hotel, had been waiting—God bless his soul! So the nurses told him it was finally okay to visit me. He brought paper and a pen and said, "Habib, write a letter to your wife, telling her that you are recovering." I said, "I can't even hold a pen, I am so weak." I had lost so much blood, that I had to have blood transfusions.

I wrote, *Dear Siham, the operation was successful. This is just the second day after the operation. I hope I will recover soon. As soon as I do, I have to go to downtown London and buy a present for you and the kids. As soon as I feel well, I will send you a cable that I am coming back. Don't worry. I am okay. The doctor told me that I am okay and that the operation was successful. And don't worry—I'm okay*. I wrote that part many times! The businessman took my address and promised me that he would mail it right away. My family got it and they were so happy.

I stayed in the hospital for two weeks. The nurses came in and changed the bandages and the drainage bags. Some of the nurses had very gentle hands. They had to peel off the plastic that was over the stitches, then remove one stitch every day. The doctor also visited. He explained that my stone was like a big rough-surfaced brown bean. When I asked him if I could see it, he said, "No, Habib." I responded, "It's mine." He said, "It's not yours anymore, Habib. You signed, agreeing that whatever we took out was ours. We have to study it to help other people."

While I was still in the hospital, my passport expired. I told the doctor, and he called the Immigration Office. They sent an officer on a motorcycle, who took my passport, and had it renewed for three months. He was so nice. When he returned, he said, "I have added three months for you, sir. If you need more time, tell the doctor, and we will give you as much time as you want. Even if you get out of the hospital and want more time in London, you are welcome. We like people like you, and respect you."

After 15 days, the hospital told me that I needed to leave, because they needed the room for patients who were waiting. They said that I would do very well, comparing me to a Pakistani man who had the same operation but was still very sick. Even after one week, he was not out of his bed, walking, like I was. I was walking, getting dressed, and doing well. The doctor told me to come to the hospital every day to be checked and keep having the stitches removed. The operation, doctor visits, and hospital charges totaled about £400 in those days; and there was no such thing as medical insurance!

One day I was going across the road to the hotel, and a car was coming toward me very fast. He was going to hit me. I was walking very slowly, because I was not yet recovered, and I was still hurting. I gave him a nasty look, and cussed at him in Arabic. He kept going, but then stopped and came back. He said, "I am sorry." I told him that I had just had an operation. He apologized several times more.

Some of the hotel guests that I had gotten to know wanted to fight with him. I told them, "No, he said he was sorry."

The hotel guest who didn't talk with us was from Saudi Arabia. He was there to have medical treatments. He had just gotten married, but was unable to consummate the marriage. He was a young, strong man, but something was wrong, maybe mentally. Maybe he was shy or scared and he didn't want to talk about it, because he was embarrassed. The doctors told him to find girls in London, and to practice. He followed the instructions and he recovered!

Two people came to the hotel asking for Said. We told them that we didn't know of a Said, but that there was one man who sat alone and did not speak. They exclaimed, "That's the one; that is the man!" His brothers asked him why he did not speak to the other guests, pointing out that they were Arabs like him. He then came to us and apologized, saying he was ashamed of his behavior. We continued to visit with him. That is how we learned of his story.

It was close to Christmas, and London was getting very cold, like Lebanon. I only had seven or eight stitches left, and I told the doctor that I wanted to go back to Africa because I could not take the weather. It was costing me two and three shillings very often to turn on the heat in my room, or in the salon downstairs. The doctor said, "Habib, you can go back. Do you have nurses and doctors there?" I replied, "Of course."

I made plans to return to Africa. I asked the hotel manager to call the airport and reserve my seat, because I had been holding a return ticket. He called a taxi to take me shopping for my wife and children. I bought gifts that filled two cases. For Mama, I bought a suit—a skirt and jacket. I remember: They were three colors, white, beige and blue. Even though I stayed in the hospital or hotel during my entire stay and bought many gifts, I returned to Africa with an extra £200 pounds left. It was amazing how inexpensive things were then! The exchange rate was 10 Lebanese pounds to one British pound.

It was an easy flight back to Kenema, Africa. My brother picked me up, and we went to Siham's sister's house in Freetown. Because my wife had to take care of the store while I was gone, her sister had helped by taking care of our little girl, Suad, who was four or five years old. When Suad saw me, she hugged me, and cried, "Papa!" The next day we took the airplane from Freetown to Kenema—a little less than an hour's flight. I met my wife. She was so happy. I asked Siham to find me a nurse, and the doctor gave me all the supplies for taking care of the incision—the bandages and cotton. The first day, the nurse they sent me pulled the plastic covering off roughly and removed a stitch. It hurt, and the wound bled a little. The second day, I told the Siham, "Call the doctor and tell him to send me a different nurse." Siham said, "Don't worry. I will do it for you." Believe me, she did it very slowly and carefully. It didn't hurt me one bit. She was very nice.

The doctor had given me a diet. He told me to only drink one cup of coffee a day, no tea, and no hard liquor. If I wanted, I could drink one or two pints of good, imported beer. The doctor instructed that, for one year, I couldn't have hot peppers, black pepper or salt—and no sex, either. He said not to eat too much; I should eat just a little bit four, five, six times a day, or my belly would split open. He explained that, although the outside healed more quickly, from the inside the healing would take one year.

Every day, I went from my bed to the store. I sat all day in a chair with a table in front of me. The only time I got up, was to go out to the restroom. Siham did all the shopping, and all the work. She took care of the kids. If I started to get up, she would say, "No. Don't go. Sit down!" For one complete year, she did not let me do anything. After the year, I started to move goods around the store. But the doctor told me not to do it too quickly. My wife and I agreed to continue this for two years to make sure that I was completely healthy. So I gradually started adding hot peppers, more food, and even started to enjoy my wife again.

I was very lucky to recover completely. When I first came back, Dr. Aboud told me about a man who had the same operation as me in Freetown. The doctors were all trained in London, so they were good, but the blood was bad and they didn't have supplies. He died after only about five months. The London hospital was just so clean.

The floors shone. Everything smelled clean. That is one of the things that impressed me the most. Dr. Aboud was such a good, nice man. He had recommended that I go to London, and gave me good advice, God bless his soul. I brought him a gift from London to thank him. When I saw him he hugged me and cried—he was so happy for me. After that, I tried to take good care of myself.

I promised Said £1 when he learned to walk. That was a lot of money for a child back then. After exactly nine months, Said walked, and I gave him the money. Said was growing, and then Haidar was born about two years later. When he was about three years old, Haidar had an African boy that was a nanny, or babysitter. Haidar wanted to go outside to play. I told his nanny not to let him go far, the road was busy. I went inside and was busy with customers in my store. Then I heard the screech of a car braking. Haidar was very close to the car. A very nice doctor was there. He said the boy was not hit. I was very athletic in those days, and I just put my hand on the store counter, leapt over it and was outside. I saw that Haidar was okay, and saw his nanny coming toward me. I was so upset, that I slapped the nanny with my hand. I said some bad words. I do not forgive myself for that, because I lost my temper.

The doctor came over and said, "Habib, nothing happened to your son. Take it easy. Never mind, everything is okay." Then another man, Kamara, who was my friend and neighbor—a diamond dealer who was considered the African chief in the area—came over to me and said, "You Lebanese people come to this country and make yourselves bosses." He started to talk abusively to me. I started to get upset with him. I didn't ever tell him that I was sorry. I should have apologized to him, because I should not have slapped the African boy who was our nanny.

Everything was confused and I was upset. The African chief wanted to demonstrate his power in the community, so he went to the court and summoned me. I was surprised because we had been good friends—I had given him money and vegetables from the store. He hired a lawyer from his party, so he didn't have to pay anything. So I hired a lawyer, but I had to pay. He was the best lawyer in town. He was educated in Cambridge, London. He was married to an English woman. We went to the court and the judge knew me. But all these people are sorry for me, but they cannot acknowledge that they know me. A Lebanese friend of mine did business with Kamara, the diamond dealer and area chief, so he went to the chief and asked him, "What's wrong between you and Habib?" Kamara explained, "Habib, I like him, but I have lost £50 because of the court costs." My Lebanese friend countered, "If I give you the £50 will you finish with this problem?" Kamara replied, "I have nothing against Habib, but he made me lose £50. I have nothing. If I get that £50 pounds, I will forget everything. I make friends. He is my neighbor, he is my good friend." And it was true that he was a good friend. When I traveled to Lebanon, I left my family in his care. So the next day, I went to the court. I waited for Mr. Kamara to appear.

The judge, who knew me well, asked, "Habib, why are you here?" I explained that I was waiting for Mr. Kamara. The judge said, "The case is dismissed. Go home." I said, "Okay, Your Excellency." When I arrived back at the store, Kamara was sitting on the veranda. I said, "Mr. Kamara, how are you?" He said, "I am good, Mr. Habib." He stood up and got me a chair. I said, "How did you do that for me?" He asked, "What did I do?" I explained, "I went to the court, I didn't see you there. You made me go for nothing. I waste my time, and leave Mother working here." He said, "I'm sorry. You are my friend. We have to forget this. We are friends. I am sorry, Habib. You are upset. Your child is my child. I don't know what to think. We are brothers, we are friends. I beg forgiveness." I said, "Oh, my Kamara," and we hugged each other. Kamara said, "No more trouble between me and you! No more fighting!"

I was feeling fine, and we were starting to make money again. I called my family in Lebanon and asked them to send my kids back to us, during one of their school holidays. Siham and I decided to expand, and that we would order a good ice cream machine. The man who we were buying the ice cream from was charging us too much. He also had 60 or 70 bicycle ice cream carts. I offered £50, but he insisted on £100. I told him I would give him the £100, but I didn't have the money. We made a deal and I was able to purchase some of the carts to extend my business.

Adding the ice cream business and my older children coming to live with us in Africa meant enlarging the house and the store. We wanted to extend the house behind the store by adding a fifteen-by-sixty-foot space. I divided the space into two bedrooms, a bathroom and kitchen. I moved my original ice cream machinery into the area on the side where we used to sleep. The equipment could not produce enough—I needed more production capability. Coincidentally, I had been going to visit Said and his cousin, Amir. (Sometimes I don't tell people what I want, but I am very lucky because it happens anyway! When I think of something I need, God helps me get it!) When I arrived, I said, "Hello, Uncle Said! How's business?" Then I went looking for Amir, the cousin who helped him. I was looking everywhere, and I saw Said's own machine—an old one, stored on the veranda. He had purchased a new system, ordered from Europe. He was in the process of expanding his business, and had 40 or 50 boys who bought ice cream, and then went to the outlying town and other villages and sold it.

I decided to ask Said why he had purchased the new system. "Uncle—congratulations! I see that you bought a new ice cream machine. What's wrong with your old one?"

"Nothing," he replied. "It is still working. If you want it, you can take it."

I replied, "I may not have the amount of money you would ask for it. I need it, but I manage with the one you already gave me. You know, I have my wife and children here. I had to go to London for an operation. I am so poor now."

Said said, "Habib, who is asking you for money? You just go get your truck, grab it and go." I gratefully said, "Oh, thank you, thank you. Okay, I will take it. It will make more room for you. Space is a big problem in your store?" He said, "Yes, it is a big problem. I want to use the space for something else. If you want it, take it. Don't tell me your 'this and that' story too much!"

I ran out of his store and hired a truck to transport the machinery, before Said could change his mind. I asked a very big African boy to help load it, because it was very heavy. Besides making the trip to visit Said, I was on a buying trip for my store. I forgot *everything* because I was so happy and excited about getting the additional ice cream machine!

When I returned, I told my wife that I was going to repair and install the ice cream machine, and throw the old one away. My little old one always gave me trouble and it was too small. Every half hour it made only one or two kettles of ice cream. I needed more production. I had lots of boys who started out with my ice cream in the morning. But they wanted to make more than one trip each day; they wanted to return to purchase throughout the day, making two or three trips.

Some Swiss people had a cold storage business; they contracted to hold meat and other products that needed refrigeration when transported from London and other European cities to Freetown. They had a smaller branch in Kenema and had trained an African man, Phillip, to manage the facility and make repairs to the refrigeration equipment. He had told me that anytime I needed help, I could call him. So I sent my boy to get him.

He came, and I explained that I wanted to fix the machine and install it. When I took the machine from Said, I brought all the pipes and fittings—everything! The compressor was about five horsepower. We poured a square of cement about 18 inches by 18 inches and four inches high, and let it cure for three days. Then we bolted the compressor to it, to control the vibration. We ran the pipes, and Phillip soldered the connections. We strung the electrical wires and connected them. Phillip knew how to do everything about this. I learned so much from that boy!

Then we were ready to make ice cream. I put the water and the salt in. Then I put the heavy bottle of mix in the kettle and started the process to make the ice cream. There were two, three, four kettles coming out every half hour! I had to go buy more containers to hold the ice cream in the freezer! I told my wife, "You see, we now have ice cream. But we are still buying the cones, and they are very expensive. What shall we do?"

I had a German friend who worked in a repair garage. I had an English friend who had a store for selling cloth. I had lots of friends, including the manager of the bank. Every Sunday, I opened my store for half a day, and all my friends came to drink beer. Siham made Lebanese food for them—they all loved our Lebanese food. I told them that I needed to have less expensive cones. The English friend said that he had been to Italy, and had seen very good ice cream machines that made better ice cream. My ice cream was local and could be sold cheap. But the Italian machine made very soft, smooth ice cream. It required only a five foot by five foot space, and was a self-contained system.

The German man said that he could order a machine from Germany that would make the cones, at about 100 for 10 cents. I shouted, "One hundred for 10 cents! I am paying $1.00 for 100 cones!" I moaned, "Guys, leave me alone. Don't tell me about these things. I have no money. I just borrowed money from the bank manager." The bank manager, whose name was William, said, "Habib, take it easy. Wait, wait! Don't cry. I know you like to cry too much when you need something."

He asked the English man how much the Italian ice cream machine cost. The English man said that he didn't know, but that he could bring the catalogue from his house on the next visit. The German man said he had the information for the cone machine at his house. They agreed to bring the information the following Sunday. They said, "If Mama Fakih will make good Lebanese food for us, we will bring the catalogues and figure out how to get this machinery." I replied, "You guys—you are joking. Go away!"

The next Sunday, they all came and sat down together to discuss the ice cream systems. They acted like I didn't have anything to do with it, and said, "Habib, you stay out of this. You go away and wait on the customers. Leave us alone." They talked and talked and talked. Then they called me over. "Okay, Habib," they said. "We are going to order the ice cream machine and the cone machine for you."

I asked, "Where am I going to get the money for this?" The bank manager said, "Don't worry, Habib. You can pay £20 per month." My wife said, "No, how about £25!" I replied to her, "You be quiet! He said £20, you said £25." She responded, "Okay, Papa." But I said, "Okay, we will do what Mama said—we will pay £25 each month. Don't worry." I chuckle when I remember this.

After four or five weeks, the ice cream machine arrived at the wharf in Freetown. One week later the cone machine arrived. My German friend took his van, drove down to the Freetown wharf, and unloaded the two machines. On the second day of his trip, I opened the door of my store in the morning and saw the truck with the two machines backing toward my store.

I said, "What are you doing? What is that?" The driver replied that it was the ice cream machines and asked me to call some boys to help unload them. We arranged room for the machines and connected the pipes and electricity. They all said, "Make one kettle of ice cream, Habib." After only about fifteen minutes, we had beautiful ice cream—very good ice cream! Then we started working on the cone machine. It required a three prong plug for electricity, like an oven. The batter was poured into three molds that were positioned very close together. The batter spread and came together at the seams during the baking process. After the baking process, the cones moved to the end of the machine. You had to take them off, or they would fall and break. The cone mix for the batter was for 100,000 cones, which was what the machine was designed to produce. I called the Englishman, the German, and the bank manager, and asked them to help me reduce the recipe to make about 1,000 cones per day. They said, "Let's make it to 2,000." I said, "Okay, 2,000." They said, "No, make it for 5,000." I bantered back with them, "5,000." They started to calculate it out—so much flour, salt, etc. The family who originally got me started in making ice cream would not share the recipe for the cones, and they always mixed it before I arrived in the morning, or after I left in the evening. I tried to figure out what the ingredients were from the boxes and bags of supplies they had. I knew flour, corn flour, and starch had to be in the recipe. We went through 10 or 15 bags of flour trying to get the recipe right. We wasted so much. It kept not working. One day, my friends came. They brought two cases of beer, and we tried all day to make the batter. They stayed until nine or ten o'clock, and it still wasn't right. One day, after we had been trying, they got fed up and went back home by about six o'clock. I was sitting, sweating all evening—it was hot.

Siham and I started talking. I said, "Siham, I want to try one more thing. We did not mix the batter well enough; we need to mix it better." Siham said, "Oh don't worry yourself. Let's go to bed. You are so tired. Look at yourself." I was so tired. My face was red from the fire near ovens. I also thought maybe we should let the batter rest for awhile. I didn't throw the whole kettle of batter away after using some for a sample. So I let the remaining batter rest for at least three hours. Before I went to bed, I said to Siham, "I am going to try one last time." I took the long paddle and mixed it really well. I left it to rest. I turned the machine on to warm it up. I opened up the pot and prayed, "Oh God, are you going to help me this one last time?" I put the batter in the mold, called, "In the name of God," and put the lid down.

After a few minutes, it made a *shhhhh* sound. This sound was much different! I pressed the top down, and some of the batter dribbled out. I waited and saw that the batter on the sides was getting brown. So I lifted the lid and it made a *bock* sound, a *pop* sound. I opened the lid and saw that the batter had worked. I started yelling, "It works! It works!" Siham came in shouting, "What is wrong? What is wrong?" When I told her it finally worked, we started dancing around and laughing. Siham called our three friends who had been trying to help us, to tell them that we finally got the cones to work. It was very late and they were all asleep. They all came over. The bank manager and his wife came over in their pajamas. They stayed until one o'clock in the morning, celebrating. I still had whiskey and other alcohol in the house for my friends. We made the recipe several times while we celebrated!

When Mr. Said learned I was making my own cones, he was upset. He complained, "Habib, you are competing with me. I used to make money from you, and now I won't see your money at all." I responded, "Well, you were charging me too much." I told him the whole story about my friends getting the equipment for me. He said, "Okay—good luck."

I had bought a refrigerator case for the store from him. I carried bacon, cheese, and yogurt on the top section, and bottles on the bottom, accessible to the customers. The engine and compressor were on the back side of the unit. The compressor I had eventually broke down. I called London, gave them the number of the compressor and asked how much it would cost me to ship a new one to Sierra Leone. They said it would be about £300 for the compressor and another £100 for shipping—altogether almost £400. I bought the whole refrigeration system for £200. I said, "Okay, never mind."

I started thinking, *What should I do?* At that time a company was building a very large cold storage unit to store fish so that people in the town could buy fish for themselves, or for resale. The manager/engineer for the facility was an Italian who was very friendly with the Lebanese community. He knew how to drink the Arabic coffee, and eat kibbee. When he wanted ingredients for Lebanese food, his friends sent him to me. He came to me, "How are you, Mr. Habib?" I replied, "Good. Who told you my name?" He responded, "Oh, I know Lebanese people and I am here to build a storage building for holding fish." I thought "Oh, how lucky I am!" I asked, "Do you like Arabic coffee?" and he said, "Yes, I love it and I have been here almost a week and haven't had any." So I told Siham, "Quick, make the coffee." I turned to the man, and offered, "If you want coffee every day, you come here, and we will make you some." Siham brought the coffee and we sat down to talk. We talked for a long time.

After a while I came to the point. I said, "My friend, I want to ask you something. I bought that refrigerator for £200 in Freetown." I explained that I called London, only to discover that the cost was too high. He said, "Why do you call those Englishmen? You haven't seen English marry French, French marry Italian, Italian marry English." I said, "Yes ..." He said, "Why do you think that way? You are Lebanese. I know Lebanese; you have a brain to think with!" I said, "Okay ..."

I still didn't understand. My wife was listening, and asked me, "What is this marriage business? If he wants to go marry, let him. What is this business?" I was sitting and thinking about what he said. Finally, I shouted, "I got it!"

"What do you get?" Siham asked. "What did he mean?"

"Goodbye," I said. "I am going to Freetown." Siham asked again, "What is it that you understand?" I replied, "Never mind, never mind. You won't understand. It is men's business, Mama!"

I took money for gas and opened the door. I called my driver, Sedu. When we drove to the gas station to fill up, he asked where we were going. He thought we were going to the country or something. When I told him we were going to Freetown, he said, "Freetown! Wait, I must go tell my wife!" We drove during the night to get to Freetown. We reached my brother's place, where we slept.

In the morning I went to Mr. Said. He had a big store and could get anything we wanted. We greeted each other. I told him that I came to shop for vegetables and other things. I said, "But I wanted to say good morning to you and have a cup of coffee with you. You are like my father. I love you." I walked around his store and, my God, I saw about 20 or 30 compressors, from very small to very large! I saw a few that were the right size for me. When I went back to sit down with Uncle for my coffee, I asked, "What are you going to do with all these things? What would you do with all this inventory if you wanted to sell this place?"

Mr. Said replied, "Who said I was going to sell this place? Who's going to buy this place? Who would pay me?"

I responded, "I don't know. On this trip, I didn't buy too many fruits and vegetables. And you know that I would have to go back with the van partially empty. Why don't you give me something to make the van heavy on the road?"

He said, "Okay, you go pick some things on the veranda—some engines and compressors." I agreed, and asked for someone to help me because they were heavy. I picked three compressors, exactly the same as what I needed. I looked at them and they were not broken. I gave the boy helping me load them £1 and told him to pick a good one for me in case one day I will use it. I told him to put them on the outside end of the truck to make it heavy. My driver, Sedu, came to me, and said, "Master, let me put them further inside." I whispered, "You shut up. After we go, we will put them inside. I don't want them to know that I need them. This is going to replace the one that doesn't work in our refrigerator. I was able to get it for nothing." Sedu said, "Ah, Master, you are able to take it for nothing! You will have to give me good money so that I can eat. I am so hungry."

I went back to Mr. Said and told him what I was taking. He said, "You are only taking three? Take all you want." I joked, "That's enough. Do you want me to take all of your trash? Each time I come, I will take something from you. Eventually, I will take them all." He said, "Okay, Habib, go." When I returned home in the evening, Siham was just getting ready to close the store. She saw the compressors and asked where I got them. I told her the story and we laughed together.

The compressor was made in Italy. Now we understood the story the engineer told us. The next day, we removed the old compressor and cleaned the new one. We added oil and started it. It worked! We had to drill and change various parts because it did not fit. We also had to change pipes, because the sizes of the connections were different. We opened the hole on the top to draw the air, and started the engine. It started with a loud *TCHU, TCHU, TCHU, TCHU, TCHU*. It started to quiet down—*tchu, tchu, tchu, tchu, tchu*. We were ready to close it and lock it. We let the gas pass in a little at a time. The valve was like the heart of a human being, and as the gas passed through the machine, the compressor transformed it, creating the cold temperatures.

One time the building material store in the town near our house blew up. This was in the late sixties. Siham and I were out of town visiting friends. There were propane tanks stored in the shop, and they exploded, one after the other. Someone had been smoking. It shook the ground and frightened all the kids. They were home alone. They jumped out of bed and stood at the back door, watching the glow in the sky. The younger kids were scared, but the older kids thought it was exciting. They stayed at a neighbor's house for a little while. Siham and I didn't know about it until we arrived back in town.

The children were growing up. One time, I called my father to see if I could arrange to go to Lebanon and visit the holy land. But he told me not to come then; the fighting in the area was too bad. The road to Damascus, the holy area, was blocked. He suggested that we wait until things calmed down. We waited five or six months.

Meanwhile a Muslim preacher came to visit in our area and had a meeting for us. During the meeting, he asked if anyone had anything to say. I said, "Yes, Your Honor. I had four girls and no sons, so I promised God that if he would give me a son, I would take him to the holy land. I finally did have a son, but have not been able to make the trip to keep my promise to God, because of all the fighting in the area. What should I do?" I had been letting Said's hair grow until we made the holy trip. The preacher told me to cut his hair, weigh it, and send it and an equal amount of paper money to the religious site, as a donation for the poor people. I called the barber and had him cut Said's hair real short. We put his cut hair from the towel into a paper bag, weighed it on a scale, and put paper bills to equal the weight of his hair. I remember that it was about £400. We put everything in one bundle and gave it to a friend who was going to Lebanon. He gave it and a letter explaining everything to my father. When the fighting calmed down a little, my father made the trip to donate the hair and money at the holy site for me.

From the time Said was born until we cut his hair, people thought he was a girl. The local people always gave Said a hard time, "You're a girl." And he would respond, "No, I'm a boy." One day I was in the store and I saw Said running toward me, with two young African men pursuing him. One of them explained, "Sorry, we don't want to harm this boy. But we made a bet for £1. I say he is a girl and he thinks he is a boy. We want to know what this boy is!" Meanwhile, Said was standing off to the side, listening. I turned to him and said, "Said, show them!" Said pulled his pants down. "Now look!" he said.

"What do you say now? I am a boy." We all laughed and they left. Everyone in the area knew him, and knew that he was a boy.

In 1971, when Said was nine or ten years old, he and his mother traveled to Lebanon to see my father. While there, they drove to Damascus with additional hair and donations. Said remembers the visit, and how beautiful and ornate the burial site of Mohammed's granddaughter was. During that visit, he met my brother Joe's wife for the first time. She was pregnant with Lena, who would become Said's wife many years later.

Said was very lucky, because in 1985, I was in Lebanon (without Said), and realized that the many sons of my sisters were all interested in Lena. By then, she was about 15 years old, and growing up very beautifully, and very clever in school. At that time, a religious ceremony was coming up, in which the participants needed to wear black. Lena explained that her friends were all wearing black—but she didn't have any black clothing. I gave Suad, my sister, and Lena's aunt, some money. I asked her to buy the articles for Lena. Everyone asked Lena who bought the clothing for her. She stated "Uncle Habib bought them." I added, "She is my daughter-in-law to be. She is going to marry my boy, Said!"

I was completely joking, but kept the joke going. Whenever I introduced her or talked about her, I said that she was going to be my daughter-in-law, the wife of my son. The husband of one of my sisters wanted Lena for one of their sons. He insisted that Joe give Lena for his son. Joe told him that there would be trouble. That family was a good family, but they were strong, and they fought if they wanted something. My brother, Joe, was afraid. He didn't want to be involved in a family who fought for what they wanted. He didn't want his daughter to marry into a family like that. Joe talked to our brother, Mohammed, who told him not to worry, that he would help. In a visit with the husband of my sister, Mohammed told him, "How can you ask for Lena? My brother, Joe, promised Lena to his brother's son, Said." My sister's family in Lebanon respected me. Her husband said, "What did you say?" Mohammed explained, "I remember that my brother, Habib, talked to Joe and told him to keep it secret.

He wants his son to marry Lena. They are waiting for Lena to grow up and then Said and Lena are going to be married."

During this time, we had the girls in a Catholic convent school in the town. I knew the sisters and the priests in the neighborhood because they came to me to buy their meats and vegetables because of my cold storage. I explained to the sisters that my three girls had just come from Lebanon and had been educated in French and Arabic to that point. The head sister said, "Never mind, Habib. We have people who will teach them good English." The Catholic schools there were much better at the time than the local schools. I wanted each of my children to have a good education, because I didn't get a chance to have one. Since the Catholic school was for girls, we had the boys enroll in a different school in town.

I was going to Freetown during this period for many of my supplies. I decided to look up a friend of my father, Mr. Jabar, who sold all Lebanese goods—baklava, crushed wheat, cheese. I knew him in Lebanon when he ran a cinema next to my father's store. When I first went to see him in Africa, I said, "Hello, Uncle." He asked, "Why do you call me Uncle? Do you know me?" I said, "Yes, I know you—you had the cinema back in my hometown. I never had to pay one cent to watch when my father took me in."

When I told him who my father was, he exclaimed, "Are you Habib?" When I told him yes, he hugged me and kissed me. Then we started to talk, and I told him about my store in Kenema, and that I made ice cream, and the kinds of goods I carried. I explained that I did not have any Lebanese food. I told him I had a van. Mr. Jabar said, "You come back in one hour with your van. I will show you how to make good money. You do what I tell you." I agreed, so I left to do more errands and returned in an hour with my van and driver. His boys loaded my van with so many things that I hardly had room for anything else. He gave me an invoice and pointed out the costs of the items. His selection was so complete—it was just like in Lebanon. He suggested what to charge the customers so that I would make a profit on top of his wholesale price, and told me that I could pay him when I sold the products he gave me. He said, "If you don't bring me my money, I won't quarrel with you; I will go straight to your father!" I agreed, and left to drive back to Kenema.

When I arrived, I saw Mama sitting on the veranda, drinking coffee. We backed the van up to the store and started unloading. When Siham saw all the familiar Lebanese goods she said, "What are those?" I explained, and she said, "Oh, *Rajol* (husband), where did you get this?" The cinema had been only a couple hundred feet from the house she grew up in, and so she also knew the man who sold me the goods in Freetown. I did exactly what Mr. Jabar told me to do. Siham said, "Leave the unpacking to me so that you can do the paper-work." She arranged the rice, cheese, and all the other items in the store. I made a list of those items, but did not write down the pricing.

I asked my driver, "Do you know all the Lebanese people in town?" He said, "Yes, sir, I know them all." I told him to show the list of goods to all the Lebanese people before the evening. He said, "Yes, sir," and left with the list. In about 15 minutes someone came to the store asking "Do you have Lebanese food?"

"Yes," I said. The customer went through the store. "Give me one kilo of this, give me two kilos of that …" and in one or two days I had sold all the goods. I made £200 or £300.

So within four days of getting the Lebanese supplies, I left for Freetown again. When I arrived at Mr. Jabar's store, he greeted me, "Hello, Habib. What are you doing here?" I told him that I had sold everything he gave me. I gave him his money, and he said, "Oh, Habib. You are a good boy! I will give you everything I have here. Let the people here have to wait for a new shipment of goods." We made an arrangement that every month when he got a shipment from Lebanon, he would call me to come down and get the goods I needed.

I needed more cold storage space to hold the increasing sup-plies. I went to my uncle, who had a cold storage building because he ordered fruit from overseas. He bought hundreds of cases of eggs and apples and grapes. I greeted him and he said that he understood that I was now carrying Lebanese food. We chatted about Mr. Jabar, our mutual friend. My uncle told me that he talked to my father about how I was doing. I thanked him for helping me and keeping in contact with my family in Lebanon. (I call it a sweet mouth: complimenting and thanking someone.) I asked him what he had for sale. He said, "I don't have anything for sale. What do you want?" I replied that I didn't know what I wanted.

I wanted to look inside. I went inside and when I saw the door to the cold room, I thought, "Oh, how I wish I had this cold room." I opened the heavy door to look inside and—nothing was inside! My heart was full. "Thank you, God!"

I went back to my uncle, trying not to appear too happy, and said, "Uncle, why is the cold room empty and hot? Is it broken?" My uncle said, "Nothing is wrong with it. But the government won't let eggs and other items be brought in from out of the country so I don't need it." I responded, "Oh my God—that is bad news. What are you going to do with this room? Why don't you sell it?"

"Who would buy it?" he replied. "It is built up, it isn't a self-contained box. It has a cement base and is part of the building. It cost me £5,000." I responded that I needed cold storage at my store in Kenema for when I got shipments from Mr. Jabar. I discussed that I didn't have money to move it and rebuild it in Kenema. My uncle said, "You can have it if you pay for the freezer inside and the compressor." I asked, "How much does the freezer and compressor cost?" He said, "£1,000."

I replied, "Oh, I wish I had £500, and I would take it."

My uncle said, "Okay take it for the £500. Whenever you get the money, you can pay me. Take it."

"Really?" I said. "Are you are talking truly?"

"Yes, whenever you get the money you can pay me."

"You can wait for your money?"

"Habib, you always say that, but then you always pay me quickly. Take it, and if you have money, you pay me. If you don't, I don't want your money. Just take it from the store." I went outside and declared, "Oh, God, you are the best. I love you. When there is anything that I want, I say 'God, I wish …' and you listen to me. You are the best, God!"

Since the cold storage room was built into the middle of my uncle's building, it was going to be very difficult to remove. We would have to break up the cement. The plaster on the wall was four feet by two feet by six inches thick, and was strengthened by chicken wire in the middle. The front and top had a layer of wood. I went to find my driver and asked him to get another worker for me. I bought some tools: pliers, a wire cutter, a screwdriver, and an electrical tester. First I took the fuses out and hid them so that nobody would put them back in. I followed every wire—the red wire, the yellow wire, and the black wire. I cut each one, leaving about six inches. I covered them all.

Next I worked to detach the compressor. Then I went inside the freezer and detached the fan. Now it was time to start breaking up the cement, which we did from outside and inside the structure at the same time. After that, we removed the wood. There were about 10 panels that were two inches by 12 inches. As we disassembled the storage room, I labeled everything before putting it in the truck. After we removed the wood, we uncovered the cement blocks and started removing them. It took us all day. I put them in another truck that I rented, to get them back to my store. Then I said, "Uncle, I thank you. I cleaned up everything for you. Go see." He went inside and did not see the storage room. He exclaimed, "How did you do that?" I laughed and said, "This is Habib. You know how good Habib is!" He responded, "Oh, Habib, I wish you could work with me, here." He had asked me long ago to come work for him. But I hadn't wanted to leave my store. I didn't want to work under somebody.

We drove back to Kenema with the cold storage equipment and building materials, and rebuilt it using my detailed numbering system. I reattached everything and started running the compressor. I put watermelons and garlic in, and whatever else I had in my original cold storage unit, and ran it all night. I didn't know what temperature I should have set the gauge for, so I set it at 20 degrees. I didn't know then, but discovered the next day that it was too cold when a customer came in to buy a watermelon. I opened the freezer, and brought out the melon. I tested it, and it was like stone. "Habib, is this stone or a watermelon? It looks like a bomb." So then the customer asked me for eggs. I gave him a dozen eggs and he left. A little while later he came back. "Habib, I like eggs with garlic, but tell me how you put the garlic inside the eggs!" I went into the cold storage room and put the thermostat up to 30 degrees. But it was still too cold. Then I raised the thermostat a bit more and it worked fine. My uncle had not been using the thermostat that I had bought from him.

A Swiss man came to me and said that he had heard that I built a cold storage room. He didn't know that his African boy had helped me rebuild it. He said, "Can I come and see it?" I said, "Yes, come inside." By then I had filled it with vegetables, cauliflower, lettuce, melons, eggs—everything. He saw that I was keeping the temperature at exactly 40 degrees. He asked, "Who did this for you, Habib?" I replied, "I did it myself. The work on the wiring, everything I did myself. The African boy helped me install the gas pipes." He asked, "What kind of college did you go to, to learn this?" I said, "From God. God College." He was puzzled and asked, "There is a God College in your country?" I laughed and responded, "Yes, of course."

I explained that I bought the Italian compressor and attached it to an English refrigerator. He didn't believe me, so I showed him. He again asked, "Who fixed this for you?" I laugh now when I remember what I said to him. "Hey you!" I said. "Open your eyes good! Know who you are speaking to. I am an expert in this business!" He said, "Oh, I am sorry ... I am sorry." I said, "Look, if you need any help in your cold storage, and you don't know how to fix it, just call me." He looked at me and said, "The company will fire us, and give you the job down here. I don't want that!"

I had to be very creative in fixing things in those days. Supplies and replacement parts for machinery were very hard to come by in Africa. So many things had to be ordered from Europe or America—if they could be ordered at all—and they took a long time to arrive. An example is the cone-making equipment. The electric elements lasted a long time, but the ceramic parts failed due to the high heat. I wasn't sure what to do. The local Africans made themselves clay pipes, and they were dirt cheap. I got the idea to break the long pipe end, and fed the element in through the hole. Said and Mona and I spent many evenings when a machine broke, taking it apart, and rebuilding it with the African pipe material. It was a very precise effort, but it worked, and we were able to keep the cone machines working. It sure proves that necessity is the mother of invention!

By then I had many men acting as distributors, selling my products to other companies and in the bush. I had been making enough additional money to enlarge my house. I had extended it in the back by adding a five-foot extension in cement, with five-foot walls and a wire fence around it. I had covered the roof with zinc panels. According to the building codes, that was the only way I could extend the house, because I wanted to add two bedrooms for the kids. I had a carpenter do it, and it didn't cost me too much. One day I was shaving, and heard two of my girls chatting together. The older girl, Elham, said to her younger sister, Lila, "Our friends have invited us to birthday parties many times. Now, my sister, your birthday is coming next week. Shall we call them to have a party?" Lila said, "Hey, be quiet." My older daughter asked why. Lila responded, "Their house is upstairs. It has nice chairs and nice things in it. And our house is behind a cold storage building, an egg storage building, an ice cream building! How can we invite them here? It is an embarrassment to us. No, no. I am not going to invite anybody to our house." Elham said, "Well, never mind. We have a yard behind the house that we can play in."

So I heard this conversation with Lila telling Elham that they shouldn't invite people to our house; that other Lebanese people had nice, free-standing houses with nice furniture, not connected with their businesses,. I had put all my focus and money on building up the business. All the extra money had gone into improving the store. I originally had the girls in beds in one room of the house, like a dorm room. We ate outside in the evenings on the veranda, and spent a lot of time in back visiting with friends after the store closed at night.

So I heard what the girls were saying, and I thought, "Oh, God, what should I do now? The minute I finish one thing, I get another thing! I had the store working well, the freezer working well, the ice cream machine working well, the cold storage working well, business working well—but now, what should I do?"

I kept thinking. I couldn't sleep that night. I went to Siham. "Why do you look so worried?" she asked. "Why are you not so happy?" I told her that I had heard the kids talking about our house. Siham replied, "Don't you worry. If they call their friends for a party or if they don't, it doesn't matter." I said, "Okay."

The next day, I had an idea. As I have mentioned before, high-ranking Kenema government workers came to my store. I sold them Mexican wine. Santa Maria, Santa Anna, Santa Theresa—all kinds! It was very cheap, costing about one-half to one shilling; about the same price as a pint of beer. They came practically every day: the judge, the chief of police, the civil engineers. The town planner, Mr. Tucker, was my friend. He was in his 40's—a very nice and quiet man. He never hit anybody, or caused anyone to get in trouble or lose their money or business. But he liked Santa Maria too much! So I said to myself, *I want this man to help me make a plan to build a new house behind the store.*

Mr. Tucker came early the next day, before anyone else had arrived. He asked, "Where is everyone?" I said, "Never mind, I wanted to talk to you. Come, sit down." We sat down on the one-hundred-pound bags of rice and sugar that I sold to the people to take to the diamond miners living in the bush. I explained, "Mr. Tucker, my family is getting big. We are sleeping with the rats in the house attached to the store. I would like you to help me make a plan and build a house on the space behind the store." Mr. Tucker said, "Are you going to make the plan?" I replied, "No, I want you to make the plan." I wanted to make sure that it would be acceptable under the city requirements.

He instructed, "Habib, go build the house. Do what you want. When you are finished, make the plan for me, and I will sign off on it for you." I exclaimed, "*What!* Then I can build the house without a preliminary plan?" Mr. Tucker said, "Yes, I give you permission. I am the man who makes the town plans. I am the man who gives the permissions. As long as you have this kind of wine here, nobody will come near you!"

I said, "God bless you. Okay, I will make my plan." He reiterated, "Okay, make the plan how you want. I know you. You are a nice man. You will make it for your family. You will make a good house. Make it very strong. Don't make it in a way to save money. If they tell you to use one, put one and one-half." I said, "No, I will use two!" He laughed and said, "Much better."

Then our other friends started arriving, so he said, "Keep this secret between me and you. You are building your house because you already had the plans signed by me, and they are in your safe. Right?" I said, "Yes, yes, of course."

In the town, there is a hiring hall, like an unemployment office, where diamond mining and other companies can hire laborers. The hall is closed on Saturday and Sunday, and the laborers came to my store to buy tobacco, rice, cigarettes and other supplies. I knew one of them to be a good builder, and explained that I wanted to build a house and that I wanted to hire him. He listened and said, "Yes, Habib, we will help you. We are doing nothing on the weekends." I explained, "I want to make a plan first, with your ideas and how much I can afford." I told him that what he saw in the store was not mine – I borrowed money and paid for the inventory when it sold. He said, "Habib, yes, I know." I took him outside and showed him the yard. He said, "Look, we have 40 feet on this side and 60 feet on this side." I told him, "I want to build a house that is 30 feet by 40 feet. Will it work?" He said, "Yes, of course. Why don't you build a house that is 35 feet by 50 feet?"

So we agreed on the dimensions. He was going to put the wooden stakes in the next day and start work that weekend. He told me the amounts to order of stone, sand, cement bags, and iron rods. They would start the foundation that weekend. I said, "We have to build a strong foundation because I may want to add a second story when we get more money." He assured me he would, and told me that he had lots of wood at his house, so I didn't need to buy wood.

Living near me was a man who had a "tipper," or dump truck. I called him. "I don't have money," I said, "but I want to build a house. If you will transport the stone and other building materials for me, I will provide you goods from my store." He asked how many trips I needed. I said, "As many as it takes. You can dump stones and sand in the front and side of my store." I gave him tobacco and other supplies that he wanted. The next day, he came. I saw the truck and heard the *ggghhhrrrrrr* of the motor. My wife yelled, "Somebody is dumping stone in the front of the store! Go tell him to stop!" I calmly said, "Oh maybe, Mama, maybe somebody didn't have a place to put it. Maybe the truck broke down."

Then the truck left. It came back and started dumping sand. Again Siham came running, "Now they are dumping sand all over the place!" I chuckle when I remember that I hadn't told her about my house plans yet!

There were two people in town selling building materials. One was from my town in Lebanon, and had a very big store. The other one was from the north part of my country. He was a nice man. They were both customers at my store, buying Lebanese food and paying me each month. I still needed iron rods and cement, so I went to the one from my town first, Hassan. We were schoolmates back in Lebanon. We greeted each other, and I said, "God likes you!"

He laughed, and asked, "God likes me? Thank you, Habib. What is happening good to me to make you say that?" I explained that I was building a house for my kids, but I didn't have any money. I said, "You have the building materials that I need, and I have the food in my store that you like to eat. You eat, and I take the iron rod and cement. I won't pay you one cent, and you won't pay me one cent. Every month we come to the table. If mine is less, and you have to pay me, I leave the debt to the next month. If yours is less and I have to pay you extra, you leave it to the next month. Do you agree?" Hassan responded, "Yes, Habib. You are from my town—my friend and schoolmate. If I denied you, what would you say?"

I replied, "I would say, you are the best stupid man I have met." He said, "Don't say that! If I agree, then you have to say I am your best friend." I arranged the deliveries with him. "Send me 20 bags of cement, I said. When they finish that, send me another 20 bags, and so on. Also, send me some iron rod for the pillars. I don't know how many I need—I'm just trying to build a house! Send me six pillars." He said, "How many are you going to need? I will send 10 pillars for your house."

The delivery of the cement came to the back of the store, and the iron rods arrived. Siham yelled at the driver, "You come here! Why are you putting those supplies here? Is your truck broken?" He replied, "No, ma'am, Master told me to put them here." Siham asked, "Which Master?"

Every time we got something delivered she started shouting. I wasn't right there; I was outside in the front, or maybe sleeping. Siham found me and said, "Come and look! You had the driver put things there!" I whispered, "Mama, we are going to build a house behind. Now you can rest." Siham questioned, "You want to build a house?" I explained, "The kids want a house. I am going to build that house from nothing." Siham said, "Where are we going to get the money?" I said, "You just take it easy. The building supplies owner is going to eat and we are going to build. That is how we are going to do it."

The contractor started digging and preparing for the foundation. We discussed how many pillars we needed on each side. The foundation was poured in the first month. The pillars were added in the second month. Then it was time for the cement blocks. I went back to Hassan to ask where I could get them. He explained that I could buy the cement and sand from him, and he would send over the machine, the wooden frames, and a man and his brother to make the blocks. "They can make as many blocks as you need. It will be very cheap. Just give him five or six shillings a day, and a cup of rice, and that will be enough. They will make a thousand blocks, 12 inches by 6 inches. They are good boys and will not cheat. I will tell them to make the blocks strong for you. Put them inside the house to work. Don't put them outside in the hot sun." So the men came and made the blocks on the weekdays, so that they would be made and drying in time for the weekend construction crew.

After the walls were complete, we had to build the roof. I called Hassan to ask how much cement was needed. He suggested 60 bags. The roof was made by first putting wooden beams across the space, with supporting pillars. Then iron rods were crisscrossed throughout. Then cement was poured on top. It took almost 50 men to pour the concrete for the roof. They worked throughout the night, because the job could not be interrupted partway through. The roof was flat, so that a second story could later be added. The kitchen was on one side, with the bathroom and cement water reservoir. There were two salons. One was for the casual use of the family. The other salon was the good one, for entertaining visitors and guests. I made the stairs just like an arrow to the roof. Since Hassan was eating more every month, I had decided to go ahead with the second floor. It had four rooms, one full bath, and one half bath, with just a toilet and shower. It was going to be a big, strong house. It took two or two-and-a-half years to finish. When we moved to Los Angeles, we sold it to a woman doctor who converted it into a small hospital.

We continued to live in the old house until the new one was completed. The children were so excited and happy as they watched the new house go up. But it took a long time, because I could only afford the workers part time, on the weekend. We gave them food and tobacco in place of cash sometimes.

When the house was complete, we needed to furnish it. An English friend of mine who was an officer in Palestine when I was there was the manager of the Forest Department of the local government. His wife was the daughter of another English officer in Palestine, and was born there. She spoke Arabic exactly like me, and liked to smoke hubbly-bubbly and play backgammon. One day I put my aim on them! I thought to myself, "Boy, make good friends with them. Go for the wife first; she can do everything."

So one day they came to buy cheese and whiskey. I had all the good whiskeys. I asked the woman, "How about if we play a game of backgammon?" She said, "Are you serious? Do you have a table?" I said, "Yes." She replied, "But why didn't you tell me?" I told her, "I didn't know you liked to play backgammon!" (I said this even though I had known of her interest for a long time!)

I had been telling Siham that the only one who could help us get furniture was the manager of the Forest Department, because that is where the wood for the furniture could be purchased. "You can invite them over for shish-ke-bob." Siham called to invite them both, "You must come. I am making shish-ke-bob and some good Lebanese food. My husband will make hubbly-bubbly for you and we will play backgammon." They made arrangements to come on a Saturday. That Saturday morning, we bought one whole lamb. Siham started cooking and I got the hubbly-bubbly going. They came in the afternoon and we ate and drank and visited until about ten o'clock that night.

On one of their visits, we showed them the newly finished, but very empty, house that we had built. As our friendship developed, we continued to invite them over. After several visits, the wife asked, "If your house is completed, why do you not move in?" I replied, "This house is ready, ma'am, but I have no money to buy furniture." She said, "What! What furniture?" I explained, "Like a chair, like a dinner table. You could talk to your husband and see if he could supply me and I could pay him little by little. I don't have much money. We are saving money until we can buy all that we need."

She called her husband and explained that we weren't using the house because we could not yet afford the furniture. He said, "Really, Habib? Where is the key?" I replied, "The house is open." He said, "Come on, let's go see the house." They opened the door and saw the beautiful house, the black and white tile, the kitchen and four bedrooms. He said, "Habib, give me some paper and a pencil." He wrote lots of numbers and did lots of adding. Then he put the paper in his pocket, and said, "Okay, we will talk in about one month." I said, "Alright."

He didn't tell me anything more, and I didn't mention or ask further. I was scared to say anything, or ask how much I would have had to pay. Siham asked me if I thought we should have mentioned it. But I told her, "Wait. Did he ask how much we could pay, or tell us the price?" She said, "No." I explained, "Well, when he comes and brings the furniture, if he says, 'Where's the money?' I will tell him to take his things and go if he won't wait for the money. That's it. Why do you worry? I didn't tell him, I didn't talk to him. He just asked me for the key and he went inside the house. We have no problem, Mama. You just keep quiet."

In almost one month, the officer called me and told me that he had everything and asked when he could deliver the furniture. I said,

"I want it in the morning after the kids have gone to school, so that it will be a surprise for them when they arrive home." The kids had been begging me, "Papa, can we go sleep there; take our mattresses and put them on the floor?" But I had continued to tell them, "Nobody will go inside and use the house until we have bought the new furniture."

The next morning, three trucks pulled up, packed with furniture. The officer said, "Give me the key." I told him as I had before, "The place is open." He went inside, and called the drivers to bring the furniture into the rooms. He took the furniture to the upstairs rooms first. Every room had two beds, dressing tables, and closets—except for Said's and Haidar's. They only got one closet.

It was very hot in Sierra Leone, especially in the upstairs area of the house. I needed to air condition the house. Between two upstairs rooms, I opened a hole and installed the air conditioner. I did the same thing for the other two bedrooms.

After each of the three trucks had unloaded and gone, the officer called me inside the house. I went inside. The house looked big, with the nice furniture. There was a cabinet model radio and record player, and a big dining table that sat ten people. The kitchen had a nice, big stove and oven, and all the other appliances. I went upstairs and saw that every room had beds and dressers. In the sitting room outside, there were tables and chairs. Everything was completely done. I kept saying, "Oh my God! Oh my God!" The officer asked, "Habib, do you like it?" I responded, "Very much—but where am I going to get the money to pay for it?" He said, "We're not worried about the money. Here is the bill. How much ever you are able to pay, you can pay every month—£100, £200, £300. You go pay the cashier and he will give you a receipt. And when the debt is finished, I will stop it. Don't worry about that." I responded, "£100, £200; that's good, I can afford that." We said goodbye. I took the key to the house, locked it up, and went back to the store.

In a little while, our driver left to pick up the kids from school. We used to have a Volkswagen van that he drove. He went to the convent school to pick up the girls, and then to the other school, to get Said and Haidar. They were always hungry, coming from school, so they went straight to the kitchen like they always did. Mama always had a table ready for them out on the veranda, and the kids were about to start eating. I told Mama to call the oldest one, Elham, to me. Mama went to our daughter. "Elham," she said, "your Dad wants to talk to you." Elham jumped up and came, "Yes, Dad, what can I do for you?" I said, "I have a surprise for you." She said, "What kind of surprise, Papa?" I said, "Here is the key to our new house. You go open it, and you will see the surprise." Elham questioned, "What kind of surprise? I know the house is nice but it is empty; there is nothing inside." I raised my voice and said, "Will you do what I am telling you to do?" She said, "Yes, Dad."

Elham finally went. Meanwhile all her sisters and brothers were sitting at the table, eating. Elham was hungry and wanted to eat, too. As she passed by them, she said, "Father says I have to go open the house. Everybody keep my chair. Don't anybody sit in my chair!" She didn't want her sisters and brothers getting any part of her snack!

Elham walked to the door and opened it really quickly because she wanted to come back to eat. As she started to open it, she realized that she had seen something! She did a double-take and yelled, "Wow! Everybody come look! Nice new furniture!" All the kids scrambled up from the table, "Nice what?" They left their food and slowly entered the house. They saw all of the tables, chairs, and cupboards. They all said, "Let's go see if we have beds!" They went running up the stairs and to see their completed bedrooms. They opened the doors, and saw the beds, cupboards, and dressing tables. "Oh, wow! We should go thank Papa!"

They all rushed to the store. "Thank you, Papa!" they said. "Thank you, Papa!" The customers in the store asked, "What is going on? What have you done for your children?" I explained, "I built them a new house, and bought new furniture." They said, "You are joking! Where?" They hadn't seen the house being built behind my store. The house was completed in about 1971. Said was about nine years old and Mona was only about two when we moved in. Even Mona was born in the old house, before we moved into the big new one.

Every once in a while, after we were closed, people would come looking for me, because they had learned that we lived behind the store. One man, the head of the Lebanese community, was a good friend of mine. One day, he came through the gate and opened the door of the store, just as I was about to close. He saw the building and was very surprised. He was used to seeing only fruit trees. Then he saw my wife and said, "Hello, Mother Said." (Out of respect, our custom is to use the name of the first-born son when addressing the mother.) She knew him, and responded, "Welcome." He asked, "What happened here?" Siham explained, "We built this house over a couple of years." He asked, "Where is Habib?" My wife explained that I was asleep.

The community leader said not to wake me up, and the two of them continued talking. Siham invited him and his wife to visit overnight. She said, "We are happy to see you, because you invited us many times. But when we were in our old house, we were ashamed to invite you. But now we are proud. We have a good house. Maybe it is equal or not equal to your house, but we can receive you here." He said, "Oh, I will go tell my wife." He was married to a mulatto woman. She and Siham were very good friends. He told his wife about our new house, and she was excited to come see us. We enjoyed their visit and welcomed many people in town into our house to visit while they stayed with us.

After we furnished the house, I called Elham and her sister to me. "Do you remember that you talked to your sister about not wanting to invite friends over for your birthday because you were ashamed of our house, and it wasn't like their houses? Now, look around. Is this house like their houses?" My daughter said, "It is *much* better!" I said, "Now, can you invite your friends over for your birthday?" They said, "But it's not our birthdays!" I responded, "Well, call it your brother's birthday, or your sister's birthday. They won't know. Plan a party and invite everybody. Show everyone that you are proud of your father and mother." They agreed. "Okay, let's do it!" The girls called their friends, and invited them to a party to celebrate one of their brothers' birthdays. All their friends were surprised and said, "Oh, we thought you lived behind the store." But my daughters were able to say, "Not anymore!" They all had fun at their party.

I estimate that I built that house for about £13,000. Our little store didn't look like it could produce that much income for us. But the money came out of it; we didn't expand or change anything to be able to afford the house. God is good, and helped us. There is a saying in our country that if we want to get married and to build a house for our family, God will help us in any way. He encouraged us to do that. I believe that He sent me so much—Siham, money that I needed for a family, and then my family. I didn't dream of being a landowner when I first moved to Sierra Leone. God caused that man to sell me my first house for £1,000, and maybe He listened to my two daughters talking about wanting a better house, and then helped me get it.

Each day at about noon, one of the boys who worked for us, helping Siham in the house, would bring lunch in a big round tray to the store for Siham and me. In the morning, before going to the store, Siham would explain to the African boy we hired to cook how she wanted the food prepared. We also hired a boy to keep the house clean. They worked about six hours a day for us. We had a few helpers over the years, but the ones that we had the longest were Santiki and Molai. We had five small dogs in the house. They would bark if they didn't know someone, but they were smart. They wouldn't bark when I came in the house, or when our friends visited. The kids in the neighborhood always teased them with sticks. In Africa, the children were not taught to be kind to pets. There was enough poverty that the Africans saw the dogs as competition for food. If the dogs did something wrong, the boys who worked for us would beat them with sticks. We had to tell them they could not treat the dogs that way.

One night the dogs started barking for a long time. The guard must have been asleep. (He was better for running errands!) Said and Haidar jumped out of bed and ran to the landing on top of the stairs. Siham yelled at me, "Wake up, wake up! I think there are thieves here." I jumped out of bed, grabbed my shotgun, and ran downstairs in my pajamas. I put the belt of bullets on. Said and Haidar came running toward me. I whispered, "What are you guys doing? Get back, get back!" Somehow Said was hanging onto my pants and the belt, and Haidar was hanging on to Said. I said, "Get your hands off my pants. Go back inside." I wanted to move fast to see what was happening, and to catch the thieves. I ran out the door and saw the thieves jumping over the fence. I yelled, "You! You! Over there! Who is there?" I cocked the trigger of the gun, and took a shot in the air. It was a big, powerful double-barrel French-made shotgun, and the kickback caused me to fall down. The two kids behind me tumbled onto the ground with me. We started laughing! My wife and daughters were all standing at the top of the stairs.

After lunch each day, I went home to take a nap, and Siham stayed in the shop. Then I would return later in the day when the kids got home from school. One very hot day, with a little breeze, Siham, the shopkeeper, and our driver all fell asleep in the shop. A burglar came and picked up a box of sugar, left the store and started walking down the street in front of the other stores. One of the Lebanese store owners, Kamel Amin, called to him, "Hey, come here." He was caught with the sugar. The owner knew he had stolen it because he didn't have money for it.

After my nap each afternoon, I usually returned to the store about 4:00 p.m. The driver would take Siham shopping and then home. The children would be home by then, doing homework, and playing around the house. Lila often came to the shop directly from school, to be with me. Said would come also, after he finished his homework each day. Said liked to imitate me—closing the shop around 6:00 p.m., and putting the big padlock on the door in the evening. Then we all would walk home together, or take the car. We had a guard, Kaikai, who had been a soldier. If we didn't see him at the shop when we were closing up, he would stop by the house to report for duty. He didn't like to come into the yard because of the dogs, so he would stand at the gate and get our attention, every single night. We would give him some food, and a few schillings so that he could buy some kola nuts. The kola nuts kept him awake. I used to eat them when I had to travel all night in the African bush.

We all sat down to dinner at about 7:00 p.m. each night. Sometimes Said and Haidar would be missing. My daughters and the African boys working for us would open the door for them later in the evening and let them sneak in. The girls would smuggle food upstairs for them when they came in late.

I opened the store for a few hours on Sunday, starting later in the morning. On weekday evenings, my friends would come over to the store when I was closing. The door was a metal sheet that rolled down. If the door was half-closed, that meant that no customers could come, but my friends could meet me there. My friends included the chief of police; the cinema director; Mr. MacIntosh, the Scottish man who was in charge of water distribution and had a bright red Karmann Ghia; Mr. Masaquoi, the town's resident administrator; the drug and pharmaceutical dispenser; and several other business men in the town. By then, the driver would have taken Lila home. Said loved to be there listening to me talk to my friends, and hearing the jokes that we all exchanged while drinking our Heineken beers. Sometimes it would get late and dark. The lady who sold peanuts would come by, carrying her brown or roasted peanuts on her head. My friends and I would talk about the town happenings. By the end of the evening, I was always surprised that Mr. MacIntosh could find his way home. Said always enjoyed those evenings, listening to the conversations.

I kept the books by hand, in a big, thick ledger. The adding machine worked by pulling a handle. I wrote each employee or distributor on a line in the ledger. I kept track of how much they were supposed to be paid, and any draws they made for food during the month. On a Friday or Saturday at the end of the month, I had each employee put their thumbprint on the page to show that they had received their earnings.

On Saturdays and Sundays in the mornings, our wives would get together and cook serious meals to eat in the afternoon—African or Lebanese dishes, or Indian curry with lots of condiments. Our friends would come over to eat with us; Lila and her husband would, too. After the meal, we would turn on the fans and air conditioners, and all take naps. Said and Haidar liked to go to the cinema matinees. Usually on Sunday evening, I would ask the family what they wanted to do. We usually had picnics and met with friends.

One time we were visiting my daughter, Lila, and her family. I was backing up in her driveway in our Volkswagen van. Lila was waving goodbye, but her neighbor, Ali Kazem, who was standing behind the van, started yelling that it was on fire. There were six kids and Siham in the van. We all piled out and discovered that the engine had caught on fire.

During this time, I bought my goods from wholesalers. Each time I bought, they would give me more credit, because I always paid them the next time I made purchases. I would leave my wife in the store, while I made the buying trips. On the way, I would stop at the bank to get or deposit some money, and to tell the bank manager to pay the bills that came in. That was the way we did business in those days in Africa.

One day, I saw an African arguing with the bank manager, who was refusing his request for 1,000 Leones. I interrupted the argument as I dashed in, leaving my car running, to tell him that I would need checks covered for my buying trip. I said, "Maybe 5,000 or 10,000," and saw him write it in his ledger. The African said, "What! You give him 10,000, and I am here arguing with you for one hour for 1,000! He is Lebanese and you are my brother. We are two black people." The manager explained, "He is a businessman. He has almost 10,000 in the bank. When he goes away and buys 10,000, he comes back at the end of the month with 10,000, maybe 15,000 that he puts in the bank. And he has a house. You told me that you could mortgage your house, but I found out that you have 10 sisters, and 10 brothers. But he has his own house, his own store, his own car. He is honest. When he tells me that he wants 5,000 for a week, he returns it before one week. You see the difference between you and him? It isn't because you are black and he is white. He is white, but he is straightforward. If I give you 5,000 for a month, maybe you will pay it in three or four months—maybe one year, before I get the money. Then I get in trouble with my manager. That's why, my friend."

The African man looked at me and demanded, "Mr. Fakih, where did you get all that money?" My response was, "I worked for it. I brought money with me, and I worked for it." Honesty is the most important thing. When you want to do something, you have to think of the consequences.

Once my store was offered wholesale watermelons. I agreed to buy all they had. Watermelons were very popular, and I didn't want to lose the sale to anyone else, or have the farmers sell directly to my customers, leaving me out. They didn't tell me the quantity, and I ended up with three truckloads of watermelons! I had them put the melons in the store, on the veranda, and even out in the street. So many! I had to put the price really low, at about $2.00 each. All my customers bought two or three each. Everybody sent their young African boys to take them in the middle of the night. After two weeks, they started going rotten; we had to get rid of them.

Even though I know I am clever, I like to go to people older than me, who have more experience. I ask them their opinions and take their advice if I think it is good, but reject it if I don't like it. It is just like when I arrived in the United States: I am older than my brother, Mo, but he is "older" in terms of his experience in the U.S. because he came here so much earlier. I would listen to his advice and follow it sometimes. Sometimes it would work out, and sometimes not. My son, Said, does the same. We must all look back at our families, and what we all believe. We have to find a balance when we make our decisions.

After I came back from working in Palestine, I worked with my father in Lebanon for a short time. My father and I respected each other. Sometimes my friends were jealous of our relationship. One time they told my father that I had been smoking. One day, when we were home, my father and I decided to take a walk. We got to a store that sold groceries, and my father bought a pack of cigarettes from the shop owner. I knew he didn't smoke cigarettes; he liked his hubbly-bubbly. We walked out of the town, into a pretty, green area of trees and bushes. We stopped and my father held out the pack and said, "Take one." I took it, said thank you, and threw it into the bushes. My father said, "No, we just left the house together. I haven't seen you smoke." I asked, "Daddy, is this a joke or what?" He said, "No, it's not a joke. I know you want to smoke, so I don't want you to hide anything from me. You are not a boy anymore. You are a man.

You are working, and earning money. You can do anything you want. So I don't want people to come tell me, 'Habib smokes,' or 'Habib goes following his love.' Habib, you are working and earning more money than me now."

I said to him, "Papa, why all these words? I don't like this kind of talk now. You are hurting me. You have taught me to be serious and honest with you. How can you listen to all these people talking about me? Papa, I am going to be upset. Please next time, whatever you hear about me, don't listen, just come and ask me. I never smoke. Maybe when we were young boys playing, someone forced me to put it in my mouth, but I threw it away, just like now." My father asked, "You are not smoking now?" I replied, "Papa, if I smoked, I would tell you that I smoke. Anything I want to do, anything I plan, anything I make, I always come and ask you first." He said, "You're right. He crumpled the packet of cigarettes and threw them away. I shouted, "Why did you spoil them? Leave it. You could have given them to my uncle." He finished the conversation by saying, "I promise you now, my son. I will not listen to anybody else. I trust you and we work together. We trust each other. Whatever you want to do, you can do it not in secret."

He started to smile and began telling jokes. We continued on our walk and found a beautiful place to sit down. We sang Arabic songs—my father had a very nice voice. He read a lot, and he knew many stories. I told him some good jokes, too. Then we went to my aunt's house in Nabatieh and she made tea for us. She was the one who gave me eggs for the soldiers a few years before.

Our driver would take the children to school each morning. We sent the girls to Catholic school. We used to like to go to the cinema for entertainment in the evenings.

Everything was going nicely for a time, but the business started slowing down a little. More people were moving in, building more stores. I wanted to enlarge my business. Hangha Road was the main road through the town, and clothing, food, and supply stores lined the street. One day while I was going to visit a friend, who had a business there, I passed a store with three metal doors that rolled up, like garage doors. But now the doors were closed, even though it was business hours. That store had sold potatoes, flour, rice and sugar. So I asked my friend, "Why is that store closed? Who is the owner?" My friend explained, "I think that the man, an African, got sick. He fought with his brothers, who were partners with him. So he closed the store."

My friend introduced me to the owner, and I told him, "I want to buy that store from you." He said, "What do you want it for? I don't care what you want to do with it. I have the key in my pocket. Here is the key." I commented, "We have to talk." He asked, "What do you want to talk about?" I said, "We have to talk about the rent and the rental time, and you have to write up the agreement papers. I don't trust you." He responded, "You don't trust me, but I trust you!" I said, "No, let's talk seriously. How much were you renting it for? I will pay you exactly that amount." He said, "No, I have been renting it for £500 for the whole year. I will give it to you for £400 for the whole year." I asked, "Why would you do that?" He said, "Habib, I know you are a nice man. Any time I want a beer, you would give me a beer. Any time I want some onions, you would give me onions. For that £100 savings I will take £200 from you."

I said, "Not bad. Let's go sign an agreement. I want it for 20 years." He exclaimed, "Oh, 20 years! Habib, maybe I am not going to live 20 years!" I countered, "But *I* am. I know that. I am still young. And you are still young. Unless you follow a woman too much and drink too much, you will live a long time." He said, "Okay, make the papers, Habib. I will sign them, and bring the money with you. And there is the key, anytime you want to get in." I agreed, "Okay, but you have to give me one month free. We need to make it start from next month. I have to clean the place, paint it, put the shelving up, arrange everything. Do you think I want to move my good stuff in here like this?" He said, "You are right, Habib. Make it start from next month."

We completed the paperwork, and I moved in. I didn't know exactly what I was going to do with the space. People wanted to rent it from me, but I kept turning them down.

One day, one of my kids suggested, "Papa, the cinema is good. Why don't you make it a cinema? It is big." The space was big. It was 90 feet long and 40 or 50 feet wide. I thought a cinema was a good idea. People liked movies; I could make good money. I had a nice African neighbor whose uncle was a justice in Freetown and was a good friend of the president of the country. I visited him and asked, "Mr. Scott, I would like you to help me when I complete the application." I discussed my ideas with him. Mr. Scott said, "Habib, you make the application and get the place ready. You have to go through the whole site and make it good, and we will help you. Why not?"

I responded, "I will make you a partner. I will give you 10 or 15%. How about that?"

He said, "Very good! I agree!"

"You don't have to pay anything. I will build it and do everything else."

"Where will you get the money?"

"Don't worry—we work, we sell groceries. Don't worry, we will do it the same way as I built my house."

He just laughed. "Whatever you say, Habib. I am with you. Even if the people laugh at me, or laugh at you, I agree with you."

We completed the application and demolished the old place and poured the foundation. Mr. Scott took the application to the community magistrate. They told him that they would study it and let him know. I started building on the site. An inspector came and I tipped him a couple hundred pounds. I passed the inspection; the inspector said the place was good for a cinema. But just outside the town was another big, new cinema, owned by a very rich Lebanese diamond dealer. We would all go there on Friday nights; he charged $1.00 or $1.50 for each ticket. He brought in Lebanese films, American films, Egyptian films. People told the owner that I was building a local cinema, right in the town that would compete with his business. I decided to charge 50¢ per ticket. The people told him what I was planning on charging. He asked all about my business.

Then he went to the community magistrate and asked for more information about my application. He met with the people who were going to review my application and give me a business permit. He put some money into their hands—thousands of dollars. They sent me a letter saying that they rejected my application because the cinema would be too noisy—too this, too that. They stated that if I wanted to apply for land outside the town, they would consider it. Of course, they knew that I wasn't going to do that, since I had this site and had already done work on it. Also, if I had tried to buy land around the town, the other cinema owner would just offer more money for it—I didn't have a chance. I had spent good money—about £2,000 at that point. He had spent £5,000 against me—getting nothing for it, but keeping me from having my business. Mr. Scott asked what I was going to do, and I said I was just going to leave everything as is. I planted trees, and made a small orchard of plums, figs and other fruit.

By that time it was getting near the close of school for the summer. While I was working in my store, my children told me, "Papa, you have to go to the school to see the certificates presented." (These were achievement certificates for reading and writing achievement, religious studies, etc.) The governor of our town, Mr. Masaquet, was my good friend. At one time, he was the liquor distributor for my store and the other local stores. He transferred the business to his brother when he was appointed the governor. Mr. Masaquet was always invited to the school ceremonies to make the awards. The school my daughters attended had about 300 children enrolled, and it taught only in English. Although mostly Lebanese children attended, no Arabic or local languages were taught.

The ceremony started. They announced the first certificate, for best behavior: "Elham Fakih." Elham stood and walked up to shake hands with the principal and other officials. When she came to Mr. Masaquet, he said, "I know you. I know your father. Congratulations! Your father is the best citizen in this town." He gave her the award; I think it was a book. Elham accepted the award and walked back to her chair to sit down.

The ceremony continued with the next award, to the girl who excelled in the English language: "Elham Fakih." This time, while the governor was congratulating her, he laughed, and said, "Well, Elham,

I have no doubt. Your father is very clever. He always tried to cheat. He comes to buy 50 boxes and always tells me there were only 49. When I go back to count them, there are 50. Afterwards, I see him and he is laughing. He is always giving me trouble! I know he's joking when he gives me a problem. You deserve this award." Elham took the award and went back to her seat.

The third award was for the best student in the Catholic religion. The award was a Bible with a golden cover, from the French Ambassador. When the name "Elham Fakih" was called, the governor jumped from his chair and shouted, "I know that man! Her father is a Muslim! And she is a Muslim! How can she be the best in this religion?" The principal explained, "If you come on Sunday morning, you would see that she is the girl who calls all 300 girls to prayer. She asks questions about Jesus Christ, and we answer her." Mr. Masaquet turned to Elham, "What are you?" Elham replied, "What do you mean, 'what am I'? I am Elham Fakih." He asked, "What religion are you?" She responded, "Your Excellency, religion is about God. We all pray to one God. We all pray to the people He sent us. Mohammed, Jesus Christ, Moses—they are all messengers of God."

Mr. Masaquet asked, "What do you think of Jesus?" Elham said, "Jesus is a person just like Adam. That is what my father told me. God told Adam, 'Be a man from the dirt.' He told him to become a human being. And that is just like Jesus Christ. God told him, 'Be a boy born to Mary.' God told him how to cure leprosy and perform many other miracles."

Elham was speaking to Mr. Masaquet on the loudspeaker. People watched and listened. He asked, "How do you know all that?" Elham responded, "What is in the Bible, is in the Koran." Mr. Masaquet asked, "Why are you telling me that?" Elham answered, "Because I love the Christian religion just like how I love the Muslim religion. And this community is a mix of Muslims and Christians." All the audience clapped for Elham.

Mr. Masaquet shouted, "Impossible! Now I am going to talk to your father!"

After the ceremonies, Mr. Masaquet had his driver take him to my store, in a car with the flag flying from it. He didn't wait for the driver to open his door. He exploded out of it, pushing his driver aside, and came striding into my store. I was busy with a customer at the time. He asked, "Tell me, Habib, what are you?" I asked back, "What do you mean, your Excellency?" He said, "I see that your daughter has won three awards, including the one for the highest achievement in the Christian religion. I don't agree with it. Are your children Christian?"

I responded, "Mr. Masaquet, you know me. Your father was Muslim, but you are a Christian. Why did you do that?" He looked at me and said, "You I cannot argue with." He shook hands with me, "Habib, I thank you very much. You are the best citizen in this country. We would like lots of people like you here." He began talking to the African people, encouraging them to shop in my store. He told them, "I have known this man a long time. He was in Nigeria first. He is a good friend to Africa." He said to me, "Habib, you are an African boy now. You aren't Lebanese anymore. Your family and you are one of us. You eat like us, you sleep like us, you talk like us, you do everything just like us. What do you think? Are you Lebanese? You don't need to go to Lebanon anymore."

My mother was sick during this time, and I had not seen her for four or five years. I left Siham with the kids in Sierra Leone and flew to Lebanon to see her for two or three months. She had not been able to walk—but when she saw me, she stood up and walked. While in Lebanon, I was told that there was rioting in Sierra Leone because of the elections. I was not too worried about my store, because I was a friend of everyone there. I always offered a cow and killed it for a barbecue for each of the holidays—whatever religion was celebrating. Siham always gave the clothes that the children outgrew to poorer people. I gave money to all the old people. I was good, you know. People in the town loved me. There was one man in particular, who was the town head of the party whose president was in power. His house was across the street, opposite from me. One time when the president was coming to visit, he asked to borrow chairs, carpets, etc.

I took everything from my house and loaned it. When the president came, they called me and I went over and shook his hand.

In spite of my good works, my Lebanese friends knew I was out of the country, and were concerned for my family. They came to Siham and told her to keep the door locked. They told her that if she wanted anything, they would bring it to her. They went across the street to my neighbor and asked his help. He said, "Don't worry about the Fakih family." He brought about 10 of his people to my house, instructing them to surround the perimeter to guard my family. I shortened my visit with my mother in Lebanon by about a month. When I returned, my neighbor told me that he had armed all of his people with machetes, and that they were ready to kill for my family. I was so happy and appreciative of that man!

One or two months after I had returned to Sierra Leone, my mother passed away. Since I had just been there, my brother, Mohammed, flew from the US to Lebanon to help with the funeral arrangements.

By the time Mohammed arrived in Lebanon, our mother had died and the family had already taken her to her grave. My oldest sister, Fatimah, who is younger than me by two years, told Mo, "Your mother said that if you come here, you have to marry." I had to decide what to do with Elham, as she was very clever and needed to continue her education. She finished high school in the convent, but there was no college in the area. My brother, Mohammed, had left Nigeria and was living in Chicago. He had planned to learn mechanical engineering for diesel engines. However, he changed his major to accounting. While he was in school, he met and married an American girl who was a nurse. He was also working for a company who was making snacks, so had some money saved up. He met and became friends with an American lawyer from Israel who spoke Arabic. This lawyer helped Mohammed get his green card.

At the time, Hassan was still in Freetown selling clothing under a quota-limited visa. Mohammed told Hassan that he would help him move his family to the United States also, with assistance from his lawyer friend. Mo wanted to find his brother a job, but didn't want him to have to work under anyone. They heard that the donut business was a good business to be in. Mo took a loan out against his house. Hassan brought money from Nigeria. They invested in a Dunkin' Donuts franchise so that they could work together. That is how our family started our long work relationship with the Dunkin' Donuts organization. Chicago was very cold and windy. Mo went to Lebanon when our mother died. My mother had told my sister to find Mo a wife. She didn't know that Mo had married and divorced an American girl when first in the US. Our sister arranged for a Lebanese wife from our town for Mo. Her brother was living in Los Angeles.

Later, Mo and his wife visited her brother in L.A., and that is how the family eventually moved to L.A. He liked L.A. and the warmer weather. Mo found a Dunkin' Donuts store for sale in Torrance, near L.A. He called Hassan and told him about the weather. Hassan sold the Chicago franchise to a Palestinian, rented an apartment in Los Angeles, and moved his family there. So Mo and Hassan owned and operated the Dunkin' Donuts in Torrance.

From Sierra Leone, I called Mo in Chicago and talked to him about Elham, explaining that she wanted to go to college to learn pharmacology. I asked him if I could send Elham to him, to have him arrange the schooling. I assured him that I would take care of all the money that was needed for expenses. I took Elham to the American Embassy in Freetown to get the visa for education in America. They asked me her name. When I said it was Elham Fakih, they said, "Yes, we have heard about her. She was very good, and she won the Bible from the French Ambassador. Is she the one?" I confirmed, "That's the one. If you want me to prove it, I can show you the Bible." They said, "No, we believed you once you said your last name, because there is only one Fakih family in Sierra Leone." They agreed to give Elham a visa to visit her uncle. I asked what would be needed and the cost, in case Elham wanted to stay and enroll in college in the US. I wanted to tell the consul the truth, and make it so that if Elham didn't like it, she could easily return, but also make sure that there was a way for her to stay and go to school if that is what she wanted to do. I said I would transfer $5,000 or $10,000 to Mohammed for Elham.

For Elham's trip to America, I bought traveler's checks from Dick

Duncan, the bank manager. I kept money in a little safe under the table in my store. I used to buy some diamonds and gold from people in the military. I kept my collection of these things in that safe too. My safe was getting full, so I had arranged to buy a bigger safe. My friend knew that a new safe was going to be delivered, so he offered to buy my little one. "Habib, how much do you want for your old safe?" I said, "I will sell it to you for £150." He said, "I will give you the money; I want it now." I replied, "I can't give it to you now because my other safe has not yet come. I have to wait until I get my other safe." He said, "No, please. I have people coming to my house with diamonds and I want to have my money in a safe." I asked, "What do you want me to do? I have money, I have traveler's checks and the passport for my daughter, who leaves for America tomorrow." He begged, "Please, please, please." I thought, "Well, what could happen in one day? It wasn't likely that the store would be broken into this night." He finally got me to agree to take my things out of the safe, and give it to him that day. I put the few thousand pounds and the gold and diamonds in a drawer.

The people working in the store and the customers had ears, and someone must have overheard this conversation. In the back of the store was a hole with iron bars across it in the outside wall to allow more ventilation for the cooler motor. That night someone came through the bushes in the back and cut the iron bars. They squeezed through the hole and took everything and left. They took the boxes of diamonds, and the gold, and the money—but luckily, they left Elham's passport. I called the police. I called the manager of the bank. He said, "Don't worry. I can stop payment on the traveler's checks and reissue you some new ones." He did that, but the money, gold and diamonds were all gone.

Elham and Mohammed did not know each other, so Mohammed wrote, "E L H A M" on a big piece of paper and held it up to the debarking airline passengers when she was supposed to arrive. Elham read the sign, looked at the man, and yelled, "Uncle!" Mo said, "Are you Elham? Can I see your passport?" He was joking with her. It was a nice meeting. Elham stayed with Mohammed and his wife in Chicago. Elham started college at Loyola University in Illinois. She called after two or three weeks and sent us a nice letter about her experiences in America. I had a friend who had been a diamond dealer in Africa who was then living in New York. Back in Africa, he would get provisions from my store before he went to the bush. Our families were friends, and we traded dinners back and forth. I trusted him, and when Elham needed money, I would write a check and send it to him for her tuition and living expenses.

It was very important to me to give Elham a good education. If it were not for the wars, I would have liked to stay in school myself. I liked learning, and wanted my children to have the opportunity to be exposed to many things, and to think broadly. As I have mentioned, my father used to travel to different villages in his saddlery business. Some of the villages were Muslim, some Christian; in some, Muslims and Christians mixed, living together. When I had been in school, the schools wanted to us to learn about religions. So they had a Muslim teacher come one day, and a Christian teacher come the next. Each of the teachers told us that if we didn't want to stay to hear about their religion, we could leave. When the Christian teacher said that, all the Muslims left, except for me. I wanted to stay because I had a Christian friend named John. The Christian preacher, who knew my father, said, "Habib, did you not listen to what I said?" I said, "Yes, Father. Can I stay?"

He answered, "Yes. If you like, you can stay." So I stayed. That evening I asked my father, "What is the difference between a Christian and a Muslim? The preacher said I could leave the class. But why would I want to do that? It was raining; the weather was bad. Why should I go out into the rain when I could stay inside in the classroom? And I wanted to listen. I like to understand the difference between Christians and Muslims. They both say to be nice to neighbors, respect your parents and brothers and sisters, and respect anyone older than you."

My Papa said, "If I were you, I would stay and listen to both of them, and at the end of the year, compare them. Ask yourself which one is better. Then follow that one." I asked, "But what if the

Christian one is better?" He said, "That is no problem for me. You can go, make yourself a Christian." I asked, "How can you tell me that?" He said, "Muslim, Christian—they all follow one God. We all go for one God. They have their messenger, Jesus Christ, and we have Mohammed. Jesus Christ came before Mohammed. They don't believe in Mohammed, but we believe in Jesus Christ and Moses." My father helped me understand religions. At the end of the year, I got better marks in the classes. Before that I was the fourth or fifth student, but at the end of that year, I came in second in my tests.

I continued to be happy in my new store. There was an annual harvest celebration in the country, when the coffee and cacao beans were ripe. All sorts of important foreign delegates from various countries were invited to the festivities. When Abdullah, the head of the Lebanese community, was asked to find lodging for some of these visiting dignitaries, he asked me if I would have them as guests in my house. I said, "Of course. I have four bedrooms. I can squeeze the kids together. Who are they? Are they good people?" Abdullah replied, "Yes, you are lucky. They are the American ambassador and consul. Can you keep them one night?"

I said, "Oh, American! I can keep them one week. I will give them food and entertain them. Yes, of course. I have my brother in the United States, and my daughter is there." In the evening, they came to my house. My wife prepared Lebanese food. We offered mixed nuts and whiskey and brandy. We had a good dinner. They were so happy. After dinner I showed them around. We sat down and drank coffee and talked. I told them that my brother was in America and that my daughter was in college over there too, staying with my brother, to whom I sent money for Elham. I explained that Elham went over as a visitor, but wanted to learn pharmacy. I said, "I hope I didn't do anything bad." The ambassador responded, "You did what was best. Maybe, if you would have come and asked us, we would have said no—but what you did is now good. I am happy you did that for your daughter. But next time if you want to do it, don't say it." I said, "Okay. If you want, I can send for her to come back. I don't want to get a bad name. Maybe I will be there someday myself."

He said, "I am sure you are going to be there. I am sure you will take all your family and be there. Habib, the United States doesn't ask what color you are, what religion you are. There, it is against our laws. You are a good man. Our country's people would love you. You would be one of us because you are good man, you take care of yourself and your family. Your kind of people is who we want in America. We don't want people who make trouble."

The next morning my wife and two boys who I had hired to help her made a nice breakfast for the ambassador and his group. Then their car came to take them to the celebration. They stayed a second night with us, said goodbye, and left to go back to Freetown.

Said had finished high school the year before. I hated to see my children without education, because I didn't finish my own. I thought to myself, "If I had enough money, I would spend it to get a good education for my children, because education can protect them from trouble, and from bad people. They will behave, they will be nice, and they will be respectful and respected." I told Said, "Let's do the same as Elham." I hadn't seen Hassan for four or five years, just before he left Sierra Leone for America, but I hadn't seen Mo for about 20 years, when I left my brothers in Jos, Nigeria. We never seemed to be in the same country at the same time; we kept crossing paths without seeing each other.

So I decided to take Said to visit my brothers. By this time they had moved from Chicago to Los Angeles. They sold their Dunkin' Donuts store in Chicago because the weather was too cold for them. They bought another Dunkin' Donuts in Los Angeles and moved to Torrance. Elham came with them, transferring to Cal State University in Dominguez Hills. At that time, I had good money. I had saved about $40,000 and had transferred the money to America to keep it safe and have it available if I wanted to send other family members to America. Mo had opened a savings account for me with the money.

Said and I went to the American Embassy with our passports. We asked to see the consul, and he asked what he could do for me. I explained how long it had been since I had seen my brothers. I told him that my son had done very well in school, and that I wanted to take him to visit his uncles. Then we would come back to Sierra Leone, or I might send him to Lebanon. The consul was the one who stayed overnight at my house during the harvest celebrations. He remembered the story I told him about Elham. "Mr. Fakih, how are you?" he said. "I know you want to visit your brother and you have a business here. But what is Said going to do there? Is he going to go find an American woman?"

I laughed and said, "No, no! He is too young." Said was eighteen at the time. The consul said, "Okay. Give me your passports. You also need to bring documents that say that you have no problems, and have a good record." This was to prove that I didn't have any debts or other outstanding obligations.

Then we went to the travel agent, Mr. Yazbec, and told him that we were getting visas to go to Los Angeles. He said, "Los Angeles. Where in Los Angeles do you want to go?" I replied, "You just send me to Los Angeles." He said, "How can I send you to Los Angeles? Los Angeles is *big*! It is bigger than Freetown, and Nigeria and … You will be lost. You go talk to your brother and have him give you the address."

I called, but my brother wasn't home. His wife told me to tell Mr. Yazbec that they lived in Torrance. We all started looking at a big map of L.A., and finally spotted Torrance. Mr. Yazbec said, "Okay, you still have to go to the L.A. airport, then call your brother and he will come to get you, going from here to here," as he traced the trip on the map. I said, "I don't care from where to where. Just get me the tickets. Tell me how much it costs. I still have to get the visas. If the consul asks you where I am going, you explain it to him for me." The travel agent said, "Okay, he knows me. Give him my card."

We went back to the consul. He was preparing the documents. He said, "Now tell me the address of where you are going."

I said, "No, don't ask me. Ask Mr. Yazbec. I called America and they told me Torrance." He said, "Okay, okay, I don't need any more. Here is your visa, Habib. It is good for five years. It is a multiple entry visa. For Said, the visa is one year." I asked, "Why is Said one year and I am for five years?" The Consul said, "Said is going to fall for some girl there. He is going to get married. He is not going to come back. But if I give it to him for one year, there is a chance that he will come back and not go again. Habib, you don't know me yet?" I said, "No." He said, "Are you sure we haven't met?" I again replied, "No." He said, "Of course you know. Remember the Cacao Celebration two years ago in Kenema? You had two people from the American Embassy as guests in your house."

I exclaimed, "Oh, that was you? Oh, hello, my friend!"

We hugged each other and laughed. We were so happy. He said, "I am going to give you the visas and just keep it quiet between you and me." I said, "Don't tell the ambassador." The consul said, "The ambassador already knows. I told him and he said yes."

We went back to Mama and told her that I was going to go to Los Angeles for one month, and would leave Said there—or he could return with me if he wanted. We boarded the plane in the tropical weather of Sierra Leone and arrived at JFK airport in cold weather, with ice on the ground. We were right behind an African couple from Nigeria in line to go through Immigration. They opened their suit-cases and the officer carefully searched the contents. Then it was our turn. We had two or three suitcases each. The customs worker asked us where we came from, and we told him that we were arriving from Sierra Leone. He asked, "Why are you coming to the United States?" I told him, "Oh, I have my brother here in Los Angeles." He said, "Okay, go." I said, "Just like that, we can go?" He impatiently responded, "Yes, I said, go. Go."

I was about to argue with him about why he didn't open our bags! Said said, "Papa, he said to go. Let's go."

It was the end of December, 1979, and we were still wearing trop-ical suits with interlining! We were told to go to another section of the airport for our flight to L.A. on American Airlines, so we jumped on the first bus that we saw, and a man grabbed our suitcases to put them in the back. We told him we were going to Los Angeles, but he told us that his bus was going to La Guardia or some smaller airport. We said, "No, no, no—we want to go to Los Angeles." He wasn't really very nice, but he opened the door, told us to get the other bags out of the way, get our bags, and put the other ones back in. Said was working frantically to get our two bags out. All the people were waiting for us. We had never seen a bus so huge. I waited outside in the cold. Then we had to go back inside, and ask to find the right bus, since we had arrived at an international terminal and had to take off for L.A. from a domestic terminal.

Our flight was just about to touch down at the L.A. airport. As the plane came down, we saw lots of cars. I told Said, "Oh, look how many cars they have! If you want to buy a car, you can pick any car you want. Maybe they are auctioning them."

We met my brother, Mohammed, wearing his pink Dunkin' Donuts jacket at the airport, and Elham wearing her Dunkin' Donuts uniform. I didn't recognize them at first. But Elham recognized me and shouted, "Hello, hello, Papa!" My brother and I didn't immediately recognize each other, because it had been 20 years since we had last seen each other. For three years, L.A. had very little rain, but it had been raining hard in the few days before we arrived. It was sunny and clear when we landed. I told my brother that he should tell the mayor to respect me because I brought the rain!

We picked up our baggage and went to my brother's house to visit with friends and relatives. The first food we had in America was Kentucky Fried Chicken. Our family told us that we had to drink something with it—fruit punch or coke or milk. Said said, "That's weird!" We weren't used to having anything except plain water with our meals.

Mo had developed a liking for football. The first time we went to a game, I commented, "What kind of football is this?" They said, "This is American football." I watched the players run with the ball, then hold each other and hug each other! I was sitting near him, watching. Then he jumped up and shouted, *Allah rabbo! Allah rabbo!*—which means, "God be with you." I didn't know what I was doing, but then I did the same thing. My brother looked at me, and asked, "Do you understand the game?" I replied, "What game? Why do you do that? Is somebody going to send you money for jumping up and down? What are you going to get for that—a bag of sugar or flour?"

One evening we were talking and I asked, "What is this Las Vegas that I hear about? How far is it from here?" My brother said, "Yes, it is far. It's about four or five hours by car, and by plane it is about one hour." Mo asked if I would like to go to Las Vegas. I said, "Yes, of course. I came here to see the world!" Up to that time, he had just taken me from the airport to the house to the store. I wanted to see more of America. So Mo said, "Okay, let's go." I put about $1,000 in my pocket. He called his Armenian-Palestinian friend, Steve Carey, and the three of us arranged to leave that night at 10:00 p.m. to drive to Las Vegas. Said didn't go, because, at 18 years old, he was too young to get into the casinos. We filled up the gas tank and arrived in Las Vegas at about 1:00 a.m. Oh my God—the casinos! Wow, I had never seen anything like it. We looked around, gambled, and then drove home the next day.

Mohammed's wife's family was living in Glendale, near L.A. I used to call it Agadir, like the town in Algiers. The house of my brother is his brother-in-law's house, because the two of them married two sisters. I called it the White House, because every Sunday, Mo and his family gathered there. I liked hanging around with my brother, and missed him on those Sundays when Mo left to visit his wife's family. I came from Africa with different habits; men spent much of their free time with their male friends, and women got together with other women. In America men and women stayed together more of the time and when visiting; they went dancing and golfing together as couples. We didn't have those practices in Africa.

One day we were at my brother's house, playing blackjack. In Sierra Leone, we used to play those same games for a shilling or two, maybe a few quarters. In the US, it cost one, two, or even five dollars. But as the saying goes, "When in Rome, do as the Romans do"—so I had to join my brother's friends. In this particular game, Mo lost and I lost. His brother-in-law and other friends kept winning. It was getting late, around midnight, and I went to the bathroom. When I returned, the women were taking the cards away from the table, because they were tired and wanted to go home. They put on some music and one of the ladies started dancing on top of the table. Since I was down about $200, I said, "Hey, where are the cards?" The lady started singing, "No cards, no cards, no cards." I was so upset that I came toward the table, tipped it, and scared the lady. She jumped off and onto her husband. They said, "Abu Said (meaning father of Said), you are going to kill that woman!" I yelled, "Get that woman away! Bring the cards here! We have to get our money back! Where is the whiskey? Bring the whiskey! Bring the brandy!" They got upset and they left.

Now I am going to talk about Steve Carey. He is the Armenian-Palestinian who went with my brother and me to Las Vegas when I visited America with Said. He is a nice, good man, and a very close friend of my brothers. He worked at the Dunkin' Donuts store with my brothers, and stayed with them. He had his own car. When I was there, he took me around, showing me the town. My brother's wife, my sister-in-law, liked to cook soup and rice, vegetables and rice, beans and rice, and so on—after a week of staying with my brother, I had gotten tired of the same dishes. I asked Steve, "Don't you guys have Lebanese food, or Arabic food? Don't you have different cheeses, sausages, fruits, oranges, grapes—a variety, like we have in Africa?"

Steve said, "Oooo, we have too much of it here. The whole world brings their food products to the L.A. area." I said, "Then where are they? You need to show me!" Steve said, "Come on. I will show you." He drove me to an area in the middle of L.A. All the stores in that area were Lebanese-Armenian. They spoke Arabic more than they spoke Armenian. I went inside one of the stores, looked at the huge selection and exclaimed, "My God! Now you are my friend!" I held Steve and hugged him! I went around the aisles and picked eggs, bacon, sausages, vegetables, grapes, oranges, tangerines. I bought $100 worth of groceries—a lot at that time. We carried all the bags to the car and drove back to my brother's house. Luckily, his wife was not there, and my brother was working at the store. We started bringing the groceries into the house.

Elham arrived home from her day at college. I told her, "Elham, look. I am fed up from eating soup and rice, soup and rice, soup and rice! Now I want you to make a nice, good dish, which I love—fried eggs with garlic, tomatoes and black pepper." Elham said, "Okay, Papa, I like this dish. How many eggs do you want?" I said, "Put in one dozen, half dozen. Make it big so we can eat as much as we want!" She cooked one big plate that looked like a pizza, but it only had eggs, parsley, tomatoes, sweet peppers and black peppers. I ate it with two Lebanese breads. Elham ate too, but still there was more than half of the plate remaining.

My sister-in-law came home, and asked, "Habib, would you like to eat?" I said, "Oh, thank you. I already ate, and I left some for you in the fridge." She opened the refrigerator, and wow! It was full!

She called to her husband (my brother): "Come, look what your brother did!" He came, and she showed him. "All this he brought." He said, "So what! He always brings things to us. He is the boss of the family. He can do what he wants." I said, "Brother, come eat." He replied, "I will eat, but I don't eat onions and garlic." He is the only one in the whole family that never liked onions or garlic. I said, "Good, then I will fill the fridge with only onions and garlic. You go eat in your mother-in-law's house!" His mother-in-law lived in Glendale, too. She had two other children who lived and worked in the area.

When I first came to America, I saw on the television that all the ads for products quoted prices that ended in "99"—like $8.99, $29.99, $47.99. I was sort of intrigued by that, and my brother, Mohammed's wife, started teasing me about it. Whenever she bought anything, she would tell me it was "$99.99." When I was shopping at K-Mart, Ralph's, or Bi-Mart, I would ask the salespeople, "Isn't this $99.99?" The answer to the value or cost of anything and everything became "$99.99." It became a running joke in the family, and I told all my friends in Africa when I returned there.

One rainy day, the brother of one of my sisters-in-law, Fehmi, and I were walking in the parking lot near the Albertsons store in Torrance. He had come from Lebanon about a month before to visit his family. Suddenly we found a beautiful young girl just lying on the ground, alone. There was no one near her. I said to Fehmi, "Look at this girl who has fallen down!" He said, "Why, what has happened?" I replied, "I don't know. Maybe nobody wants her, nobody cares about her. Come, let's see if we can take her—me and you. If you want her, you take her. Let's take her to the hospital. Maybe you want her. I don't have a wife here and you are not married! If you don't want her, I will take her myself!"

I was just joking, but he acted like he believed me. A few more people finally came by, and were standing around her. Then the ambulance came, put a brace on her neck, examined her, and took her away to the hospital. I said to Fehmi, "You see, nobody picked her up. You let her go, and now we don't have anything!" Later, he told my brother, "Do you know what your brother wanted to do? He wanted to pick up a girl who was lying in the parking lot and rent an apartment!" My brother knew that I was joking, and he carried it on, "Well, why didn't you do that? Was the girl nice and good looking? Sixteen or seventeen? Wow, that would have been a good catch!"

After that, whenever I see Fehmi, I always remind him, "Remember when we lost that good-looking girl?" Now he is living in Lebanon, and recently had heart surgery.

We had good times with Steve, seeing the town. We spent a lot of time in the Dunkin' Donuts, watching how they were made and sold, to understand the business. When it was getting time for me to return to Africa, I shopped for my family, buying clothing for my wife and children. I spent about $2,000 on the presents.

I asked my brother to sponsor me. I gave him the necessary documents—my birth certificate and identification. I explained to him that I knew the people at the American Embassy; they had been my houseguests and were nice people. I wanted to be allowed to travel and live in the US, and told him to do everything legally. I didn't want any trouble. I wanted to do this because I wanted my children to have an opportunity to go to college in the United States, since there were no good colleges where we lived. If any of my children wanted to learn more, I thought it was my duty to help them get more learning, more education.

So Said stayed in L.A. with his uncles and cousins. After my month-long visit with my brothers and their friends, I boarded a plane in L.A. to fly to New York. We had to change planes there, and flew on to Monrovia. Then I flew in a single-engine plane to Free-town, back to Siham and my children in Africa. But my luggage did not arrive with the plane. When my brother arrived to pick me up, I filed a report with the airlines for the missing luggage. They had me make a complete a list of the contents, which included all the gifts I had chosen for my family. When I came home, they were very sad that I came empty-handed. The luggage was never found, and the airline reimbursed me about £200 for each of the two bags, which was not nearly as much as the gifts cost me. But I did give the family some good news. I told them that their uncle was going to sponsor the whole family to visit America, to visit Disneyland and Universal Studios. I did have a few things to give the family that I had carried with me on the plane.

In Sierra Leone, there were members of a religion called Ahmadiyya that originated in Pakistan. The people were Muslim. It was founded by Ahmad, who titled himself the prophet. It seemed to have attracted the wealthy people in the area. They built a building and a school on the side of a hill overlooking the entrance to Kenema, but later abandoned it. There was a big field that was part of the property. On many Saturdays or Sundays, our family would go to the field and meet other Lebanese families there. We would bring tabouli and chairs. The children played together, our wives talked among themselves, and the men would visit and smoke cigarettes.

We also used to picnic on the air field, which was grassy land. Only one plane flew in, once a week, with carrying 10 ten or 12 passengers. We drove to the picnic areas in my Mercedes 220. When Said was little, I put him on my lap so that he could see to steer the car. One summer day, I had parked the car on the side of the road. I always left my keys in it. Mama was busy getting the tabouli ready to eat. I saw Said get in the car. He started it and slowly drove to the end of the field where a villager was walking. The villager saw the car moving but could not see little Said. He yelled, "Oh, God. This car is moving alone. The devil is driving the car!" Said was scared. He drove back across the field and parked near where I was sitting.

The villager came running up to us, "Hey, Master! Did you see that car?" I said, "Yes—so what? What happened?" Frightened, he replied, "The devil was driving that car. Didn't you see that?" I replied, "No, I didn't see it." The villager came back with, "You didn't see that?" Again, I said, "No, I didn't see that. See, the car is parked right here. Don't you see? There is something wrong with you, Mister. Go away—go away, go!"

Lila was my first daughter to get married; Elham was still in America, living with my brother and attending college. Next door to my house was another building that I had wanted to rent for my business. But as I mentioned earlier, the old man wanted to let one of his sons try to run the business. The son didn't do well at the job, so he moved on to another job. Our neighbor in Kenema was so nice—a good man. He planted roses in his garden, and would come over to give vases of flowers to Lila. He had another son, Ahmad, who we didn't know very well. We had only seen him a couple times, but we knew his father and mother well, and some of their relatives. One day Ahmad came over with his cousin, Mariam, who was a close friend of Siham. We invited them to sit, and they explained that Ahmad liked Lila and wanted to marry her. He was a nice boy. He worked in a pharmacy and knew medicines. He had attended Beirut University. He was honest in his work. He was young, and Lila was young, so everybody thought they fit each other, and that they would make a good couple.

We decided to have the ceremony at Kamboi Hotel—a Lebanese club in Kenema. It was named after the Kamboi hills that surrounded the town. The hotel was built by a Lebanese-African mulatto, but he was not able to finish it. He put up only the walls and the ceiling, but he did manage to get the bar going. The Lebanese community rented it from him for special occasions. On many Saturday nights, we took our food there and visited with other families. Sometimes well-known musicians came through town and performed at the hotel. The wife of my brother, Hassan, was a tailor, so she made Lila's beautiful dress.

Dick Duncan was the bank manager we used in Freetown. His wife was a mulatto, and related to Siham through her father. When he learned that we were arranging the wedding celebration for Lila, he and his wife offered to do the cake. They brought the six- or seven-layer cake to Kenema from Freetown by plane! We invited 500 people! Guess who made all the food for the wedding? Siham! She started more than one week before the celebration. She bought the meat and put it in the freezer and cold storage room of the store. In the evening, people asked if we needed help. I always responded, "Thank you. If we need any help, we will let you know." Meanwhile, I was busy in the store.

Said and others helped bring all the food to the club. We arranged the tables in a "U" formation, 15 to 20 feet long on each leg. We set out kibbee, rice, grape leaves and desserts. Nobody believed that Siham was able to do all that food preparation alone! There was so much delicious food. We had much left over. I went around and asked the guests, "How do you like the food? Was there anything that you did not get?" They complimented us on the food and were very happy.

The next day, Lila and her husband went to Freetown to stay in one of the hotels for their honeymoon. On the second day, Lila called to tell me that she missed me. I started crying and then she started crying. I gave the telephone to Mama, and she spoke to Lila. Lila was very close to me. When she was growing up, she would come home after school, change clothes, have a snack, and grab her homework. Then our driver would bring her over to the shop. She never left me until closing time; she stayed with me and did her homework at the store. She also helped with the office work, telephoning customers, and taking cash. Said started doing all of this also, as he got a little older.

Lila felt very homesick when she was first married. I felt like I was missing something. Here my first child was, a long ways away in America, and Lila was now married and no longer living with us. Over the years, Ahmad moved from pharmacy work, to photography, and then to import-export. He is very clever. Lila told her husband about how nice it was in America after one of her visits here. The fighting was getting worse in Sierra Leone, so they decided to move to America. Ahmad got a job teaching Arabic and English. Later he went into the printing business. They got their green cards and are very happy living in Portland.

About every other Sunday, we used to visit friends who lived in Ngelehun. Ngelehun is in the middle of the bush jungle. The roads were partly paved and very rough. It took us about 45 minutes to get there. I would pack all the kids in the van or the Mercedes. One of the boys and Mona would sit in the front, and the rest of the children would be in the back. There was no electricity. We would leave early in the morning so that we could have dinner with our friends around 3:00 or 4:00 in the afternoon, and get home before dark. People used generators and candles for all their needs in the village. The Hausa people living in that town were immigrants from Nigeria. I used to reminisce with them, speak Hausa with them and buy some of the barbequed meats that I had learned to enjoy when I was in Nigeria. One of the first times we ever had turkey was at one of these friends' homes. They also cooked African dishes.

On many occasions while we were visiting and eating, the man's house guard would let him know that customers had arrived. He had an office in back of the house and he sold uncut rock diamonds. He would be gone from a half hour, up to two hours, while he was removing diamonds where they were kept in little papers folded over and over, then weighing them on his scale. I accompanied him, as the business was interesting to learn about. He had a big safe and the dealings were all in cash. It was fun watching our friend's methods to negotiate and try to get the best deal for the diamonds. If he liked the customer, and a sale was imminent, the customer would be served sodas and food. We would leave our friends in Ngelehun about 8:00 or 9:00 in the evening I would drive home at night through the dark and dangerous bush of the African jungle.

One time when the friend went out of town on vacation, he gave me the key and asked that I open his office in case there was some diamond business. Of course, most people knew he was gone, so they didn't show up. They went some other place, or they just waited for him to return. I drove over and opened the shop from about noon to 6:00 p.m., hoping that someone would buy diamonds. I think only one time did I get lucky and make a couple hundred dollars. But I always had hope! When I came home, I admitted to Siham that I hadn't sold any diamonds, and she laughed. Siham had a good sense of humor, and she always had little sayings and proverbs that our family still uses. She probably learned them from her mother and father.

One morning while we were still living in the old house, I opened the store for the day. I saw a big black cat. It looked at me and went, "*Meeeoww!*" I drove it away. After about 10 minutes, an African man came to the store. He said, "Master, I have a *big* diamond." He showed me a big diamond—red, brown, and very pretty. I bought it from him for £60. Then I took it to an expert. He looked at me and said, "Habib, this is worth £10. It is no good." He showed me how he knew that it was not very good. When I got back to the store, I took that black cat and put it in a box. When a customer came, who was on his way out of town to a village, I told him, "Here's £5. That cat is bad luck! You take him and throw him as far away as you are going."

During this time, we were waiting for the completion of the green card process. We were counting the days. Every month I would check at the American Embassy in Freetown. My friend in the embassy assured me that he would process the documents as soon as he got them. I kept calling my brother, and he kept telling me that he was trying, and that the paperwork was on its way. But I know he was lying to me. For almost one year he told me that it was on its way. I went back to the American Consul. He said, "Look, Habib. I think your brother is not completing the paperwork. If he did, it would only take a couple weeks. He would only have to fill out the forms, send it to Immigration, and Immigration would send it to us here. We would do all the work here. Why don't you go back there? You have a five-year, multiple trips visa." I responded, "Okay, I am going back to L.A."

I flew back to L.A., and when I landed at the airport, I called my brother. "Hey, brother! Can you come pick me up?" Mo answered, "Pick you up? From where? Freetown?" I said, "No, from L.A." They were surprised to have me arrive in America. Said and Elham came to get me at the airport. When they asked why I came to L.A., I told them it was to see about the immigration papers. I sat down with my brother and we talked and talked, but nothing was coming out. He said he lost my identification—that he put it in the car but couldn't find it. When I asked why he hadn't told me, so that I could have written to my father in Lebanon and gotten another copy, he said he didn't want me to worry. "I kept thinking that I could find it," he said. "I didn't want to make you worry."

I countered, "I have been waiting for one year, and you don't want to make me worry!" He said, "Well, Brother, we will find it." At this time, the war in Lebanon was very hot. There was a lot going on politically, and the country's money was significantly de-valued. As my father was acting as the mayor of the town at that time, it would have been especially easy to get a copy from Lebanon. I kept thinking that my brother had not done my paperwork for some reason other than that it was lost, because he *was* doing his brother-in-law's immigration documents. The brother-in-law's sister already had her US citizenship papers, so the situations were different. I thought maybe my brother was afraid that issues would come up with his immigration status.

I reminded my brother that the political climate in Freetown was getting hot, and that if he didn't want to sponsor me to the US, I was going to take the family back to Lebanon. But in Lebanon, it would also have been dangerous for children 14 years old to 20. Either the armies would have wanted my older children to fight with them, or they would fight against them. They would have to fight with one side or the other. I was so scared! So I saw that the best thing would be for me to get my papers to allow my family to go to the US. It was calmer and easier for them there. They could study and go to colleges. They could have their lives. Everything was available there. The future was open.

Your future is a very big space in front of you. Behind you, you can only drift downward. If you go back, you will hold on, not knowing what will happen to you. Maybe you will be safe, maybe not. But in front of you, it is open, with nice green grass—beautiful! So you have to go to the side that you see is nice.

Mo said, "Okay, Brother. We will work on it." I responded, "No, now! You sit down with your wife and drink your whiskey. Steve and I will look every place in this house to find the documents. They might be lost inside of this house. Steve is going to go to your family room and your bedroom. I will go look in the children's bedroom. We will all go look to find the identification papers. If we don't find it, then ... We have to find the papers! Maybe you looked in some places, but still didn't see them, because your room has so many clothes and other things."

Steve worked for TWA in Palestine, cleaning and maintaining the planes. He was very experienced at finding lost items on the planes. I warned Mo's wife, "If you come back without the documents, then we will have to check ourselves, whether you agree or not. That is what I say." She turned to her husband, but he said, "He is my bigger brother; he can do anything he wants. I can't tell him no." She jumped up and went to her room. Five minutes later, she came out with the identification papers. She said, "Look where I found it—in one of the kids' books!" I said, "Oh, maybe he likes to read about birth certificates." (Their child was about seven or eight years old at the time.)

The next day, I said, "Come on, Brother, let's go." We had to go to the Immigration Office to prepare and file the papers. At the same time, Said applied to stay in the US as a student, and Elham's student visa needed to be renewed. I had to take care of immigration status for Said and Elham—all three of us. Steve was such a good friend and so clever. He recommended a lawyer downtown, but said that he charged high prices. I said, "Never mind, I have money in the bank. Whatever he wants to make my children be able to stay in America and continue in college. I want them to be able to walk on the streets, not hide in the streets—just live regular lives."

The next morning we went to the lawyer. He made an appointment for us in the afternoon, when he said he would be less busy. That lawyer was a German, and on the Immigration Board. We were very lucky. He said, "I want $700. I can give you the permit. Tomorrow morning Elham needs to go to her college and apply for another four years for a student visa. You will have to sign that you will support her." I confirmed, "Of course, I will sign." Then he asked for my bank account number, and I showed him my bank passbook, with the money that I had sent to my brother to deposit for me. He said, "No problem," and completed the papers for us. He said, "Now, I want $700." I had the cash in my pocket, gave it to him, he made a receipt for me and I thanked him.

We told him about Said. The lawyer said, "About Said—it is a bit more difficult." When I asked why, he said, "Said came here for a visit, and now you want a visa for him. You have to fly to Canada and see the American Ambassador. We will show him the $30,000 balance in your savings account." I said, "That account is in my brother's name, and he is a citizen." The lawyer said, "Very good," and told us it would cost $2,000. We said we would think about that. After we left the lawyer's office, Steve said, "Why should you pay the lawyer $2,000?" We can do this ourselves and take the $2,000 and enjoy ourselves for a few days in Canada."

We drove back to Mo's house. "Mo, we have good news for you. Here is your permit for college, Elham. Tomorrow morning you go to the college and push open the door with your foot. Nobody will tell you differently." Elham exclaimed, "Oh, Papa, thank you, thank you!" She had been upset, worrying about whether she would be able to continue in college. She wanted to finish. She was a very good girl. She liked to study. She enjoyed learning. She didn't want her time to be wasted. She is very smart—like her Dad!

Mo said, "Really—you did all that?" I said, "Really. While you are sleeping down here, afraid to do anything. Okay, Brother, now get ready for the second one: We are going to fly to Canada." Mo yelled, "Canada?" I asked Steve to explain the plan. Mo thought it was a good idea and asked "Who is going?" Steve answered, "Me, Said, you, and Abu-Said."

I replied, "I don't know if I have to go." But Steve insisted, "You have to go." Steve liked me and respected me, like a big brother. He was so nice. I decided that we would fly from L.A. to Portland, then rent a car and drive to Vancouver, Canada. We would stay overnight in a hotel there, and the next day, Said and I would go with Mo to the embassy. We would stay and see the city for a couple days after that. Mo said, "Okay, that is a good idea." When I told him to call for the airline tickets, Mo shouted, "Now?" I said, "Now, now, now. We don't want to waste any more time. We have already spent too much time."

Mo had Said working in the Dunkin' Donuts stores. Said complained, "Daddy, I am not doing much. I am only learning how to bake." I laughed and told him, "Okay, Son. Never mind. You have to go to school; you have to go to college. We came all this way, and spent all this money just for your brothers and sisters to learn—not to bake, not to do that kind of work."

Steve didn't need anybody to tell him what to do. He called the airport and asked when the next plane to Portland was leaving. Steve also arranged for a rental car in Portland. The airlines told him that a flight was available in the afternoon the next day. Then my brother's wife, Feryal, said she wanted to go, too. I said it was okay, and by then we had four or five passengers.

The next day, we left the car in L.A. and got on a plane to Portland, Oregon. In Portland we picked up the Mercury Cougar rental car. Steve knew the directions. He had experience driving that trip. We reached the US/Canadian border and a woman agent approached the car. She asked, "Are you all citizens?" We said, "No, one visiting, one green card, and three citizens." She said, "Okay, good luck."

We got to the Sheraton Hotel in downtown Vancouver very late, and had a three-bedroom suite. The next day, we went to the American Embassy at 8:00 a.m., to wait for it to open at 9:00 a.m. We had eaten at a small café, and while waiting, I wanted to take a walk with Feryal. She was worried, and said, "I'm afraid we will be late." I responded, "Don't worry, we will just take a little walk and come back. I need to have a little exercise. You walk with me and let them study what they are going to say. They have work to do." I took her to a café and we had coffee. We talked for a while, and then noticed that it was 9:10 a.m. "Oh, let's go! Hurry!" We got back and didn't see anybody there. They had already left. We sat down and waited about an hour. Feryal was very nervous the entire time.

Finally the three of them came back. As they walked toward us, we saw that they were very upset. Feryal said, "Uh-oh—they look sad. Maybe they didn't get the authorizations. They were not lucky." I said, "No, they were lucky. They are just joking. Don't worry. I know their tricks." When they got close, Said started smiling. I said, "You see? You two are lying and Said is smiling. That means it is okay." Said showed us what they had arranged. "Congratulations! We have all our visas." We were so happy! I took them to a good restaurant and enjoyed a good lunch. Vancouver was very pretty, with lots of flowers, and our hotel was very nice. The people dressed like English people—formally, with jackets and ties. If we saw people dressed more casually, like we were, we knew they were Americans. We spent two days in Vancouver before starting back.

We got to the border and were checked by the American immigration agents. They thanked us and waved us through. They were so nice, not having to check everything like they do now. We drove to the Portland Airport and turned in the rental car, caught the plane and landed in L.A. In L.A. we got our car out of the parking lot and came back home. Said was happy then. Right away, we went to California State University, Dominguez Hills campus, to register Said for classes. It was roughly a half-hour drive from Mo's house to the college.

The next step in moving the family to America was to complete more documents. Steve suggested that we go to Manulkin Glaser, a good firm. We met with a lawyer, and I explained that my brother was a citizen, and now I wanted to apply for a green card. He said, "You will have to give me the names of all of your family members. I will charge you $200 for each person, totaling $1,800, but you can pay me $300 each month." I had to write to my family and get all of their identification papers, since I only had mine with me.

Next he asked me where I had been. I explained my travels from Palestine to Nigeria to Sierra Leone. As soon as he heard that I had been in Palestine, he asked me if I had Palestinian identification. When I said yes, he asked, "Where is it?" I said, "It is in Lebanon.

Why?" He explained, "If you can send it to me, you don't need any other paper. I will be able to get you the green card right away, and you will be able to bring your family all over here." The US made a regulation especially for Palestinians so that they could easily leave their country and come here. I said, "I will try to get it. That is a good idea. Why didn't you tell me?" He responded, "How would I have known that you have Palestinian citizenship?" I wrote to my father, asking for my identification, but he could not find it. It would have been a very big help. With my Palestinian citizenship, I might have been able to get a loan or subsidy to help start my business. I knew I had the documentation when I was in Lebanon, but I didn't want to carry it with me all the time. There may have been trouble if one of the governments or military found out that I had dual citizenship. The lawyer said that it was okay to have more than one country in identification records in America.

In the end, I did have to get all the identification papers for my family. They had to be started in Lebanon for the two littlest children, as they did not yet have them. They were sent to my brother's address in Torrance. I took the documents to the lawyer and he started processing them.

I then made plans to return to Freetown. When Steve was going to make the flight arrangements, I told him, "Don't put me in a plane that changes in Monrovia. I want an American plane that goes directly from L.A. to Freetown."

Steve said, "Yes, there is an American plane with a direct flight. But let's talk. You say that there are lots of problems in Africa. You say that your children are finished with high school and need to go to college. You can sell your property, your store, and your house. You have said that your wife can take care of the sales of your businesses. Why don't you stay here, and send for your family to come? If you go, you will spend more money on the ticket over there and then back again. Your two children here are not together; they are separated, living with two of your brothers. Why don't you rent an apartment, bring your children back together and send for your family to come over here? Tell your wife to transfer your money here and send everything over. Believe me, and listen to me. You already have two children here, and you have secured them in college. They need someone to stay with them here. Your brothers, their uncles are okay, but they have their own families and children. I like you like a bigger brother, like my father—I love you and am ready to help you in everything you want."

I said to Steve, "You are making sense. Let me think." He said, "No thinking, Mr. Habib. No, Abu-Said. I want you to listen to me. Let's go find an apartment."

I agreed, "Let's go find an apartment!" I just drove with him; my brother didn't know anything about this arrangement. So, Steve and I went to his apartment complex, which had 15 or 20 units. The building belonged to an old man, in his 70s or 80s—Mr. Snowden. He was so nice.

Steve introduced us, "Mr. Snowden, I would like you to meet my bigger brother." Steve explained that I had two kids and that I needed an apartment while waiting for the rest of my family to arrive from Africa, when we would need a three-bedroom apartment. Steve explained that I wanted to stay near him, and wanted to rent from Mr. Snowden because he was a good landlord. Mr. Snowden liked Steve because Steve helped him around the apartment. He said, "Okay, Steve. I have one bedroom right now, and if he can wait for one or two weeks, I may have a two bedroom apartment become available." I said, "Okay, give me the one bedroom now." Mr. Snowden said that he was cleaning the apartment and it would be ready to move into the next day. Steve and I agreed not to tell anyone of this plan.

LOS ANGELES

Steve was able to spend all this time helping me because he had been injured at his job, working for TWA at the L.A. Airport, and was on medical leave for two or three months before returning to work. This was very good timing, because I needed someone to help me while my brothers were at work all day. I told Steve that God sent him to help me. He said, "Really?" I asked, "Do you have any better ideas?" He said "No," and we chuckled.

Steve came to pick me up in the early morning to rent the apartment and start moving in. Feryal, my brother's wife, asked me why Steve came so early that day. I said, "Because we have to go to Dunkin' Donuts, eat some fresh donuts and drink coffee." She said, "I want to make a breakfast for you." She was so nice, cooking and cleaning for me. Feryal was surprised because usually I got up in a leisurely way, shaving and dressing before one of my brothers came to take me to the store, about three or four miles away.

I went with Steve to Dunkin' Donuts and ate donuts and drank coffee. Around 11:00 a.m., we went over to the apartment. Mr. Snowden said, "You guys are lucky! The person who had the two-bedroom apartment is leaving tomorrow. Do you want to wait until tomorrow when the two bedroom will be available, or do you want the one bedroom today?" I replied, "No, we will wait for the two bedroom—it will be better for three people." I asked Steve what we needed to do about furniture. He said, "Let's ask Mr. Snowden. Mr. Snowden, what furniture do you have in the apartment?" He answered, "We have a refrigerator and oven; that's all."

Steve said, "I will take you to a Jewish man who sells furniture. He is very nice. Do you mind?" I said, "How can I mind? They are my cousins! Muslims and Jewish are more closely related than to you.

You are Christian!" We laughed together and Steve said, "I love you, Habib!" I said, "I don't care, as long as you are a good person. Who has told you that I distinguish between religions? We are all good people. You look like me. You are my brother." Steve responded, "Oh, Mr. Fakih, Abu-Said. I love you. I have learned many, many things from you." Whenever I discussed anything with Steve, he would say, "Oh, that is my pleasure! I have learned this, I didn't know that." I would say, "Do you know why? Because I am two times older than you. I have experience."

The Jewish furniture dealer was short, and very nice and polite. Steve introduced me, "This is my friend, a Lebanese, Habib Fakih." The Jewish man said, "What? Habib what?" I reiterated, "Habib Fakih." He suggested, "My friend, do you have another name to change to?"

"For what?" I asked.

He said, "Your last name—you better change it."

I replied, "No, I am proud of it. Do you know the meaning in Arabic? It is a good person, an educated person, like a professor."

"Oh, that is good, my friend," he replied. "But in your country, not here."

"Hey, Steve," I said. "Let's go. This man doesn't like my name."

The Jewish man exclaimed, "No, no, no! I love your name. Keep it! Keep it!"

I said, "Now, that is better." Steve explained that I had two kids, I had just rented a two-bedroom apartment, and that I wanted to buy chairs, a table, and beds. The Jewish man said, "Okay, I will give you a good price. Steve, haven't I always given you a good price? I know that you came a long way from Torrance, and I appreciate that."

He did give us a good price. We bought two large couches and two chairs, a table, two end tables with lamps, a coffee table, two double beds for the bedrooms, a dining table with six chairs, a TV, a little radio. He only charged about $2,500—very cheap. He said, "I want cash; I don't want a check." I whispered to Steve, "Shall we pay him now or wait until the furniture is delivered?" Steve replied, "No. If you have the money now, give it to him. Don't worry." I took the money and counted it out to the Jewish man. He said, "God bless

you! You are a nice man. Steve, why don't you bring me more customers like this?" He took $100 and gave it to Steve. Steve took the
$100 and put it in my pocket. I said to him, "No, Steve. Shame on
you. Since you put it in my pocket, let's go have a nice dinner. You
saved me lots of money. You deserve it."

The salesman asked for the address and when the apartment
would be ready so that he could deliver the furniture. We told him
that we would call him. Then Steve said that we had to go sign up
for a telephone.

After two or three days, we still had not told anyone that I had
rented an apartment and arranged for the furniture! I called Said and
Elham and told them that I had a surprise for them. The new furniture
was all arranged in the apartment and I had put fruit and vegetables on
the dining table. We took them to the building, and I gave them a key
and told them to go up to the unit number and open the door. They
were so excited to get to live together as a family again and thanked me
for arranging it. My brothers were a little upset, but I reminded them
that they didn't have to take responsibility for my children any longer.
Now my children had lived in the United States and could get along
fine on their own. I explained that they were still under their uncles'
control if I was not there. My brothers finally agreed.

Said and Elham were going to the same college. I told my brothers
that I wanted to get Said a car so that my children did not have to
rely on them for transportation, since they were so busy in the donut
shop. "You have your work, you have your family. They are adults.
Let them depend on themselves. They shouldn't depend on everyone
else all the time." We looked for used cars and found a Ford or Chevrolet stick shift that was a beautiful maroon color. We stopped and
asked the price. It was about $1,500. I said, "Okay, Mohammed, buy
it." I gave him the money and Mohammed drove us off the lot. I
asked Said to try driving it. He was a good driver.

The next day, I asked Steve to take us to the DMV office to take
the driving test. The tester was an African man, and Steve knew
him. He had met him gambling in Las Vegas. The African called out,
"Hello! What are you doing here?" Steve said, "My cousin has a

driver's license from Sierra Leone. He is a good driver and wants to have an American driving test." The man asked, "He knows how to drive?" Steve said again, "Man, he knows how to drive. He had the test in Africa. You don't believe in Africa?" The tester said, "No, no, no. I believe in Africa. I like Africa. I am African. My grandfather, my grandmother are African."

He took Said in the car, and in just a few minutes came back. He told Said, "You have passed the test." Said got his license and put it in his pocket. I told him, "You drive behind us." But he said, "Papa, you come with me." I replied, "No, it is too soon for me to come with you. You just follow us." He followed us and got home without any problems. We celebrated. We called Mo and Hassan and played poker, betting five or ten cents. We got hungry and bought chicken from Kentucky Fried Chicken. Steve asked how everything was going. I thanked him. "You were right," I said. "We have now secured the kids. Thank you." He had helped me so much, and I really appreciated him. I still talk with Steve when I go to L.A. He separated from his wife and supported his children: two girls and one boy. Now they are grown and have good jobs. Then he remarried.

I said to my brother, "Now we have to find a business." He asked, "Aren't you going back?" and I told him that I was staying in L.A., and had told my wife to finish up everything in Sierra Leone, and move here with the rest of my family. Mohammed had been running the Hermosa Beach Dunkin' Donuts, so I said, "Let's pay for that place. Let's buy it." I think we put a down payment of about $20,000 or $25,000. We bought it for less than $100,000. We were making payments to a nice, good American man who was a friend of Mohammed. We shook hands; we didn't do paperwork.

Once I had the store, Steve said, "Don't worry, I will help you." We hired people to work in the store, because Mo and Hassan had been running it. I suggested that we all become partners in the Torrance and Hermosa Beach stores, but they didn't think that was a good idea. They said, "No, you have your children and your family. You can control the store independently. You make payments using your own money. It will be better for you." Said, Mona, and Elham all came to the store to help me. They had experience and I didn't. I said to them, "You tell me what to do, even though I am the boss!" Steve was a big help. He came to the store every morning and left in the afternoon to check on his family.

I got a telephone call from my son-in-law Ahmad, Lila's husband, who sold medicines in Africa. He was helping sell my store in Sierra Leone, and he told me that it was sold, and that he had gotten visas for my wife and the rest of the family. I met my family at the airport and we were so happy to be together again.

But now the two-bedroom apartment was too small! I went to Mr. Snowden and told him that my family was all here, and I needed a bigger apartment. He responded, "Okay. Manage a few days and I might get a three bedroom available very soon." We liked this man. He did not bother us. He took the check at the first of the month. He had a box at his door that you could drop the check into. He always said that if we had any problem with the apartment, we just needed to tell him, and he would fix it. We never had any problem. It was a good apartment, almost new.

One day I got a letter from the Immigration Office. They said that I had to pack up and leave within one month because the visa period was up. I called Mr. Glaser, the attorney handling our immigration status. He said, "Don't worry, Habib. They will give us time to go to present your case. We will go to the Immigration Office and you can talk to them. Tell them that you have your lawyer with you."

We went and told an officer that I had received a letter. He asked if I wanted to say anything. I said, "Yes. Now I have my family here. I brought all my money with me, which is over $30,000 from Africa. My children are growing up and cannot get an education beyond high school in Africa. Now I have them in college. They are costing me lots of money. Imagine! Five kids going to school! I rented an apartment, I bought furniture and opened a business. And all this doesn't matter? If you don't want me in this country, give me my money back and let me leave. If my children go back, they must fight wars, because all young people are required to fight. I don't care. Just give me the money that I spent here, and I will leave tomorrow!"

He looked at me and said, "Habib, no one will drive you or your family from this country. Are you Lebanese?" I said, "Yes, I am Lebanese, and they are fighting up to the neck over there." The officer said, "Habib, there you go. You can stay here indefinitely, forever!" I responded, "My brother is an American citizen. I applied for a green card. And that is my lawyer sitting over there, if you don't believe me." He looked askance at me, and then looked at my lawyer. "Do you have any suggestions, sir?" I asked. He replied, "Not at all, Habib. You and your family can stay here. No one will bother you. Here you go. Keep this document and make copies for your children. If anyone asks you anything, just show them a copy. Have a nice day. You are welcome in America. Nothing will happen to you. Goodbye! We don't have the money to repay you. And we don't want you to have to send your children to Lebanon to fight. You brought them here to learn, for their education. You are welcome. That is what we want people to do. Education beats everything."

It upset me and I started shouting. "That is why we came here! We ran away from fighting to Africa. Then they started fighting in Africa. Now we come here. Now you guys, you don't want us. Where do you want us to go? Back to fight?" He said, "No, Habib, no! That's enough! That's enough! Good-bye. Have a good day." I replied, "Do you want me to talk to you some more?" He said. "No, no, no more."

Mr. Glaser was waiting for me. He said, "Habib, I think you better come walk with me. You talked enough!" I explained to him that my frustration over all this was because of my experience in going from one country to another, always fleeing fighting and wars. My brother was so worried until I came back and explained that we could stay here indefinitely, that no one would touch us. We were all so happy. I asked Elham to go make coffee to celebrate, and we bought a big watermelon.

We moved to a bigger apartment, and lived in California seven or eight years. When we first came, I only spoke Pidgin English. There was much to get used to that was different from all the other places we had lived. We enjoyed working for Dunkin' Donuts. But there were some problems. Sometimes the baker or the morning worker didn't show up. It was a mixed up period and there wasn't always time for the kids to go to school because they had to fill in for the absent workers. Elham and Said were at Cal State. Lila and Oula were not in the country. Haidar and Suad were in junior college. Mona was still small; we put her in a parochial school. My wife was very concerned because we brought the kids over to get more education, but then I needed them to work in the store. Elham was able to finish her four year degree. But Said and Haidar would go to school one day then have to help out in the shop the next day. They learned to bake the donuts. Suad helped the customers at the counter.

With a large family, it was very expensive. I was paying about $80 each month for Mona's Catholic school tuition, plus rent and all the other normal expenses. Mona learned English in the African school and she leaped ahead when she entered the school in L.A. She was a very good student. Whenever I would pick her up from the school, the sisters would tell me, "You have a very good girl. We never see her go with the boys. She always stays with the girls or stays alone. At first we thought that she was afraid or shy, but she made friends with two girls. She doesn't mix with too many people, just the two girls." I said, "Oh, that's my girl! She is just like me when I was young."

At that time, Hassan and Mo were working together in the Torrance Dunkin' Donuts store. Hassan was renting an apartment in Redondo Beach. Mo was younger than Hassan, but Mo had already bought a house in Torrance. Hassan started thinking he wanted to buy a house in Redondo Beach. He found one he and his wife liked for $150,000. Hassan and Mo discussed that from the $300 to $500 Hassan was getting out of the store each week, he could afford the $1,200 monthly payments. But he didn't have cash for the down payment. I had about $30,000 in the bank at the time, and that was just about the amount of cash that Hassan needed. Mo told Hassan that he could get the money from me. But Hassan replied, "But what if our brother needs that money tomorrow?" Mo assured him, "I don't think he will need that money. He told me that if you want the money, you can use it." Hassan said, "Now I can use it. But maybe in the future he might need it. I could make payments back to Habib."

If I have money and my brother needs it, I give it to him. If I need money and he has it, he would give it to me. If he doesn't have any money, he can't give it to me, and that is okay. That is the way my family is, and our Lebanese culture is this way. There are few pension funds, and no government-funded social security payments in old age. We rely on ourselves and our families. Even if my children were not able to pay back a loan in my middle years, when I got old and couldn't work, they would bring me money and food, just like a beggar.

Hassan kept refusing the money, so Mo and Steve and I took him to a bar. We thought a few drinks would help him accept the money. First we ordered beer, then wine, and finally some whiskey. It was about 10:00 p.m. We went back to the Dunkin' Donuts in Torrance. Hassan's wife had been asking about him. She was worried, because he was usually home at about 8:00 p.m. I told Steve, "Uh-oh! I see Hassan's wife inside!" I said to Hassan, "I better go inside before you do." I was hoping that respect for the older brother would make things go more smoothly with Hassan's wife. She asked, "Where is your brother? Where did you take him?" I responded, teasing her, "He is with me, here. I took him to a bar. He liked all the women in the bar. We were trying to talk him into buying the house."

Hassan did not buy the house. The interest at the time was 16% or 17%, and he felt that it was too big of a risk. Hassan and his family continued to rent their apartment.

A young Korean boy came into my store almost every day for coffee and donuts, and occasionally talked to me about buying the store. One day he came to me and explained, "I have a brother here. Could you hire him for work? I want him to work and learn to support himself. He just came from Korea." I said, "Okay, bring him." He was a very nice boy, about 20 years old. We taught him how to sell to the customers. Then he learned how to fry the donuts. He said he wanted to learn to make the muffins, and he learned to bake. After about a year, he knew all the jobs in the store.

One day his brother asked to talk to me again about buying the store. He said he would buy the store, but his brother would manage it. The only thing he had not learned was the paperwork. He asked, "Do you want to sell it?" I said, "Let me think about it. I will call you."

He responded, "Just tell me how much you want to sell it for, how much cash you want and how much you want in monthly payments."

At this time, Steve was working with an Afghan man who had worked with the Shah of Afghanistan as a customs officer. He had run away to L.A. with his family during all the fighting with the Russians. He was well-educated and spoke several languages. He had met Steve in Dunkin' Donuts and explained to him that he had money but was looking for some work. He and Steve decided to open an ice cream and sandwich shop, called the Ice Cream Bar. They each spent about $30,000, as the business cost $60,000 or $65,000. They were both friends of my brothers and me.

One day, they had a fight—an Armenian and an Afghan! They were both greedy and liked money. Steve is a good man, a nice man. Both came from good, rich families. They came to my brother and explained that they were not getting along and wanted to sell one of the positions in the partnership. Steve said, "Why don't you sell your Dunkin' Donuts and buy my Afghan partner's share in the ice cream store so that you can send your kids to college?"

Steve knew that my wife and I were arguing because we didn't bring the kids to America to bake; we wanted them to have college educations. I was tired of the argument, but I was listening to her. At the same time my brothers encouraged me to keep the donut shop. The Korean came into the store and I told him that I wanted $130,000 for the store. Without argument, he agreed to the amount, with a cash down-payment, and $1,000 a month for seven years. I had paid about $90,000 for it three or four years before.

The store was still in my brother's name because the immigration process had not been completed. I told my brothers about the sale and I paid everyone off. I bought both Steve and the Afghan's shares in the ice cream store, so it belonged entirely to me. It went very smoothly because Mo was a very good accountant, a CPA. (He also had his realtor's license.) In the long run, selling the Hermosa Beach store was a mistake. The property has become so valuable over the years, and it was a good location for a business—five minutes away from the beach. There was an annual "Saturday market" that lasted for three days, where we were so busy we had to keep runners going back and forth from the store to the booth to replenish with fresh donuts all day. We made $500 or $600 every day at our booth.

I had arranged it so that Haidar and Said would attend college in the morning. Elham and Suad went half a day also, until Elham graduated. Then I hired people to work. I had to learn to sell ice cream in this country and how to make sandwiches—it was all a little bit different than in Africa.

Once Elham graduated, she started looking for a job in the genetic science field; she is a cytogeneticist. All the hospitals wanted experience, and she didn't have any, since she was a new college graduate. She looked in the newspapers every day. She said, "Papa, I am tired of looking, and I'm worried that I am going to have to go back to making donuts." I said, "No, wait." Elham mentioned that the only person she hadn't approached was an Indian lady who had a lab. I said, "No, don't go. Does she have a telephone number? Listen to me. Before you go, you call her and tell her that you just finished college. Explain that you came from Lebanon to go to college, but that you want to work and get some experience before you go back. Tell her that you will volunteer to work in her lab for two or three months."

Elham called her, and the Indian lady said, "How soon can you come?" Elham said to me, "But Papa, there is no money!" I replied, "Don't you worry. You just go one month, two months, three months. If she likes your work, then I will have a new idea." Elham said, "Okay, Papa." After about two months, Elham explained, "All the work that she gives me, she says I am doing very well. She said that I will do well in Lebanon, when I return. She gave me all the work. She likes my work better that the people that she pays."

I said, "Okay. Now, are you sure you are doing a good job?" Elham confirmed, "Papa, I am sure I am doing a good job. The woman likes me and my work." I asked Elham how much she thought the employees were being paid, and she said $15 to $16 per hour. I said, "Would you like to work for $10 an hour?" Elham said, "Oh yes, Papa. If I work for eight hours that is $80. I never dreamed of making $80 in a day!" I responded, "Go back to the lady and explain that there is a war in your country and that you need to find a job until the war stops. Explain to her that you applied at a hospital in L.A. and they will hire you for $10 an hour. Tell her that you are leaving her at the end of the month and that she will have to get someone else because you have to start making some money. Tell her, 'I have to help my dad. I have to get some clothes for myself and my family.'"

I used to talk my way into jobs like this, and I taught Elham to do the same! Elham went to the Indian lady, as we discussed. The lady offered her the $10 and Elham was so happy. I told her not to show her excitement to the lady, but when Elham got home she had a big grin on her face. "Papa, Papa!" she said. I said, "You got the job!" Elham said, "She accepted! I got the job. Thank you, Papa. How did you know?" I said, "From the way you came in."

One day Elham introduced me to Nazmi, a man from Sidon, Lebanon. She told me that he wanted to marry her. The family of my brother's wife, Feryal, was friends with his family. Elham had met him at her uncle's house. He was from a good family, a well-to-do family in Lebanon. His uncle owned a hospital and his cousins and other family members were doctors and lawyers. They had lots of acres of oranges and bananas. I started discussing the possible marriage with my brother, Mo. He cared a lot about my daughter and my family, and he liked this man.

When Nazmi came to meet me, he came with lots of gold in his hand, and was very well dressed. I was concerned because he wasn't working, but Mo commented, "If a person has money, why should he worry about work?" I responded, "But one day that wealth will be gone. If he doesn't work to make money, that money will be finished. His wealth won't last." I discussed this with my brother. I liked the man but he was not a serious man, not a businessman. My brother had been in the United States longer than me. I am older than him, but he had more experience living in the US and knew more about things here.

At that time, Elham was about 28 years old. When girls get that old, they want to marry and have a family. We arranged the marriage in a hotel in L.A. His family from Sidon came for the ceremony. At the reception, I heard his family talking among themselves, saying that Nazmi was not very responsible. One man said, "Oh the bride looks nice. She must be sick, or have something wrong with her. Or maybe her parents are poor and want to get rid of her because they are tired of feeding her." I heard this, but it was already too late. When I told Mo what I overheard, he said, "Oh my brother! You are very concerned about that person." I said, "Do you want to tell the people?" Mo replied, "No." So I told him, "Okay, you are responsible from now on for this marriage. If it is successful or not successful, you are responsible!"

At this time, Mo had a territory franchise for buying and selling Dunkin' Donuts. He had a partner, his brother-in-law (Feryal's brother), plus Steve, the friend from Afghanistan, and two lawyers, working to set up and develop the business. Steve had a lot of money from his country, so he helped with about $30,000. They intended to buy and sell the individual stores to Koreans, and other immigrants looking for work. My brother had lots of money at the time. He paid for Elham's wedding ceremony and the $2,000 to $3,000 hotel bill. My brother was so nice, so generous.

After the wedding, we all went back to our jobs, and I went back to work at my ice cream bar. We got a telegram from Lebanon that my wife's mother had passed away. My wife loved her mother. She kept crying, so I offered to send Siham with Suad to visit Lebanon. But we did not have the green cards for them yet, so I told them to go for two months or a year, to visit Siham's father and brothers. I would wait for the green cards, and planned to go to the American Embassy in Beirut or Syria when the cards were ready. That was a big mistake. They were stuck there for three years. The Israelis raided Siham's father's house and took money, jewelry, and other things. This is why Siham had her first stroke; she was only in her early fifties. Our town in Lebanon was a big city, so the family ran away to stay with good friends who lived in a little village. They welcomed them, and Siham's family stayed with the friends for about a month until everything calmed down. The Israelis were blowing up towns on their way to Beirut, and occupying the area.

Siham had two brothers in Abidjan, West Africa. She said she might be able to go there and get the visas and come back. Siham went there, but her visas were denied, so she had to go back to Nabatieh. During the three years that Siham was there, she continued to suffer small strokes; she suffered a lot. Also during that time, Suad met a nice, good man who was an interpreter, working with computers for the airlines. She married him over there. I finally was able to start making plans for going to Lebanon. We called my brother, Hassan, in San Diego and told him to come to L.A. My two brothers and I went to a Jordanian travel agent because he represented a Jordanian airline that regularly flew into L.A. from Beirut. My brother and his mother-in-law already had tickets, so he told the travel agent that he wanted two more seats for his brothers. The agent explained that there were no more seats, but that we could get on the next flight a few days later. But my brother asked that his original seats be cancelled so that we could all go together. So the travel agent rearranged all the tickets.

Then we went back to my house and met Lila and her husband, who were visiting from Africa with their children. Luckily, they knew the office manager in Sierra Leone for the Jordanian airline who was also involved in imports. His family were very good friends. They both had children and visited each other many times. Lila said, "Papa, wait a minute." She had his telephone number in Freetown, since they used him for arranging their trips, so she rang his office, and caught him there. Lila said, "Look, I need a favor from you." He replied, "What do you want? You just give me the order."

Lila explained, "I have my father and two uncles here. One uncle, Mohammed, is flying to Beirut with his mother-in-law, and he already reserved tickets for the Monday flight. My father, with my other uncle, wants to go with them. They went to the office in L.A. and were told there were no seats available for the other two. Can you put them on that flight, or do they have to wait?" He responded, "Lila, you give me the order and I will obey. Just give me your telephone number, and give me twenty to thirty minutes." Lila thanked him, and hung up.

He called back in about an hour. He said, "Tell your father and your uncle and your other uncle that they should go on Monday morning to the airport desk and give them your names. Your tickets will be ready and everything will be okay." This was Friday. We called Hassan and told him that we would be flying on Monday. Oh, how nice! We were all happy. Mohammed's wife said, "This is impossible! Lots of people try to get reservations, and can't get them. How could Habib get seats?" My brother bragged, "Habib's daughter knows many important people!"

My lawyer told me that in order to get my green card, I was going to have to make a trip to one of the countries in the Middle East, and have my documentation processed, so that I could re-enter the US.

I used to play lotto and gamble to make money. I met with my daughter and asked, "Can you clean this can?" Elham emptied the can of olive oil and asked, "What do you want it for, Papa?" I explained, "I need it. Just clean it." I took the can and put it in my cupboard. I checked in my pocket and had about $20 that I would have used to play lotto. Instead, I put it in the can. Every day, I put the money from my pocket in the can. Finally, when we got ready to make the trip to the Middle East, I opened the can. I found $750 in the can! It was like a gift! I exchanged the cash for travelers' checks for the trip.

We got to the airport Monday morning and were sitting, waiting for the gate employees to arrive. When they arrived, they called for my brother, Hassan, and me. All my family were looking and whispering, "Hey, he is going to get the tickets." The ticket agent said, "We have an order from Mr. Ahmad to reserve two tickets, and we have them all ready." I asked if we could sit next to the rest of my family, but they said that they were giving us tickets for people who didn't show up and we had to take their tickets. The ticket agent asked, "Is Mr. Ahmad your family?"

Irritated, I responded, "Why? If he is not my family, if he is not my friend—he is interested in me. He can do this for me!" The agent replied, "No, thank you. I'm sorry, sir. I'm sorry." We gave her my brother's credit card and she said that when the plane arrived, she would call us first. We sat down, and in half an hour they announced, "The plane is ready for boarding. May we have the Fakih family first." Everybody looked at us like we must be V.I.P.s! My brother asked, "Are we V.I.P.s?" and I told him, "Of course. If you walk with your brother, you are always a V.I.P." So we went first, and even had special service and better food. My brother, Hassan, was next to me. We were drinking coffee. The stewardess came by to give us refills. I was on an inside seat, so I held my cup on my brother's leg so she could pour the coffee. Just then the plane experienced some turbulence and the hot coffee spilled between my brother's legs. He yelled at me about not being careful. The stewardess ran to get a cloth and was about to wipe my brother's pants. He shouted, "What are you doing? No, no, I will do it myself." We laughed and laughed.

While on the plane, my brother Mohammed's mother-in-law was tired and wanted to sleep. Mohammed loved his mother-in-law. She was old and sick, and he tried to take good care of her. There was no place to lie down in the plane, so Mo offered to give her his seat too, but she did not accept.

We arrived in Amman, Jordan in the evening. Lila's husband's friend was responsible for meeting V.I.P. people at the plane. Before the people started to disembark, he entered the plane and told the captain that he was expecting V.I.P. people on that flight. They announced, "Fakih family, please come to the front of the plane." So we got up. I said, "Come on, brother. You are a V.I.P. man!" The man introduced himself as the brother of the manager in Freetown. He asked, "Who is the father? Let me see your passport." We shook hands and we followed him to a very important place. He told us that a person would bring coffee, tea, juice, and snacks, and that we would wait while the workers took care of the suitcases, and processed the tickets.

After a little while he drove us in his van to a hotel about an hour away. The hotel was so nice, with beautiful trees. We reached it by 10:00 p.m. They brought us a dinner of steaks and soup, but we were tired. We ate as much as we could, and went to the elevator to go to our rooms. My brother and his mother-in-law were in one room, and my other brother and I shared another. I started talking to the boy at the elevator, who was a little bit dark. Since the Jordanians are a little dark because their country is hot, I wasn't sure whether he was Jordanian or African.

My brother told me, "Don't make trouble for us. Let's be respected; we are V.I.P.s. Respect yourself, my brother." I spoke to the boy in Lebanese—but in Jordan, it is a different dialect of Arabic, so we didn't understand each other. The people who come from Amman speak exactly like the Lebanese, because they travel between the big cities in the Middle East so much. But this boy came from a town outside Amman. In the towns, the houses are covered in mud and don't look like much from the outside. However, on the inside they have marble floors, flowers, and trees, and are very beautiful.

We went up to our rooms and slept that night. In the early morning, the doorbell rang and the waiter arrived with coffee, tea, and a big pot of milk. My brother liked to drink coffee with his milk. Sometimes I drink coffee plain, and sometimes with milk. My brother who was escorting his mother-in-law knocked on our door and said that she didn't drink coffee; she just wanted milk. He took all of our milk for his mother-in-law, and so my brother, who was sharing a room with me, didn't have any milk for his coffee! When we got dressed and ready, the man took us in his van again, to the airport to leave for Beirut.

In Beirut, we were met by my youngest brother, Joe, and my nephew—one of my sister's sons. They were only expecting my brother, Mo, and his mother-in-law. All of a sudden they saw Hassan following the porter with the luggage. Then they saw me. Everyone was so excited to see all of us. The driver asked where we wanted to go. My sister's husband managed a hotel at the seaside. He was the son of my uncle, who was the brother of my mother. He was the second husband of the sister who went to Africa, and for whom I got the divorce from her first husband. I liked him and my uncle, so I wanted to see him, and his hotel was on the way to our town.

We drove there and found him sitting in the office, relaxing in his chair with his feet up. He half opened his eyes when we got out of the car. Then he closed his eyes, thinking he was dreaming. Then he opened his eyes again, and we all shouted greetings. He ordered

Lebanese coffee, and served it in small cups. He served it to me, and then to everyone else. I told him, "You are nasty. You brought us cold coffee." He started yelling at the boy about the cold coffee, telling him he was lazy. We laughed, enjoying the visit.

After that, we got back on the road to go visit my sister and my father in Nabatieh. We arrived at my older sister Fatimah's house. It was on a hill and had a veranda in front. They used to all sit on the veranda. My sister used to put a chair on the edge of the veranda and watch everybody coming and going. They were expecting Mo and his mother-in-law to arrive that afternoon, but they didn't know Hassan and I were also coming. I sat in the front seat with Joe. I opened the front door and Joe opened the front door on the other side. Fatimah shouted, "Oh, Joe came with Mo! Oh, this is not Mo, this is my big brother, Habib!" Then Mo opened his back door and Hassan opened the other back door. "Oh, Hassan too!" she said. "All my brothers have come."

Fatimah came running to us. My father was still alive at that time, but he couldn't remember anything. He had Alzheimer's. I went to him and kissed him. I asked, "Do you recognize me?" He responded, "Oh, maybe you are a friend of the family. I know you come every time." My brother, Mo, came and hugged and kissed him and said, "Do you know me?" Again, my father responded that he was a friend of the family. He did still recognize Fatimah and Joe, because they were always right there. My brother said to my father, "You have three sons in America. Do you remember?" My father said, "Yes, they tell me that I have sons in America. I hope that they will come see me one day before I die." I explained, "Daddy, we *are* your three sons. We came especially to see and talk to you." He said, "Okay, if you want to say you are my three sons, my children, I will not deny it. I love my sons. They write to me, I write to them, we talk together." My brother, Mo, couldn't help it—he started to cry.

My two brothers could only stay for one month because they had to get back to running their stores. I still needed to go to Athens to get my immigration papers processed so that I could re-enter the country. At this time, Siham was a little better from her stroke. She could walk and talk, but slowly. Her right leg was heavy and dragging.

I went to the Greek Embassy in Beirut, and they gave visas to my wife and me. I explained that I wanted to go to the American Embassy to get our green cards. We flew to Athens and went to the President Hotel in Alexandria. We stayed that night and took a taxi to the American Embassy the next morning. We explained our business to the guard at the door and he let us in. We waited with lots of other people until a girl called me to her window. She greeted me in Greek, so I told her that I spoke Arabic and English. She started speaking to me in Arabic. I showed her my papers. She took them to another person, who was Lebanese. He came with her back to the window and explained that all the papers were in order, except that he had not received the Affidavit of Support from my brother. He said, "You have to go back and call him to send the affidavit. As soon as we get it, we will let you know." I said, "How will you let me know? There is a war and fighting." He answered, "Okay, call us in two weeks. Maybe we will get it by then. Just give it a week, if he says that he already mailed it." I agreed and we left. We decided to walk back to the hotel. It was only about a mile, and the exercise was good for Siham to help her improve from her stroke.

Siham's stroke was brought on by the stress of her mother's death, the war, and the soldiers breaking into her father's home while she was there. She was also overweight and smoked heavily. She had started smoking in Sierra Leone when a neighbor who fought a lot with her husband would come to the house and visit with Siham. They would have Lebanese coffee, and the other woman would have a cigarette. She started offering them to Siham. Soon one cigarette became two. Then it was one pack a day, then two packs a day, then three ... and so on. The doctors stopped her from smoking immediately after her first stroke. They should have had her stop smoking gradually. It was not like here, where there is intense follow-up for strokes and other major illnesses.

We got back to Beirut and took a taxi back to Nabatieh. It was very dangerous at that time. There was not a good place to stay with my family, so I stayed with my wife's family. The house was much safer. It was built with stones and had a basement with 18-inch walls that we used as a bomb shelter. We would go to the bomb shelter when we heard *Boom! Boom!* On the second night we were all packed in the one room of the basement. The only other man was my father-in-law. There were so many women—sisters, grand-sisters, little sisters—probably about 10 girls. I was about to pull my hair out!

On the third night, when Siham said, "Come down," I said, "No, I am not going down. You go down." I kept sleeping. Whatever was going to happen, would happen. I needed my sleep. When I was down there, it was just talk, talk, talk! I couldn't sleep. I would be tired the next day, but still needed to go out and do my business.

During this trip to Lebanon and Athens to take care of immigration matters, I wanted to call my brothers in the US. I couldn't do it from Nabetiah because there were no telephone connections between Nabatieh and America; I had to go to Beirut to make the call. I hired a taxi to take me to a place where there was a telephone. I came to a place where the police would not allow cars, so I had to walk.

I got to the place where there were telephones. It was usually very crowded, but there were only a few people there then, plus the workers. I placed the call and talked to my brothers about the immigration documentation. I asked how everyone was, and my brothers said everyone was good. Then I walked to my nephew's store. He sold wine, beer and whiskey. I left there. It so happened that my wife's brother and his wife lived next door, on the sixth floor. They didn't tell me that they lived there, and they didn't call to me, but they were watching me.

Later, they told me that they were afraid to call out to me because they did not want to bring attention to any of us during this period of unrest and war. They later asked me why I was there. I walked on through many streets, and many people watched me, wondering what business I had. Most people were not willing to be out on the streets during those times. I walked and walked. My nephew later asked me, "Where have you been, Uncle?" I told him where I had walked. He shouted, "Where? Alone?" I said, "Yes, alone." He asked, "Did you see anybody in the streets?" I replied, "No, that was strange. I saw no one in the streets. No cars, no dogs, no nothing!" He said,

"God helped you! Otherwise we would have had to pick you up and take you to the burial grounds." I asked, "What do you mean?" He explained that two factions were fighting. One street would have fighting and one street would be normal with people walking and doing their regular business.

He scared me. I told him that I was going to his father, Hassan's place to visit. We sat together and Hassan made nice hubbly-bubbly and a big pot of coffee. We were just starting to relax and talk. I drew three blows when—*Boom! Boom!* I asked Hassan, "What is going on?" He said, "Nothing. Leave the hubbly-bubbly. Let's go." I argued, "Leave the hubbly-bubbly? I just put the fire on it!" He said, "Come on, let's go." He told his boy to take care of the fire and we left.

We drove to his son's store, but he wasn't there. So we thought maybe he took off and went to the house. We had to cross to the other side of the fighting to get there. We got trapped on the road with fighting in front and behind us. The fighters shot at each other across the road. Cars caught fire and were abandoned by the side of the road. My brother-in-law put his head outside the car and yelled at the driver in front of him, who was going too slow, "You ****, move. Why are you going so slow? You are going to die whether you go slow or go fast." The driver was more scared of us than the shooters.

Finally we got home, but decided we should buy food and supplies for a few days, in case the fighting reached my brother-in-law's home. We bought coal for the hubbly-bubbly, tobacco, bread, cheese and sardines. When I started to pay, then Hassan wanted to pay. I wanted to pay, he wanted to pay, I wanted to pay, he wanted to pay—we went back and forth like this, with us pushing each other. A tanker came rolling by, manned with soldiers like a swat team in America. The soldiers asked, "What's going on here?" We said, "Nothing, nothing. I want to pay, he wants to pay." They ordered, "Okay, one of you pay and get out of here. Don't make trouble. Otherwise we'll take you to jail." I said to Hassan, "Are you happy? You pay."

We took the supplies up to the sixth floor of his house. There was no electricity, so we had to walk up all the flights. We started to make some food, and then the fighting came into the area. Hassan told us to go to the other side of the house and hide behind the doors. Then I heard, *Boom! Boom!* I was scared, and my stomach was upset. Hassan said, "Don't worry." He put all the tea that we bought in a kettle and boiled it to help settle my stomach. We needed to sleep, but who could sleep with all the bombs and rockets going off? The building was made of very strong cement. I remember that one rocket passed very close to us. The whole building shook, my pillow jumped up, and I landed on the floor. At 10:00 a.m. the next morning they called a truce for several hours so that the people could get out in the streets and get food and take care of their business. I said to Hassan, "Let's go down."

We got in his car to leave, but the battery was dead because he had left the radio on. While we were trying to decide what to do about the car we heard about a dead man in the area. His brother was sick, and he had gone to get medicine. One of his other brothers was a soldier, and shot him dead as he was walking to get the medicine. He did not know that it was his own little brother.

We turned our attention back to the car again. We had jumper cables, and tried to get help from the people in passing cars, but they all said, "Who cares?" and continued on. We were about to push the car, hoping someone would stop to help. Before I pushed I said, "Oh, God, please help." I started to push, and the car started. Hassan looked behind to me and asked, "Who helped?" I answered, "I called on God. He helped." We drove away.

On the way, we stopped at a baker and bought bread. Then we continued on to our town. Our family was very worried about us. We told them the story of what happened, and we were all happy. It was very good that Hassan knew the roads in Beirut and out of the town, to avoid the areas that were involved in the fighting.

After a few days, I again called my brother in L.A., and he promised me that he would complete the forms quickly. I went back to the embassy in one week, but they told me that they had not yet received them. So I had to wait a couple weeks. I called again. This went on for six months before the papers were ready. Finally Siham and I went there, and they told us we had to go to a photographer, and a doctor to get exams. This was about 10:00 a.m. The embassy told me we needed to return at 2:00 p.m. So I had to rush with my wife to get all this accomplished in time.

We went to a Greek doctor. He said, "You look like a strong man. Just give me the money and I will sign the papers." I gave him about $20 and rushed to the photographer. Rushing around was a little trouble, but it was worth it. In the afternoon we got all our papers and the visas.

I told Siham, "We have to stay here today and get a hotel for the night. There are no planes back to Beirut this late." We went to the saloon and tried to order coffee and tea. The server said, "Sorry, we don't have tea." I told my wife in Arabic that they didn't have chai. The waiter interrupted, "Do you mean chai?" I said, "Yes, chai." He replied, "Here we call it chai; we don't call it tea." I said, "Okay, bring us chai." He said, "I agree, in Greek, tea is called chai. We are neighbors. Lots of our words are the same."

The next day we flew back to Lebanon. When Siham opened the luggage, she realized that she had forgotten three fine new dresses in the hotel. I said, "What's wrong?" and she explained that she forgot to pack the new clothes we bought in Athens. The next day, I was at my sister's house, talking to a man who was a good friend of Joe, my brother. He told me that he was going to Athens the next day. I explained that my wife had forgotten three dresses at the President Hotel. He said, "I know that hotel. Don't worry, I will get them for you." In one week the man came back with the dresses. He had given our name to the hotel, and they had saved the dresses very nicely. We were very lucky! The visas were for three months, and so we had to get ready for travel.

We had to leave my daughter, Suad, there because we could not get her visa. She was in her mid-twenties at the time. She stayed with her grandparents (my father-in-law's house) and visited my father, who was staying at my sister's house. Suad had learned English, so she applied to a school that needed an English teacher. She made many friends among the other girls teaching there. One of the other teacher's mothers was very sick, and in the hospital. Suad went to visit her friend's mother in the hospital, bringing flowers.

The woman thought Suad was nice and would make a good wife for her son, Sami. So she told her son about Suad. At the time, he was employed by the principal of the schools as a substitute teacher, because the war kept him from his job at the airport. Later, he told me that he watched Suad. "When the other teachers had breaks," he said, "they sat and talked together—talk, talk, talk. But Suad usually sat by herself and read a book." He liked that.

When his mother got well enough to go home, Suad visited her there. Suad wore a gold bracelet, and when she returned to her grandparent's house from one of those visits, she noticed that she had lost it. She called back to the house and asked her friend to look for it. The next day, the father was getting in his car to go to work, and noticed that the back tire was flat. He got the jack and started to lift the wheel. Under the wheel, he saw something shiny and picked up the bracelet. He went in to his daughter and said, "Isn't this something you were looking for, my daughter? Call Suad." Everybody thought that was a sign of good luck. They all said, "We are going to get Suad here because her bracelet was lost here and we found it!"

The next day they went to my father-in-law and told him that they liked Suad and wanted her to be their son's wife. My father-in-law explained that Suad's mother and father were in the United States, and that he would have to call us. "If they say yes," he said, "with their permission, we will have the pleasure to be one family, together." My father-in-law's eldest son—my brother-in-law, Abraham—was in Africa. He told Abraham to call me and explain everything. He called and told me that Suad had a nice man that had proposed to her. I asked, "Do you know that man? If you and your father feel that this is okay, and that the family is good, go ahead and carry on with the plans. I leave it to you." Abraham told his father that I gave my permission.

My father-in-law called Sami's father and explained, "The father of the girl does not know you. He has left everything to us. We do not disagree." Sami's father wanted to discuss how much in dowry would be required. It was tradition to talk about the price and settle on the dowry amount. This money was to open the house, get furniture, a car—anything that a wife needed. If a divorce were to occur later, the wife would get to keep all those things. Also, an amount of money was usually agreed upon before the marriage—this would be paid to the wife in the event of a divorce. This tradition was especially important because 90% of the women stayed home and took care of the house and the kids. They did not have their own income to be saving and spending. My father-in-law told Sami's father that he had no goals of how much money to get for Suad. He said, "My goal is for you to take good care of Suad. I have taken good care of her. I want you to be good to her. If you promise me that, I need nothing more from you. Whatever you want to give her, whatever you want to do, I trust you. I can say one pound gold in advance, one pound gold later."

Sami's father said, "But we should put something in writing." Sami's father owned houses and land. He was a rich man. My father-in-law responded, "That is up to you. I trust you. My son-in-law made me responsible for Suad and I have taken good care of her. I want you to do the same. I transfer that responsibility from me to you. That is all I want." Sami's father was so impressed. He told everyone, "I have never seen people like that. They don't think of money. They think of respect and dignity." He told Suad, "You are very good in my eyes. I haven't met your father or your mother, but I have heard about your father. He is a nice man."

They had the wedding ceremony. Suad continued teaching to help her husband, because he couldn't go back to working at the airport during the war. Oula had married before Suad, when Said and Elham were in L.A. Now I had four married daughters. Only the baby, Mona, was still at home.

The immigration documents for Said, Haidar and Mona were sent by mistake to Freetown, Sierra Leone, instead of Lebanon. I called the immigration agents and they said they couldn't find us. The Consul had changed, so we didn't know the new person in that position. The agent gave us a date about four weeks out, and told us to send the children back to Africa to complete the immigration process. Nazmi, Elham's husband, helped to get good tickets for them.

During this time, I worked in the ice cream store, but was becoming unhappy with the situation. Steve had signed a five-year lease—but partway through, the landlord said it was not valid, because ownership had transferred to me. He raised the rent from $1,000 per month to $3,000 per month, based on fair market value. The problem was that $3,000 per month was about what we were taking out of the store each month, so continuing to do business at that location was impossible. During this time, Said was working several jobs part time. He was working for Weisfield's Jewelers, Denny's, and Dunkin' Donuts; he also delivered the *Herald-Examiner*. Elham and Said helped out and were able to pay the rent for the family apartment.

When Siham originally became ill in Lebanon, we were told in Arabic that she had suffered a stroke. But we really didn't know what was happening. We didn't get any doctors' reports or other information. We thought, "Oh, she was overweight and she needs to cut down." She loved the French fries! We really didn't follow up, because of ignorance. That was before the emphasis on diagnosis and medication within the first few hours of a stroke. Then, while I was in Portland and Said was running the ice cream store, Siham had her major stroke.

I tried to sell the ice cream store, first for $90,000, and then dropped the price to $75,000. Nobody wanted to buy it. The original landlord, who was Chinese, sold the strip mall to an Iranian man, so I talked to him. But he didn't care who was renting from him—he just cared about the $3,000 monthly rent. The store had cost me about $70,000 or $80,000 for the purchase and the additional equipment I bought. So I spent $70,000 and was offered $7,000 for the equipment! But I had no choice; I had to feed my family. When the man who sold me the video games we had in the store heard I was selling everything for $7,000, he offered to buy. I agreed and he gave me the check.

When I sold the store, Mo came to me and said, "Habib, my brother, I want to tell you something. You have lost your money and your business, and your wife is sick. How about if you go back to Lebanon, and I keep Said and Haidar to work with me? You could stay with our father, and your sons will send you the money you need every month. You go back to Lebanon and let the kids stay here and go to college and work. You have no future in this country." I replied, "Yes, brother, but I am strong. I can still do work. I cannot surrender so easily, because I have always worked. I can't sit and wait for you and my children to send me money. What happens if sometimes you can't send me money? Where can I borrow money from people in Lebanon? I don't want to be a beggar. I will never do that."

A little while after that Mo had to make a trip to Portland. He asked me if I would like to come with him. I said, "Yes, I have nothing else to do." In Portland we went around to the stores in his territory. He had a store in Raleigh Hills, in Tigard, on 122nd Avenue, and one in Hillsboro. We visited them all. He asked me if I liked Portland. He said, "Lots of people are afraid to come to Portland. They don't like strangers. There are lots of Japanese and Chinese. I offer the donut shops to them. In L.A., they like to buy these businesses, but in Portland they refuse to stay, and say it is too cold, and the local people don't like strangers. What do you think?"

I replied, "If you give me a place, I still will have some money coming in from Hermosa Beach that I can use to pay you." Mo said, "Pick any place, but the one in Raleigh Hills is run by a Chinese man. He has a store in Torrance also, and lives in the L.A. area. He might be willing to sell the Raleigh Hills store." I said, "That one is fine. I like it." Mo explained that the Chinese man still owed him $40,000, and owed the Dunkin' Donuts Corporation about $100,000. I had about $40,000 from my old Hermosa Beach store that I could use to pay my brother. I asked him to talk to Dunkin' Donuts about transferring the $100,000 debt over to me. Mo said, "That is a good idea."

Mo called the Raleigh Hills franchise owner and said, "I want you to come quickly. I have found someone to buy your store." The man took a plane up to Portland and arrived to meet us the same day. We worked out the details of the sale and planned to announce it the next day. This was at the end of January, 1987.

That evening Mo suggested that we go to the store, and act like customers, just to see how it was doing. It was a little after 6:00 p.m. in January, so it was dark in Portland. There was no help in the store—no boys, no girls. I called out, "Is anybody here?" and no one answered. I looked in the kitchen. There was nobody there. I came back out and told Mo and Haidar that no one was in the store. Suddenly a boy came out from the restroom, zipping up his pants; a girl was behind him, still putting her dress down. Mo said, "Hello. Sorry, we were just coming to get some coffee." The boy answered him, "Well, when you came and didn't find anyone, you could have walked out. You didn't need to shout." We said, "Oh, really! We are very sorry." The boy asked, "What do you want, now? Do you want a cup of coffee?" We said, "No, thank you. We have changed our minds." We left.

The next day the owner came to the store to meet with the employees, and to announce that there would be new owners. Then Mo, Haidar, and I came inside to be introduced. The boy and girl who had been in the store the night before were standing among the other employees. When the owner said, "Everybody say 'hi' to the new owners," that boy and girl just looked at each other, took off their hats and aprons, and walked out!

PHOTOS

One of my first pictures, taken when I was thirteen years old. I was working in a restaurant in Palestine to send money home to my family in Lebanon.

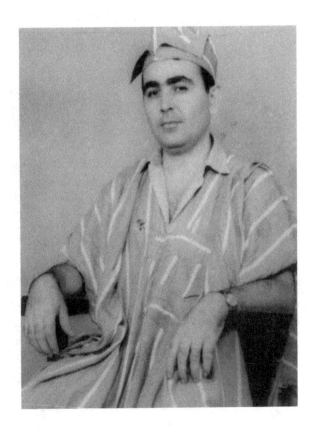

I was in Nigeria wearing a traditional tribal gown. Nigerian clothing style was beautiful and elaborate.

I am standing by my car in 1954 in Nigeria. I loved
to own the best big American cars!

My wedding picture with my beloved wife, Siham, in 1954.

We are relaxing on our honeymoon in Jos, Nigeria in 1954.

My wife, Siham, was pregnant with our first child, Elham, in 1955.

This is my first grocery store
in Kenema, Sierra Leone,
West Africa, in 1960.

I am with my brothers, Mohammed (left) and Hassan (right),
who introduced me to the donut business in America.

I am sitting second from the right, in Portland in 2007 with my seven children.

This donut shop in Portland was our first in Oregon. I am
standing with one of my sons, Said, in 2011.

Getting together with my brothers for a game of poker and smoking the Lebanese water pipe in Portland in 2004 was one of the best times of my life.

new flavor to Old Town

ANTHONY ROBERTS /The Gazette

Mayor Keith Mays (from left), and Sesame Donuts owners Habib, Haidar and Said Fakih celebrate the grand opening of Sesame Donuts with a ribbon cutting event sponsored by the Sherwood Chamber of Commerce in November.

Celebrating the grand opening of our second Sesame Donut Shop with the town mayor and my sons, Haidar, and Said (far right), in Sherwood, Oregon, in 2006.

From machine shops, trucks, grocery and ice cream store, to
the donut business in Portland, Oregon. I am standing to greet
my customers with all the donut trays behind me.

I am enjoying thebeautiful Columbia Gorge area with my sons and daughters.
The Pacific Northwest reminds me of old times and places in Lebanon.

Me, in my donut shop wearing my Grandfather's hat.

PORTLAND

WE RENTED AN APARTMENT IN LAURELWOOD, VERY CLOSE TO THE STORE. I told Said that we bought a store in Raleigh Hills and that he should send our furniture and make plans to move Siham and Mona to Portland.

We started to do the work in the store. Customers came and bought coffee. The policy had been that they were charged 35¢ for the coffee and 25¢ for refills. I didn't like that idea; I thought it would be better to charge a little more for the cup, and then offer free refills. But we didn't change anything at first. We just studied the business.

The place was filthy; there was donut batter on the ceiling and on the walls. The doors into the kitchen were so dirty. I had Haidar hire one person. They cleaned and scraped to make everything look better. I noticed that only one or two out of 10 customers would order a donut with their coffee. I would ask them if they wanted a donut. "Nah, no donut. Nah, no donut." I went into the kitchen and saw Haidar making nice, big donuts, with lots of glaze. They looked delicious. I said, "Haidar, pull out one tray for me. I am going to give each person a treat of one donut."

I gave each person in the whole house a donut and a napkin. I explained as I passed out the donuts, "We just bought this place. We are new owners here. My son is a qualified baker, trained by Dunkin' Donuts." The people ate the donuts. They started saying, "Where did you get these? They are delicious. Give me two. Give me six."

When we were first in the donut shop in Portland, Said was still running the ice cream sandwich shop in L.A., closing out the business. That was where Siham had her major stroke. Said was making sandwiches, and Steve and others were talking to her about how cold

Portland was. I think it upset her. Said explained that she stopped talking, her face got red, and she fell down. She was taken to the hospital in a coma.

After that, Said worked in the shop during the day, and in the evening, he slept at the hospital. Siham was in a coma for 10 days. When she had recovered enough to leave the hospital, my children took her to Lila's house in L.A. By then, Said and Mona were staying there also, as our furniture had already been shipped to Portland. It was a very difficult time for all of us. Siham was not able to walk. Her right side was completely paralyzed, and she was very incapacitated. Lila was the one that called me to tell me about Siham's latest stroke. I think Said and Mona feel a special bond because they spent so much time taking care of Siham during her long illnesses, and before Said and Mona married. Once Mona left, and Said got married, Lena (Said's wife) took over most of Siham's care.

Before the furniture came, and the rest of my family moved to Portland, Haidar and I would buy fried chicken, and eat on the floor of the apartment on newspapers. We would sleep on the flour sacks at the store. Because the business was so slow, we couldn't afford to hire people so that we could leave. We didn't have beds at home anyway! So much business had been driven away. When customers came in to buy a donut, we would offer them another one to try for free. We started giving free refills of coffee. They started to come back. We began talking with customers, greeting them and being friendly. One short man, who I believe has since died, one day said, "Look, you are going to make this business good. I like you. I am going to tell my friends to come back to this store. It is cleaner, the donuts are nice, and you are not charging for refills." Within one month, the store went from $200 to $300 a day to making $400 to $600 a day!

Finally the furniture arrived, a few days before Siham and Mona. When Siham and the rest of my children were finally able to move up here, Mona and Lila put Siham on the plane. The last time I had seen her, she was good and strong. When I picked her up at the airport, she was in very different shape. I had to cry.

My younger children needed to go to Africa to finally get their green cards at the embassy. Nazmi, Elham's husband, assured us that he could get the tickets cheaper in L.A. than if we got them in Portland. The children needed to get to Freetown within four weeks to pick up their green cards. Nazmi said, "Okay—within a few days, I will get you the tickets." A few days went by. Then one week. Then two weeks. I kept asking where the tickets were. Said and the other children flew down to L.A. to wait for the tickets. Nazmi couldn't get them. The children flew back up here. I had to call the embassy and ask for an extension. They said, "Okay, but this is the last extension for four weeks."

We didn't ask Nazmi again. We got the tickets from Portland, and Said, Haidar, and Mona flew from Portland. It was like a reunion for them. They stayed with Lila's husband's brother, and got to see their old friends. Said had been gone for nine years, and Haidar and Mona had been gone five or six. They stayed a month and then returned to Portland. That was in 1988 or 1989, and we were still living in the Laurelwood apartment. Lila and Ahmad moved up to Portland from L.A. during this time, and they also rented a Laurelwood apartment.

About this time, a Lebanese girl came to work for us. Said hired her. She was fluent in Arabic and English; her family had been here for quite a while. Said fell in love and wanted to marry her. She was lovely. I think I have a sixth sense: When I sit with someone, I have an intuition about them. Her father came to me, and we had coffee and talked. Afterward, Said asked me about them. I said, "Said, they are not our type; they are a different type. You are an educated boy. You are Habib's son, Siham's son. You are different from this family. So it will not work."

Said countered, "Papa, I like this girl. I want to marry her." He was giving the girl lots of presents. For a while, I didn't say anything to Said. Then I said, "Be patient. Wait. Be patient. Wait." Said started talking to his sisters, to get them to talk to me. I finally told Said, "If you want to marry that girl, you go marry that girl. But not with my blessing. I don't like that girl for you!" I spoke with Mona, who said, "Papa, my brother really likes that girl. Why don't you let him marry her?" I responded, "Daughter, maybe these people are after Said to get the Dunkin' Donuts—so that they can take over the store and kick us out." Mona said, "Oh, Papa, you are thinking bad things too much. I don't think they would do that. You are imagining things." I said, "Okay, but this isn't the right girl for Said. Leave me alone. If you want to help your brother, you can go get her. I don't want to help. She's not right for him."

A few days later, the girl's cousin, who was one of our bakers working for Said, was talking with a friend who had come into the store. He didn't see Mona behind the counter, and she overheard him saying, "I don't think that Said should marry my cousin. I like Said. He is a good boy. His father is nice. He helps a lot of people here. That girl doesn't deserve Said. The girl is not good for Said." His friend asked, "What do you mean?" Our baker explained, "I heard my aunt, the girl's mother, say that if Abu-Said asked permission for her daughter to marry Said, she was going to ask that the Dunkin' Donuts be put in her daughter's name as her dowry." Mona remembered what I had told her a few days before. She thought, *Oh, my God! How did Papa know?*

Mona didn't say anything in the store or when she first got home. I was sitting down getting my hubbly-bubbly started. You see, I only do my hubbly-bubbly when I have a lot of things going on in my mind. Mona came to me, "Papa, are you a prophet? Are you a man who knows the future?" I replied, "What kind of silly thing are you saying?" She asked, "Remember a few days ago when you told me if you asked for the girl to marry my brother, she might ask for the Dunkin' Donuts?" I said, "Oh, that was just talk. I just said that." Mona said, "No, Papa. That was true. I heard her cousin say that. They are going to ask you for the store." I laughed and replied, "Now do you believe me? I know what is going on in the future."

Mona went to Said and told him what I said, but he wouldn't change his mind. He was very upset and took off in his car. The next day, he still had not returned and we got very worried about him. We started calling his friends but he was not with them. In the evening, we got a telephone call from Elham. Said had filled the car up with gas and driven all the way, non-stop, to L.A., to talk to his uncle, Mo.

Mona called Said in California, "You have to come back to Portland. Your mother needs you. Your mother is crying." Said responded, "I'm not going to come back if your father is going to stay stubborn. It is either me or your dad. He has to change his mind. I have worked very hard. I am his first son and he *has* to make my wish come true." Mona reminded Said, "You can't punish your mother because of your father." Said's reply to that was, "No. My father is punishing me and my mother."

Said was very lucky to have his oldest and youngest sisters, Elham and Mona, talking with him about this problem. Said asked Mona, "What does the girl say? Have you talked to her?" Mona explained, "She hasn't said anything. She just called and asked about you. I told her you went to Los Angeles and she said, 'Oh, okay.'" Said then called the girl from Los Angeles, "Hi, how are you? I am in Los Angeles and I won't come back until my father agrees to ask for your hand in marriage." She replied, "Oh, okay. So you are going to stay in California?" Said replied, "Yes, I will stay here. I will talk to you; I will call you often."

Said told me later that he was waiting for her to show that she cared or loved his family. He expected her to say something like, "Your mother is handicapped, and you have your father and the business to think about. Don't worry. Let things quiet down a little bit." She didn't say anything about Said's job or his mother and me. She didn't care; she wasn't supportive. Either she wasn't smart; or she just cared about Said and herself, and no one else; or she was thinking, "Okay, good. Just stand there and don't listen to your father." This is the message that Said got from that telephone conversation. Said's concern for his mother was greater than his disagreement with me. He discussed the situation with his sisters, and thought about the recent conversations with the girl, and finally decided to return to Portland.

He continued to talk to Mo, who said, "Look, I have tried talking with your father about different things more than two or three times. If he says it, it is going to be, because he knows more than me and more than anybody else. He is good at analyzing the future and explaining it. If your father agrees that you should marry that girl, I

will pay for the ceremony, for the house—for everything! Let's go."
He put Said back in the car and they started the trip back up here. Mo
took Said to a nice hotel on the way so that he could cool down and
relax. When they arrived, Said gave me a hug. He hadn't changed his
mind, but he was still thinking about what the girl said ... or about
what she didn't say, but should have.

Meanwhile, Mo spoke to me. "Look," he said, "I came here to
talk with you, but I won't force you or tell you what to do, because
you are my older brother. You can say what you want. But why are
you stopping this marriage?" I explained to him, "First, the father
does work between here and Canada. I am not sure what it is. I don't
know and I don't want to get involved. I need for Said to have a girl
who has more education. I want Said to have a nice, good life, to have
grandchildren in the future. I want him to marry within my family. I
don't want him to marry outside the family." I think Mo agreed with
me. He said, "Anything you say. But if you change your mind and
agree about this girl anytime, I will take all responsibility for Said." I
said, "It is not the money that is the problem. What is important is
the kind of girl that I would like for my son. He is my first son. He is
going to get married, so I want to look for a nice, good girl for him."

Said was still in a crisis in his head over this girl. He was in a temporary "cease fire" with me, coming to work as usual and visiting his
mother. Said had a very good friend, Abraham, from the eastern area
of Lebanon. His family was very loyal. (If you gave them a million
dollars and told them to keep it for two years, you would get it back to
the dime!) One night, Said and Abraham were walking on the water-
front in Portland, at 10:00 or 11:00 p.m. Said was raised by Siham
and I in the old, traditional way; he didn't like seeing women smoking
and drinking, or staying out late by themselves. All of a sudden Said
saw the girl he loved coming out of a dance club with a couple of her
cousins. It was a singles bar, with drinking, smoking and dancing.

After that, Said went to Mona and explained, "Mona, this is what
I saw." Mona said, "Said, maybe you have to forget her." Abraham
said, "Said, this is wrong. I know you love the girl, I know you have
a problem. Maybe now you have to change your mind. This is really

getting bad. She never called you to tell you that you have to respect your parents and stand by your family."

Said went to the bank where the girl worked as a teller. He was so upset that he drove his car over the curb when he parked it. He told her, "It is over. You take everything that I gave you and everything that you gave me." She had earlier returned some gifts he had given her. "I don't want them. I don't want the bad memories. You seem stubborn, hard-headed. I am handling all this pressure, and besides, I don't like the way you do things. You drink too much beer. You know what? This is the end. You didn't support me when I needed you. This is the end."

She never called. Said never called. After a couple of months, Said forgot about her. Slowly, Said started accepting the things that I had tried to teach him.

A few weeks after all this, Lila and I were sitting and discussing getting a wife for Said. Lila mentioned Lena, my brother Joe's daughter. Lila said that she was beautiful, and very nice, and eighteen or nineteen years old. Joe's family was living in Nigeria at the time, having run away from the fighting in Lebanon. He was working in a hotel as a bar man. We had his telephone number so we tried to call him. It was the middle of the night there. It was really not Joe's telephone; it was his neighbor's. When the neighbor answered, I asked to speak to Joe, and he sent his watchman to get Joe. The watchman told Joe that he had a call from his brother in America. Joe was scared—a telephone call in the middle of the night from his brother in America might mean that something was wrong. We said our hellos and each asked about our families. I asked, "What are all the kids doing?" Joe explained, "There are three in school and two in the house." I asked, "Who is in the house?" and Joe replied, "Lama and Lena are in the house, and the other kids are in school." I said, "Okay, I have something to tell you. I am going to send Said to visit you. I am thinking of Lena. If they meet each other and like each other, how about if Lena becomes the wife of Said?" Joe responded, "Brother, you are my big brother. If you want Said to marry Lena, nobody can deny you. I and my family are all at your service. Do as you like. You are welcome."

I told Joe that I would complete the documents so that Said could visit for one month. "I would like you to see if they like each other, if they can love each other, and to do all the necessary things." Joe responded, "Okay, I have no problem. Just send him. What time is he arriving?" I told Joe, "We haven't done anything yet. First I had to see if Lena was still at home. That is why I asked you." Joe confirmed, "Yes, Lena is at home. Don't worry. Send Said as soon as possible."

We got off the telephone, and I turned to Lila, "Now we have to talk to Said." He didn't know anything about this. We were plotting without him. When he came home, Lila and I told Said that we found a wife for him. He asked, "Where?" We told him about Lena. I offered, "How about if you go to Nigeria for a vacation? One month to West Africa—where your father was, where your mother was, where you were born. You should go see the area. Take a month. If you like the girl and the girl likes you, everything will be okay. That is what I explained to your uncle. If you don't like her, you just go have fun and come back."

We looked all over the house to find a picture of Lena so that Said could see her. We found one from when she was about nine years old, but nothing older. Said thought that if she looked like that as a child, she would be very beautiful when he saw her grown up. Said and Haidar liked their Uncle Joe. Joe called Haidar, "Os," meaning little boy, Shorty. They had spent a lot of time with him when they were young and living in Africa while Joe was running a business in Freetown. They used to go on picnics and to a southern beach in Sierra Leone at Sulima on the Atlantic; there was lots of fish and lots of sand. We would drive there in about two hours, hike back in to an isolated area, and stay two or three days in a house that the army had abandoned. Said had not seen Uncle Joe in over 10 years. So for him, it was more a reunion with his uncle than a trip for his possible marriage. Here we were telling Said to go meet someone who we wanted to be his wife! He had never seen Joe's children before, because Joe had not yet married and started a family by the time we left Sierra Leone.

I had seen Lena a couple of times, and one time was in my sister's house in Beirut in 1973, when she was only about a year old, and I had traveled to Lebanon to visit the family. At that age, she was just trying to walk. But every time she tried, she fell down. I said, "Hey, come, Lena, to me." But she couldn't come. She always fell down. The next day, I asked the family to take me to a toy shop in the town of Beirut. When I walked in, I recognized the shop owner. He was a good friend from Lagos. He was quite a bit older than me, and didn't seem to recognize me. The girl working for him asked if she could help me. We found a "marche bebe", made with wheels, that a child can stand in and practice walking without falling. My sister had an older son, and I saw a red toy car that I thought he would like to ride in. I bought the two items and said to the man, "Hey you! Did you forget me, now that you have a fine store and some money?" He looked at me and said, "Are you talking to me?" I replied, "Yes, have you forgotten that we did (this and that)?" He shouted, "Are you Habib?" I told him that I was and we hugged. He asked, "Why didn't you say hello when you first came in?"

He turned to his clerk and asked, "Did you already charge him?" I explained to him that I recognized him when I entered the store, but that I didn't say anything, because I wanted to pay for everything. I laughed and told him, "I don't need you anymore! I am living in America." We talked and he said, "Oh, you are lucky. Can you take me to America?" I replied, "Why do you want to go? You have this big store." He agreed, "It is a big business and good money. But there is trouble going from the house to the store. You cannot guarantee that you will arrive safely. It is difficult." I replied, "Well, you better take care of yourself."

I took the toys home and put Lena in the marche bebe. In a few days, she started to walk and run. She was so happy. I told her mother, Zena, "This is the first payment for Lena to marry Said." I remember that Zena said, "Oh, I wish to God that Lena would be for Said." She had met Said one year before, and everyone liked him.

After a few weeks, I was sitting at my sister's, drinking coffee, and I called to Lena, "Lena, come. Walk to me." I think I taught most of the children in our family to walk.

That Monday, we called the airport to make final arrangements for Said to travel to Lagos. We also called his uncle, Joe, to tell him that Said was on his way. Joe's neighbor in Africa was an important man in the area, and he knew the police and other important people. Joe and his neighbor went to the airport together to meet Said. They explained that they would be picking up an American boy and were allowed to go inside the airport to wait for the plane. When Said arrived, they greeted each other, and hugged. Joe took Said to his home.

When they got to Joe's home, Lama, Lena's younger sister, opened the door for them. Said said, "Hello, Lena." Lama said, "Hello. I'm not Lena, I'm Lama." Said didn't yet know what Lena looked like, so he had mistaken them. When Lena entered the room, he was so happy to meet her, and finally see her. I had told Said before he left the US that I would call him a couple days after he arrived at Joe's. I said, "If you like the girl and you want to marry her, and think she is good for you, you answer me in Arabic, 'Tamam.'" That means it is good. I continued, "But if you don't use that secret word, then I won't talk to my brother and you can just enjoy yourself in Africa as a vacation."

After two or three days, I called my brother's neighbor's house and asked them to get Said for me. He came on the telephone and I asked him, "How is it?" He responded, "Papa, Tamam! Tamam! Tamam!" I said, "Okay, give me your uncle." Joe got on the telephone and explained, "They like each other very much. We are so happy." I replied, "Well, then, go on with the ceremony and get everything done. For the dowry, just write what you want." Joe teased, "I am going to ask for every penny you have!" I replied, "Do that. Then you will have to spend that money back, supporting me and my family!" Said and Lena got all the paperwork ready for their marriage, but they did not yet have a ceremony.

Then they had to go to the Immigration Office to get a visa for Lena, but were refused. So Said had to come back to the US alone to start the paperwork process to be able to have his wife join him in

America. While he was over here, waiting for Lena's documents to be completed, we were paying $300 to $400 each month on long-distance telephone calls between them! Said finally made another trip to Nigeria with the completed paperwork, and prepared to bring Lena to her new home in Portland, Oregon. They had not yet had the part of the marriage ceremony where all the family and friends are invited to share in the celebration. In our culture, only after the woman has gotten a house and furnished it, and after a big celebration is held, is the couple truly married. Lena did not get a house or work to furnish it, because they knew they were going to live in Portland.

While Said was in Nigeria, I got the bad news that my father had passed away. Joe also got the same cabled news. I had to call Said to tell him that he needed to come back to Portland as soon as possible to run the store, as I needed to go to Lebanon for my father's funeral. Joe was only five or six hours away from Lebanon, but it takes about 20 hours to get to Lebanon from the US West Coast. Said said a quick goodbye to his soon-to-be bride, and quickly got a ticket to come back to the US. Meanwhile, I called Lila, my daughter, and told her the news. She knew a travel agent who was able to get me a flight out the next morning. The flight went from Portland to Denver, and then to Newark (New Jersey), New York, Paris, and finally Beirut. He warned me that I might reach Lebanon before my luggage, and that I was going to have to be smart and fast at each of the transfers, so that I didn't miss any of the connections. I got to Lebanon 24 hours after I started the trip.

I had told Haidar about the death of his grandfather. Just before I left, and while Said was in flight on his way back, Haidar was driving his new Ford Tempo, crying about his grandfather. He didn't see a van at an intersection, and it hit him. Thank goodness, he was not injured, although his new car was damaged.

When I arrived in Lebanon, they had already buried our father. Our culture's practice is that after seven days, you invite people to your home, read the Koran, and offer them food. Another ceremony is held 40 days after someone's death. I didn't have a house in Lebanon at the time. We borrowed Joe's house for the first ceremony. He had closed it up while he was in living in Nigeria, so we opened it up. I stayed there, and we invited people there for the ceremonies. I ordered food. Some of the people made whole lamb stuffed with rice. Some surprised us with chicken. Some brought fruit and vegetables. There was enough food for 500 people! At least 300 people were there. Many families were very close to my father.

This was when the Iraqis were invading Kuwait. People were scared that there would be chemical warfare. Everyone taped over their windows and doors. We could hear lots of artillery noise, and everyone was afraid of the scud missiles.

Joe needed to get back to Nigeria for his business, and he wanted me to visit him there before going back to America. I said, "No, I am going to stay here through the 40-day ceremony for my father, because I was his oldest son." I knew that if I were there, people would come, because of the respect. Otherwise, it would just be my sisters honoring my father, as all my brothers were in Africa or the US. My sisters really wanted me to leave. They were very afraid for me because of all the military action in the surrounding countries. I said, "Whatever happens to you, my sister, happens to me." After 40 days, we had the ceremony. Although this was during the rainy season, that day was beautiful and sunny. People came from many villages to the place where we held the memorial. The building could hold about 200 people, and it was full—with many people sitting outside on the covered veranda.

I talked to so many people that day. People told me how respected my father was, how good his family and children were, and how nice he was. I had a beautiful marble grave marker made for him, with his name and words from the Koran on it. My sisters were so happy and proud. They said that they were respected and well-known in the town because of all the work I did to show respect for our father.

That night I had a dream. I dreamt that my father and mother were standing together. I was sitting over them. My father told me, "Now, I am resting happy. Everything went well." I will never forget that dream. The next day, I woke up and told my sisters about the dream, and that I had seen my mother and my father together. They were so happy.

Our parents are buried next to each other. The cemetery was almost full, but we were very good friends with the person who was in charge of the cemetery—so we were able to have my father buried next to my mother. Also, I gave $50 to one of my young nephews, who is a painter. I asked him to clean up the grave markers, and paint them—not whitewash, only oil paint. I hired the people who make the marble grave markers to make a new one to replace the cracked one over my mother's grave. I gave them $30. A week after the ceremony I flew back to the US.

In 1999, on a later trip, I found both of my grandfathers' graves— my mother's father and my father's father. The markers were sinking in the ground. I paid to have them fixed. I was actually looking for the grave of my favorite aunt, who lived in Beirut—she died when I was already in the US. I wanted to go pray at her grave. I had asked several people to show me the grave of my special grandfather on my father's side. I was very young when he died, and I did not remember where he was buried. No one from the family remembered, because they had all fled the town during the wars, and were not able to visit and maintain the graves of the relatives.

I was looking at my aunt's grave and standing near a grave that was encircled with iron fencing. Out of respect, I was moving very cautiously; I was scared to put my foot on the graves, because they were old and had sunk into the ground. Before I made a move, I had to look down. In front of me I saw the name "Fakih." "Fakih"! That is my family! Tree leaves and dirt covered up part of the marker. I took my hand and started to clean the cement surface off. I saw "Hassan Mohsen Fakih". The date said 1942. Oh my goodness! That was my grandfather's marker—the one I had been looking for! I was happy and upset at the same time. I prayed for him. In a few months the rains would have come, and would have caused debris to cover the marker permanently. I had found it just in time! I cleaned it very well. Then my cousin, Yassin took me to the person who makes grave markers. He told me he could make one for my family for $250. He went to the grave and copied the information exactly and made it in marble. I told my sister and the rest of the family that I had found my grandfather's grave. They were all very happy. Then I asked my nephew to paint the graves, and not in white wash—real paint. I paid him for it. I also asked him to help me find the grave of my grandfather on my mother's side. He found it and showed it to me; it was his grandfather also. It was very close to the holy place in the cemetery. The marker had been made with marble, but was flat against the ground. Just like my other grandfather, half of it was covered in mud. I made arrangements with the same man who built the other grave marker for me, to also do one for that grandfather. I was so happy to give both my grandfathers nice grave markers. They were good to me when I was a child.

When my family went to the graves on their memorial day ceremony, they saw that all the family's graves were new and big and clean. They all shouted, "Oh, who did this?" One of them said, "Who else besides Habib! You are all lazy. Habib came from America and did this." They said, "Oh, he is American. He gets too much money. American people are too rich!" I said, "Let them say what they want. Anyhow, my heart is clean." I did that because both of my grandfathers were good to me. They fed me and spoke to me nicely. They loved me. My mother's father taught me the Koran. He was teaching all the young people like me. We all sat on a mat under a big fig tree. I learned half of the Koran from him, and the other half from another man, Ali Sappah, who worked opposite my father's shop. All my uncles thanked me for taking care of the family graves; they were so happy.

Just before I left Lebanon to fly back to Portland, my daughters thought I should buy a little house so that I would have a place to stay in when in Lebanon. This was in about 1990, and we put a little money down on it and have made payments on it over the years. My nephew was living in it during this time. He was supposed to be taking care of it, but instead, he damaged it, so Oula was cleaning it and getting it ready for our visit in 2002, when I planned to take Siham back to Lebanon.

When I returned from the trip in early 1991, Said had to go back to Africa, as he was still working on getting Lena her green card so that she could come live in the US. Siham and I were about ready to move into our new house. As Mona, Lila, and Haidar were packing, they threw lots of old things away, left and right. We were going into a new house and wanted to have new things for it. Before Said left on his trip, he told Siham and me to hide behind the door, because he didn't want Mona and Haidar to throw us away too! Said is a hoarder; he likes to hang on to things.

Lena likes to repeat the story that Said told her when he came to the US from Africa, before he met her, with a new pair of cotton pajamas that his mother had bought for him. He loved those pajamas, wearing them every day for three or four years. They wore out and got torn, and he grew out of them, since he was a growing teenager at the time. One day his sister was doing spring cleaning, and while looking through his clothes, she found the old, shredded, cotton pajamas. She took them to Goodwill. When Said heard that the family was sending old clothes to Goodwill, he went straight to his closet and discovered that his pajamas were missing. "Where are my pajamas? Where are my pajamas?" He made such a big deal out of it. He wanted to know which Goodwill. He wanted to go look for them. He wouldn't talk to his sister for two days. He kept nagging for a whole month, "Oh, you threw my pajamas away!"

After that, the rest of the family started to make plans to come to the US. Joe took his passport and went to the Ambassador in Nigeria. They gave Joe a visa for himself, but not for Lena. Joe came over for a one-month visit; he enjoyed himself and went back. After a while, when school was out for the girls, he went back to the Immigration Office and asked for visas so that the family could visit Disneyland. He explained that he was first planning on going to Lebanon, but instead promised his children that they could see Disneyland. Immigration believed him and gave him a visa to take the whole family. When they arrived in L.A. in early July, they got a van and brought the whole family up to Portland. I rented an apartment in the Garden Home area to be ready for when they arrived. The plans were to have the wedding for Said and Lena, and then the rest of Joe's family would return to Africa. But I said, "No, you are not going back to Africa; you are staying here." I furnished the whole house for them. They brought about $30,000 with them. Joe started working with me at the Dunkin' Donuts.

One member of the family was concerned, and then got other people excited about Said and Lena just "dating," and not yet going through the wedding ceremony according to our customs. So Said said, "That's it! We're getting married." He felt that they had spent enough time getting to know each other. He had been to Nigeria twice to see Lena and spent $300 to $400 each month talking on the telephone every day. One day on the first visit, Joe said, "I am going to take Lena's mother to the African marketplace. You are going to sit with Lena in the kitchen and fix us lunch." Said replied, "Sure. Fine. No problem." He knew they weren't going to fix much lunch. Here they were trying to discuss their history and life plans and cook lunch! They only fixed some fried potatoes and salad. Said said he did <u>all</u> the talking. Occasionally he would stop and ask, "Do you want to say something, Honey? Do you have any questions? Why don't you say something?" But Lena would very quietly say, "No, I don't have anything to say." They talked for more than two hours in the kitchen, and Lena still wouldn't say much. Said told her his life history in those two hours. He told her about all the girls he had loved so that she wouldn't hear it first from anyone else. Joe and Lena's mother came back—Joe asked what they had talked about. Said told him that he didn't ask Lena whether she liked him, and didn't ask her to marry him. They just visited with each other. Finally, after about three weeks, her family asked Lena whether she liked Said. Said likes to say that he doesn't know what Lena answered!

During one of the visits in Africa, Said needed a haircut, so he asked Lena's brother Bassem to take him to the barber. The barber was about the same age as Said. While getting his hair cut, Said asked the barber if he was single or married. He said he was single. He asked why Said was visiting, and Said told him all about the trip to meet Lena. The barber knew Bassem and Lena. He started pouring his heart out. "I don't know," he said. "Some girls in this town don't want to get married to a barber. They want to go overseas. They want rich guys. They want money. They want to travel. They want this and that. They are not satisfied."

Said sympathized. "You know, you are right," he said. "Today's woman is hard to please. That is awful, man. So what happened to you?" The barber replied, "Well, I met a couple of girls and they were like that. They just didn't want to get married. They were show-offs." While Said was talking to the barber, he noticed that Bassem, who was sitting in a chair, waiting for him, was laughing, giggling, and acting uneasy.

On the way home, Said asked, "What were you laughing about?" Bassem said, "Oh, my God! I forgot to tell you. I didn't know that you guys were going to talk like that. But this guy wanted to marry Lena. Our father said no, and Lena said no. He was angry for a long time, because our father was rude to him and didn't give him a chance." Said responded, "You're kidding me! I was at his mercy; that guy was cutting my hair. I could slap you right now." Said had been talking to the barber, feeling cocky and sure of himself, excited about his future life with Lena.

Lama likes to tell the story that before Said came over the first time, she and Lena used to sit in their bedroom at night, and say, "What if he is ugly? What if he is bad? What if he is old?" Then Lena would say, "Then I just say 'no.' It's no big deal."

There was a friend of the family who was a Christian Lebanese man living near them in Africa. He was worried about Lena when he found out about her arranged marriage. One day he took Lena for a walk by herself, and very seriously said, "I don't want your dad to make you feel that you have to get married to Said. I just want to tell you that you have a choice to say no if you don't like him." Lena assured him, "My dad already told me that. He wants us to get to know each other." He repeated, "I just want you to make sure. If your dad says anything, let me know, and I will help you." He got Lena more worried! She thought, "Oh my God!"

At dinnertime, Lena's mother started talking about all the guys who wanted to marry Lena, who they said "no" to—you know how mothers like to show off! Said interjected, "You left one guy out." They said, "Who?" Said replied, "The barber, who almost ruined my hair!" After Said explained what had happened, they all started laughing.

When they got married, Said was 28 or 29 years old, and Lena was 20. We had the marriage ceremony for them at the Trianon Restaurant in Portland on September 1, 1991. Fred Harter, the owner, was very nice, and let us take over the whole restaurant for the evening. All of our families came up from L.A. for the celebration. We had a nice, good evening. Said and his wife went to the coast for the week for their honeymoon.

Joe and his family decided to stay in the US and open a business. Meanwhile he was working in the Dunkin' Donuts with me on a salary. His wife was working, and his sons were working. We found a business in Canby that Joe liked. The couple was selling it because they were splitting up. They wanted $30,000 for it; we gave them $15,000 down and made payments for the remaining $15,000.

At the same time, Haidar and Lama were starting to play hide and seek in the store. People would ask, "Haidar, what do you want from that girl? You are always following her." I thought, maybe Lama was taking money from the drawer and Haidar was checking on her. I had to listen to the people; I wasn't aware of anything. I finally spoke to Haidar. He explained that he liked Lama and Lama liked him. Haidar had two years to finish his Business Administration major at Portland State University, and Lama was just finishing high school. So I told Haidar that they could get engaged now, and have the marriage ceremony when he graduated.

But Haidar said, "No, I want to marry this girl now, I really like her!" It was the rainy season and Haidar kept driving to Canby late at night, after we ate dinner, at 8:00 or 9:00 in the evening. I would say, "Where are you going?" He would say, "I miss my uncle. I am going to see my uncle." I was scared for him, because the roads were wet and slippery, and sometimes icy. I thought, *Before that boy has an accident because of the late night driving ... and I see that they love each other*. So, what could I do? I had no choice. But I wanted them to be engaged until he got his degree.

He didn't listen to me. I said, "Look, my son, if you marry, the day you marry, that's it. No more college!" Haidar assured me, "No, Papa. I can be married. I will work and go to college. I promise you." I replied, "Yes, you promise me. But your uncle promised me that he would finish college. He did one year only. He didn't finish. Your sister promised me that she would get her master's degree. She needed one year more. She didn't do it. She got married. And you would be the third one. Okay, you want to get married—you go get married, before I pick you up off the street after a car accident!" Said teases me because I *sent* him to get married when he only had 30 units left in his senior year. That was true, but it was because he was driving me crazy! Every girl he saw on the street he wanted to marry. "How about that one?" he'd say. "How about this one?"

So, I went to my brother, Joe, once again. I said, "Forgive me, my brother. Before, I denied that Haidar and Lama wanted to be married. But now I know it's true. Could you give me Lama for my son?" My brother looked at me. "Now you agree?" he said. "Earlier, you did not agree. You said you did not want Haidar to marry my daughter." I said, "Please, my brother. I am scared for my son—I fear something will happen to him. Every time after dinner, he says, 'I want to see my uncle. I love my uncle. I want my uncle.' I don't know what is going to happen. I have only two sons. Please, please. What do you want? I will give you whatever you want." Joe said, "I don't want anything." Then he said, "Sit down, Brother. I am just joking with you. Whatever you say." Joe was just playing tough with me. He knew that his daughter and my son loved each other.

Haidar was very clever. He had been saving some money behind my back. He had saved about $15,000 to buy a duplex. Joe and I had told Haidar that he couldn't get married because he couldn't buy a house. Haidar responded that he could buy a house, and he bought a duplex for Lama and himself. About that time, I came home with a new car—a white Ford Tempo. When Haidar saw it, he said, "Papa, that car is for young people; not for an old man like you." I gave him the key—so then he had a house and a car, and was prepared to marry. I lamented, "Oh, my fault! I gave you the car. All my fault, I let you save that money. You want to marry? Now you deserve to get married. You have a house and a car."

Lama was after Haidar, too. She would always tell him, "Go tell your father. Cry to him. We want to get married. My cousin in Saudi Arabia wants me. I'm going. If you don't marry me, look here, I'm going to get married quick! My mother told me, 'Leave Haidar.' She wants me to leave you and marry my cousin. But you are my closest cousin. I love you."

We planned the marriage celebration. We had recently bought our house, after living three years in the Laurelwood apartments. The garage was full of junk, clothing, tables, and boxes. I had the Dunkin' Donuts truck, and so I loaded everything in our garage into it. Then we started to clean up the garage, and to paint. We rented tables and chairs and started making the food for the wedding. We roasted a whole lamb, and made kibbee and all the other traditional foods. We called people living in California— brothers, cousins, nephews— to invite them to the wedding. They all came to our house. We made everyone happy. It was a bigger, better celebration than for Said, because at our house, everyone could be *together*, talking and eating. It was very friendly, and people enjoyed themselves. Then off Haidar and Lama went to the coast, for a two-week honeymoon.

Joe worked in the store, and Lama worked in the kitchen. Bassem, her brother, worked in the afternoons, while he was in school. Joe and I would take off, going home to relax with hubbly-bubbly. One day while we were talking and enjoying our hubbly-bubbly, Bassem called. It was about 5:00 pm. He asked Joe, "Daddy, can I close the store? No one is here." Joe said no. A very short time later, Bassem called again. "Daddy, can I close the store?" Joe said no again. On the third call—"Daddy, can I close the store?"—Joe shouted, "No, eat shit!"

So we had good times in Portland, with all of us together. Joe had bought a donut shop in Canby from a woman by then, and had moved there with his family. Every Saturday all the family came to our house to eat and talk together. Every Sunday, we all went to Joe's house in Canby for the evening. We missed those Sunday visits after Joe and his family went back for a time to live in their apartment in Beirut.

Things were going so smoothly for a while, with no problems. But one day my sister in Lebanon called us to tell us that the apartment that Joe still leased in Beirut was going to be torn down by the owner. The owner was working with the city, and they wanted to redevelop it for a mall. Each lessee was going to be paid $80,000 to $100,000 to move out. I got some money for Joe to make the trip. I tried to find someone to buy his donut shop. After a few weeks, Joe's wife and his two youngest children followed him to Beirut. When Joe got there, he discovered that a cousin who was supposed to be taking care of the property took half the money; he cheated Joe. Joe took the money that he got and bought an apartment in Beirut, because rents were very expensive. He couldn't come right back to the US, because his green card had not yet been granted, and he had to wait in Lebanon. Joe knew lots of people because he had been a barman in restaurants and hotels. Joe got a job as a barman and waited until he got his green card.

In Lebanon, people were paying money down and making monthly payments on apartments even before they are built. Unlike in the US, they take a couple years to build, because they are constructed of stone and marble. They are very beautiful, but they don't hold up well in earthquakes. There is a joke that the rich people who have beautiful villas also have tents in their gardens. They sleep in the tents and put their cars and camels in the villas, because of the danger of earthquakes. I have heard that, but I don't know if it is true.

Lama had been waiting for her citizenship, and applied for her father, mother, brother and sister. The paperwork came, but only for her father and mother—so they came, and the children stayed in Beirut. Later, Joe and his wife applied for green cards for their children, and finally got the whole family back here.

Meanwhile, my daughter, Suad, was pregnant. Her baby boy, Mohammed, was born at St. Vincent Hospital, here in Portland. Siham enjoyed the new baby—her grandson. During this time, Mona stopped her schooling at Portland Community College so that she and Suad could help take care of Siham.

About six months after Suad had her baby, she began making

plans to go back to Lebanon and her husband. I thought I should go with her—otherwise she would be traveling by herself with a baby. She had gotten a free standby ticket because her husband worked for the airlines. We planned to fly from Portland to L.A., and then to Rome, and then on a Middle East plane to Beirut. When we arrived in L.A., they told us we might have to wait one or two days to get seats on the same plane, because of my standby status. I told the man, "Never mind, here is my credit card." It was important that we maintain our schedule, because Suad's husband was going to try to meet us in Italy and accompany us on the last leg of the trip.

We arrived in Italy. After we landed and went through Customs, Suad saw her husband waiting for us in the visitors' section. She turned to me, pointed and said, "Look, Papa. Sami is over there." I said, "Where?" Suad repeated, "Over there!" I saw lots of people waiting! I didn't know Sami. I couldn't recognize him. She said, "See, he is wearing white, like the airline personnel." I remarked, "Lots of people are wearing white!" We kept walking, with Suad carrying the baby while I took the luggage. We saw someone come toward us—a nice, young, handsome man. Suad said, "That's Sami!" I said, "Oh, that's Sami. I was looking for a nice, good man, and he was here, right in front of me!" So I finally got to meet my daughter's husband.

I spent about a week with other family members, but most of them lived within the boundary that the Israelis were maintaining, so it was safer and easier to stay with Suad and Sami. To visit the rest of the family, Oula had to buy a permit for me for the week. In order to enter the restricted area, we had to walk about half a mile on foot. Then a special van picked us up. It had a driver and a soldier with a gun. It had no cloth upholstery; it was all metal, to discourage hiding guns and other weapons. Each person was checked—a man for the men and a woman for the women crossing the line. Oula, my daughter, and her husband came to meet me from the other side. The officials at the border trusted my Oula, and her husband Mohammed, because they were businesspeople who crossed the border and returned each week to purchase clothing for their store.

I returned to Portland to see how Siham was doing, and to go back to work. Said and Haidar had done a good job taking care of the store. Mona was taking care of Siham, but Siham was improving a little, so Mona could return to Portland Community College to finish her degree. She graduated in radiation technology and took extra training so that she could do MRIs and mammograms. Then she had to find a job—so she started working at OHSU. She told me that she wanted to be a doctor, and that she had been told that she would only need two more years of school to get into medical school.

In about 1995, I decided I wanted to go to the Hajj, and started talking about it. All of my sisters living in Lebanon had gone. Said and the rest of the family encouraged me to do this. My mother and father had made the trip to Mecca while I was in Sierra Leone, sometime before 1970. In fact, I had sent them some money, but didn't know they were going. I later told my father that I was sorry that I didn't know—I would have sent them more money, so that they could have had a nice time on the trip. My mother wanted to go to another religious shrine in Iraq, but she couldn't go because of heart problems and high blood pressure. My nephew had a physical fight with his cousins one time. My mother was sitting outside with Lena in her arms, and the boys were stoning each other. A rock hit my mother's head and injured her, causing a heart attack.

Going to the Hajj is very important, one of the five pillars of Islam. (The other pillars are to believe in God, to pray five times each day, to give alms to the poor, and to fast for thirty days during Ramadan.) We believe that each person is required to make the pilgrimage if their health and financial circumstances allow it.

Finally, in 1996, I made the trip, and took Siham, Lila, and Mona. In order to make the pilgrimage, you have to be "free." That means that you don't owe anyone money, you don't have enemies, you have a clean heart, and you are using your own money to make the trip to Mecca. It is only okay if your children help you. If it is a son, it is okay to have financial help. But it is not acceptable to take money from a daughter unless she is working and has her own money. Any money has to come from a direct bloodline relative. We were not sure about money from the banks, because in the US, money is borrowed from banks, not relatives. But the religious leaders said it was okay as long as you made your loan payments on time. You also have to leave your wife and your family complete. You have to give them enough money to live on until you get back..

Also, before I left on the pilgrimage, I had to give 5% to the poor, or the Imam of the mosque. But our religion also says that if you have family that needs the money, you must give it to them first. It is the same as the American expression, "Charity begins at home." The Koran also says that you must help seven neighbors around you. If you see that they need money or help when they are sick, you must help them. The Koran makes very clear what actions we need to follow to maintain a good community of family and friends.

I learned that I could fly directly to Saudi Arabia or Lebanon, and then go with a guided group to Mecca. I asked Lila to get the visa for us; Lila wanted me to make the pilgrimage. She brought up that my children were grown and that I had been wanting to do this, and that my religion told me to do it, if possible. I agreed, so Lila called the Saudi Arabian Embassy in L.A. to find out the requirements for the trip. They told her that they would send the form to her business address—a Middle-Eastern video store. We completed the form and sent my passport. They returned it with the visa stamped in my passport book, so I was ready to go.

I was thinking about how I wanted to go. The people belonged to different sects of Islam. So I thought, "I will go to Lebanon, to my town, and then make the trip to Mecca from there." That way I could meet up with people from my own sect, and maybe even someone I knew—a friend or relative. I know I would enjoy myself more if I went with someone I knew. I wanted the trip to be happy. I was going to a foreign country, far away, and didn't know how they lived. In Lebanon, the preachers would often take a few hundred people on the pilgrimage. They were familiar with the route and all the requirements, and would preach to them.

I flew into Lebanon, and met up with a good friend who had been living in Kenema, Sierra Leone when I was also living there. He knew of a very good tour group. The tour was responsible for all the travel, hotels and guidance. The guidance was important, because there were several rituals to be followed to be proper, and much historical religious information to be learned. It was a very good package deal. The whole trip was 22 days, and included visits to various religious shrines. After I completed the Hajj, I could be referred to as "Hajj Habib." The "Hajj" is like a title, recognizing that I had made the trip to Mecca and fulfilled all the requirements in preparation for the pilgrimage. It is said that after you have completed the Hajj, you become like a baby. You are cleansed of all the sins that you committed; purified in the beginning, like John the Baptist, who baptized Christians by symbolically putting them in water. Then you have to stay clean. You cannot steal, lie, or do anything bad. If you do, your Hajj is gone.

We flew from Beirut to Jeddah, Saudi Arabia. There we had to go through a luggage checking process like customs to make sure that people were not bringing in alcohol, guns, or other things not allowed in the country or at the holy shrines. There were thousands of people, old and young, all standing in lines by country. There were big rooms with tent tops, designated by country. The young people pushed each other in the lines, but I didn't care. I just took it easy, and held onto my bag.

The police came because the young people were getting rowdy. I continued sitting by the side, in the American line, with my American passport and visa stamp. My American passport was blue, and the Lebanese passports were red. The police asked what I was holding in my hand. I said, "This is my passport, sir." He asked, "What kind of passport? Are you American?" I replied, "Yes, sir." He asked, "Why didn't you say something?" I said, "Why should I say anything? There are thousands of people here. Why should I say something? What happens to them, happens to me. I am waiting. Anyhow, everyone is going to go inside, right?" The policeman said, "That is why you are an American. You have calm blood." (meaning he thought that I was very patient.)

He continued, "Come with me." Then he yelled to another policeman, "Hey, Ahmad. Take that American man. Let him go through the line." I thought, "Why should I push? There were two or three hundred people who came on the plane from Lebanon. I didn't need to hurry. It didn't matter if it was one hour, two hours, or three hours. I don't need to hurry! I wasn't going any place. I just came to pray. I am going to the mosque. I am going to God. I am coming to God's house."

The policeman laughed and said again, "That's why you are an American. But how do you know how to speak Arabic?" I explained, "I am Arabic, but I moved to America. They treated me nicely. They gave me citizenship. Is that bad?" He responded, "No, sir," and yelled again for Ahmad, "Ahmad, take this man and let him pass." Then Ahmad called to other people along the line, "An American man is coming; take care of him." So I got all the way to the immigration booth with Ahmad's help. When I got to the booth, the officer yelled to Ahmad, "Hey, Ahmad, where is the American man?" I held up my passport and said, "I'm here, sir. I'm here." The officer asked, "You are an American?" I said, "Yes. Don't you think I am American? Here is my portrait with my passport papers." The officer questioned, "Why are you coming here?" Then I started to talk with him in Arabic. Finally he understood and said, "Oh, you are an American Muslim."

I went inside and saw all of the luggage. Someone was shouting, "Who is the American? Where is the American?" I said, "I am the American." The immigration officer ordered, "Show me your luggage." I showed him my luggage and he sent me on to the Customs officer. He said, "Are you American, sir?" I responded in Arabic, "Yes, sir." He asked, "You are an American Arab?" I repeated, "Yes." He questioned, "How come you are American and you speak Arabic?" I explained, "I was born in Lebanon, I went to Africa. From Africa, I got married and had children. Then I wanted to give my kids a good education, so I moved to America. I opened a business there. The American people saw that I was a good man, and they gave me American citizenship. I became an American. Is that bad?" After listening, he said, "No, sir," and he stamped my passport and said, "This way, sir." I finally took my luggage and followed the people I saw leaving. I asked a man in the crowd, "Where should I go?" He asked where I was from, and I told him that I was from Lebanon. He said, "Go straight. Keep going and you will see the tent with the Lebanese flag. Your people are there. Stay there." I said, "Okay. Thank you."

I kept going for a while. It was about 10:00 at night. Everything was lit up. I saw all different people—from Turkey, Iran, Japan, China and Iraq. Each tent section was about 200 or 300 feet square, crowded with people. I found my area and set my luggage down. I was so tired, so hungry, and so nervous. I said, "Okay, God. You have to take care of me." I lay down for a little bit. Then I heard people near me talking like they were from southern Lebanon. I saw a man speaking with, his daughter and wife talking together. It looked like he didn't know anybody there, but they were talking among themselves about Kenema. I was so tired, and my brain was not working very well. So tired. The woman turned to me and offered me kibbee and said "You must be hungry, Habib."

They knew my name! They said, "What is new with you? Where are you now?" So we started to talk and catch up from when we were all in Kenema. I told them that I was now in America. They asked, "How is your wife?" I explained that Siham was sick and had had a stroke. The family had lived about 90 miles from where we were in Kenema, in the diamond area. The husband said that he had made some money in the diamond business, so he and his family returned to Lebanon and bought a couple apartment buildings to rent out. I asked him, "Is this the first time you have gone to Mecca?" He laughed, "It is your first time, but this is my fifth!" I asked, "How come the fifth time?" He explained, "I have five kids. They all wanted to make Hajj, and I had to go with each one to help with the procedures." I said, "Thank God. What about me? I have seven kids. Maybe I have to come seven times!"

I was so happy visiting with my old family friends that I forgot about the time and my exhaustion. We kept talking until about 3:00 in the morning! Then the wife said, "We should get a little sleep." We all put our luggage under our heads and lay down to rest. The air conditioning was on, so it was cool, but we could sleep without extra covering.

At about 7:00 a.m. we got up and went to the bathroom to get clean. Then we prayed and got ready to join the tour company. They had one bus for every 50 people, so there were three buses. Each bus had two young men, about Said and Haidar's age—one manager who kept track of our names, and one preacher. When we got in the bus, he took down all of our names. He explained, "Each time we stop and people get back on the bus, I have to call all your names and make sure that everyone has returned. If one person doesn't show up, we have to hold all three buses until we find them, because we are all traveling together. We have to stick together until we get to Jeddah. And remember, it is a long way to go—a *long* way to go. We will be stopping at the grave of Ali, the cousin of Mohammed. He married Fatimah. We will start from that mosque. Everyone will need to get their clean clothes ready. We have to pray there. And we have to show you everything that you have to do when we reach Mecca."

Everyone was very good. We understood the tour guides and they understood us. Some of the young people were traveling with their elderly parents, helping them. It was so nice. We had two strong boys from the tour company assigned to help us, in case we needed it. If we needed to buy something, or if we needed help getting up and down stairs, or help getting to the bathroom, they were there to help. It was an excellent company, well-organized, and everyone was so nice. They always took 150 people and three buses. They filled two hotels with the tourists. The first floor of the hotel was used to sit, visit, and pray, and there was a kitchen where we could keep soft drinks, juice, tea, coffee and snacks. The men stayed on the second floor, and the women stayed on the third floor. Clothes washers, dryers, and a small kitchen were on the fourth floor. The tour company provided food. They provided anything you wanted—but if you wanted to prepare your own food or had dietary restrictions, you could use the small kitchen.

We gave our names and settled down for the trip. As the buses moved out, the preacher started walking through the bus, sitting and talking with each person. He asked us if we knew how to read the Shahada: I believe in only one God, that Mohammed is the messenger, that the Koran is the book of Islam, and so on. They tested us when we prayed; what we said and what we did, and who was the current person we most believed and followed in the Islam faith. If you didn't know, they gave three names. One in Lebanon, one in Mecca, and one in Iraq. You had to follow one of them. They were scholars in Islam, and had studied many years. If you had any problems, you went back to the one you followed, or referred to his book of teachings. They gave us much training. For myself, I understood much, much more than before the trip.

Meanwhile the buses were traveling through the desert. I didn't see much—only sand and old tires. There were very few trees and bushes. There was nothing alive. The road was very wide and well maintained. Every few miles there was a telephone at the side of the road, in case you needed to call for help. We drove four or five hours, but it was very comfortable in the air-conditioned bus. They came around with water and cold drinks during the trip.

When we got to the first mosque there was beautiful marble with running water so that we could wash. Behind the marble wall, there was a building with showers. There were people to assist us. They told us, "Whatever you want, just ask." It was so nice. Then they explained that we would be transferring to another bus. We would put the special clothes called *ihram*—as we would now be properly starting the pilgrimage. The women took baths in a separate area and changed into fresh clothing and covered their heads to hide their hair. They could only show their faces and hands. The other men and I took all of our clothes off, bathed, then hooked a towel around our waists and draped another towel around our shoulders. We weren't allowed to have anything on our heads. We then positioned ourselves to listen to the preacher. He said, "We have to preach, and you have to repeat what we say: 'We are starting a pilgrimage. We promise not to do bad. We promise not to make wrongs. We promise to be nice to everyone. If someone tries to do bad, we forgive him. If someone needs help, we should help him.'"

Then we were ready to go back to the buses. The tour guides explained that the women would be traveling inside the buses, but the men had to be on the outside, on the roof. Oh, oh! I couldn't believe that I heard correctly. I requested, "Can you say that again, please? I didn't understand. Do we men have to climb on top of the buses for the trip?" The preacher said, "Yes." I asked, "Why is that?" The preacher responded, "Because, that is it. We are all men. We can't travel to Mecca with something over our heads." Then I understood. The roof of the bus was over our heads. On the pilgrimage, we had to symbolically suffer like Mohammed, the prophet. "But," I asked, "What if someone suffers from diabetes and high blood pressure?" The preacher explained, "That is easy, my son. You can go inside the bus, but you have to make a sacrifice of some sort." I asked, "What kind of sacrifice?" He said, "Goat. Sheep. When you get back ... " I asked, "How can we do that here? There are no sheep here!" The preacher said, "Not here. When you go back home. You put in your mind that when you go home you will buy a sheep and slaughter it and give it to the poor people to eat. That is the sacrifice. If you cannot do that, you have to go home." I assured him, "No, I will do *two* sheep! But let me go inside the bus." He said, "Okay. Once you promise yourself, you go inside." Some of the people didn't want to sacrifice, even young ones. So they got back inside the bus. And some older people said to themselves, "I want to do the sacrifice. This is what I came here for. I want to do it exactly as the rules say." Almost half of the men rode on top of the bus, and the rest of us, many of whom were older, rode inside the bus.

It was another 200 or 300 miles to Mecca. The day was very long. We stopped every 50 or 60 miles, in small towns along the way. They had markets where they sold cold water, cold juices, cakes, breads with sugar. Everything was sweet because people need a lot of energy in order to tolerate the heat. At every stop, the tour guides would ask what we wanted, and buy the supplies and bring them to us. I usually asked for bottled water. It is water from a special spring in Mecca, called zam zam. Abraham, the prophet, had two sons, Ishmael and Isaac. When Abraham's wife Sarah didn't have any children, God told him to sleep with his servant. The servant was an Egyptian girl named Hajer. She had a son, Ishmael. God felt sorry for Sarah, and so when she was 90 years old, she had a son, Isaac.

As the two boys grew up, they fought. Sarah was jealous of Hajer, because, with the birth of Hajer's son, Hajer was no longer treated as a servant. Sarah told Abraham to send the boys away to another place. Abraham did not want to make Sarah upset, so he brought Hajer a camel with food and water, and sent her to Mecca with a guide. It took her two or three months to get there, walking with the camel. By then, all the food had been eaten. Ishmail, the boy, was eight years old. He was hungry and dirty. Hajer prayed to God, "This is your son. Kill us if you don't want us to live." The boy lay down on the sand and died, and an angel appeared. A fountain of water appeared there—zam zam. We saw this shrine. The water there is free to the pilgrims doing Hajj. It is not for sale. When you drink it you feel as if you have eaten—you are not thirsty or hungry.

In the evening, we reached Mecca. We prayed, listened to the Koran, and got instructions from the preachers on what to say and how to act. We had to walk around the shrine seven times. We had to stay up all night, until 4:00 or 5:00 in the morning. We had to drink water, but we never seemed to have to go to the restroom. When we came back, we didn't feel hungry. We went to bed and slept for just a few hours. Then, at about 9:00 a.m., we got up and had breakfast. The breakfast was a little bit of bread with cream cheese, some fruit, and a cup of tea.

Lunch was provided at 3:00 or 4:00 in the afternoon. But I didn't eat then. I had eaten in Mecca, when we first arrived—rice, chicken, yogurt and salad ... all the things we fixed at home. But I couldn't sleep afterwards, because I had diarrhea. I couldn't wait until everyone got up the next morning. I got up very early and asked the people in charge to get me a doctor. They said, "We have three doctors." They called one and he said, "Why didn't you ask for me? Why didn't you wake me in the night? I am always available. I stay with you here next door." I explained that I didn't know he was there. He instructed, "Okay, here are two tablets. Take one now, and if the problem stops by the evening, don't take the next one. If it doesn't stop, take in the evening. You cannot eat any meat in this country. You are allergic to meat in this country. All you can eat is cheese, greens, salads, breads, tea and coffee." That's why I lost 22 pounds in 22 days! I was starting to melt in the hot sun of the desert! As you walk, the fat melts onto the ground!

We went to the Kaaba—a big cube built by Abraham and draped with a black cloth with Koranic verses on it. It was in the center of the mosque in Mecca, and was the shrine for the pilgrimage. Centuries before, the Prophet had been exiled from Mecca, because he was practicing Islam. The people in Mecca had all sorts of gods and idols in a big, square room at the mosque. When the Prophet told the people that it was wrong, they told him they would kill him if he didn't leave. So he fled to Medina and stayed for quite a long time. When he knew he would be safe from the pagans and unbelievers, he came back to Mecca. There, he, his camel, and those who were with him symbolically walked around the square rock seven times. After the seventh time, the camel stopped in front of the building's door. The Prophet went in with a big stick, and broke all the idols, saying, "There is no God but one. He is the God of Abraham, Moses, Jesus, and Mohammed."

The word "Kaaba" means square. It is a small temple in the middle of the mosque. There is a big black stone embedded in the eastern corner of the Kaaba. They say that God was holding the stone when he was upset with Adam and Eve. He originally sent them with the stone to make his house. Then the people removed it, and put it where Abraham returned to the mosque to rebuild it. The buildings were always being improved, and now it is for everyone to touch—a blessing that is part of the Hajj.

In the daytime, we usually stayed in the hotel because of the air conditioning. Sometimes we wanted to go outside to make a telephone call or go to the market to buy supplies or a newspaper. We were interested in the news coming from Lebanon—at that time the Israelis had bombed the United Nations building in Lebanon, and killed women and children who were hiding there.

In the afternoons we prayed. In the evenings we prayed and waited until 7:00 or 8:00 p.m. for the buses to take us back to Kaaba. We stayed each day until 4:00 or 5:00 in the morning, at which time the buses would take us back to the hotel. We did this for seven days, carrying through the symbolism of our Islamic history.

For the next leg of our pilgrimage, the buses took us to Medina, where Mohammed went after being driven out of Mecca. The people welcomed him, and Mohammed built a mosque there. We were taken to where Mohammed's uncle was killed, and where other prophets were buried. We were each given seven stones, and taken to a shrine that is a big rock with the name of the devil on it. Thousands of people were there, wearing the two towels and flip-flop sandals. After visiting the shrine, many people threw their flip-flops in a huge pile—there were thousands of them! People threw their seven stones at the devil symbol to acknowledge the presence of the devil. Some threw their stones standing far away! The people who were standing close were in the line of fire and it was dangerous!

The boys who were our tour guides told me that I had to get close so that all the stones would get in the circle. If one didn't reach, they would give us another one to try. They pushed me very close. Before I started, a little pebble hit me between the eyes, and one hit my back. They were little and didn't hurt. But a lady with us was hit by a stone in her forehead—hard enough that it bled. The workers bandaged her injury.

While I was throwing the stones, I felt the towel around my waist being pulled! A man had fallen on the ground near my feet, and people were starting to step on him. The tour guides with me hadn't noticed; they were watching me throw my stones. The man who had fallen on the ground was pulling my towel off, and I didn't have anything on underneath! I yelled to the two tour guides who were in front and in back of me, "Hey, guys! Come help me. This man is trying to take my towel off of me." They were responsible for me, and charged with bringing me back safely. They quickly held the man so that he would release the towel. I got away from him and thanked them.

The next stop in our pilgrimage was to the mountain of Arafat. Nearby were large tents with carpeting on the ground. They were air-conditioned, with the equipment running on generators. The tent was divided into two sections for the 100 men and 50 women who were on our tour. The food service was separated also, as we were trying to reach total purity as part of the pilgrimage.

I was sitting with two or three men who were from my town in Lebanon. For the pilgrimage, Oula, my daughter who lives in Lebanon, sent Ali to me—he was the uncle of Mousa, and the brother of her husband. She told him, "Take care of my dad!" But when he got there, he got sick, and I had to take care of him! He stayed close to me during the whole trip; we were very close friends. We were talking, and I said, "Hajj, look. An ant crawling on my foot. What should I do with it?" Ali said, "Don't touch it!" Then he called the preacher and everyone around, "Preacher, come see what is happening to Hajj Habib." The preacher said, "Leave it alone," and gently guided the ant to the floor.

We continued our journey toward another place, Mina—we were going to sleep there that night. But on the way, we had to stop and stone one more devil. Eight or nine older men and two older women were taken with the preacher to the area to stone the devil during the night, so that we could avoid the large crowds and hot sun. There were still about 1,000 people, but it wasn't nearly as crowded as it would have been during the day, when the crowd would swell to 100,000. When we came back from the stoning, it was so hot. I was concerned because of my diabetes and high blood pressure. A woman in her sixties told the preacher, "Oh, I am going to die. I want some water." The preacher said, "Let's leave this place now." Someone said, "Preacher, if we leave it will take us about an hour. Who can we get to carry the woman?" We were talking with the preacher and arguing about what the best procedure would be. Someone poked me. I looked, and there was a boy about eight years old holding up a very cold bottle of water. I opened it and started to drink. I didn't even thank the boy!

Then I heard the woman, "For God's sake, give me some water." I gave it to the preacher, and he gave it to a man, who passed it to the woman. In a little while, I saw the boy again. He touched me again and gave me another bottle of water. I didn't even look at him; I was so thirsty, I just drank the water. Then I gave some to the preacher and the other people. I looked for the boy to give him something in thanks. He was a little ways away, standing with a tall man who had his arm around him, and two women behind them, dressed like Muslim women, all covered in black. I called, "Come here, boy. Thank you very much. I want to thank you; you saved our lives." The boy looked at me and smiled, but didn't say anything. The man looked at me. He had such a nice expression on his face. They left, disappearing into the crowd. In speaking with the preacher, I realized that he never saw the boy, or the man and women who were all standing together. He had no idea how I got the water, just when we needed it most. No one saw the boy who gave me the water, except me! The preacher said, "Habib, just keep it to yourself. Don't say anything about it." He didn't act surprised. He asked, "Why didn't you tell me this was happening?" I replied, "I was near you. Where do you think I got the water?" He said that he assumed that I had paid for it outside, where they sell water during the day. No one noticed; only me. I think God made a little miracle!

We went back to the tent. The guides told us that everyone had to cut their hair. They had electric razors that we used to shave our heads, as part of the process for the Hajj. Then we went back to the hotel. The next day in the afternoon, Ali and I walked to the mall to buy gifts for our family. The entrance was a few hundred feet away, and it was all air conditioned. Suddenly, an older lady in her fifties came up to me and said, "I need help." Ali asked her, "What kind of help?" She explained that she went to one of the stores to buy a Saudi-style dress with embroidery on it. She didn't have enough money for the whole purchase, so she agreed with the owner to leave part of her money with him to hold her purchases. She gave him the equivalent of $350 in Saudi money. She worried that the store owner would forget that she partially paid him if she left and came back later. She needed another $100.

I gave her the $100. Ali asked her, "How do you know my friend and me, so that you can bring the money back?" The woman answered, "I know that you are with the group, and I am with your group." I told Hajj Ali, "Don't worry about it. Don't ask her that.

Leave her alone." I turned to her and said, "Here is the $100, and good luck, Mama. Go." Then she looked at us and said, "Thank you. Can I know your name?" I told her it was Hajj Habib Fakih.

In the evening we returned to the hotel. We were with all the men, sitting outside, enjoying the breeze while waiting for the bus to take us to the shrine. An older man came over and said, "Where is Hajj Habib? Can I talk to Hajj Habib?" Ali said, "Hey, somebody called your name." He shouted, "Hey, he is over here." The man came over and asked, "Did you give my wife—"

Ali, interrupting, said, "$100, it was $100!"

The man returned the money to me and said, "Thank you very much. I thank you very much for your trouble." I turned to Ali and said, "You see, Hajj Ali. You said that maybe that woman would take the money and disappear." I had told Ali when I gave her the money, "If she is a good woman, she will return the money. If she wants to run away with the money, I leave it to God. This is God's country. We came here to give our respect to God. Why not help, if we can help!" Ali said, "Oh, you guys!" I reminded him, "Someday you may need help, and you will understand the meaning of that kind of trust."

After Mecca, we went to Medina to see the grave of Mohammed and Fatimah, his daughter, and her son Hassan, with whom she is buried. The guides took us to a very nice hotel that served very good food. There were so many of us that they put about four of us in each room of the hotel. We walked to the mosque, which was only about 10 to 15 minutes from where we were staying. The guides took us to Mohammed's grave, and while the preacher was giving a sermon and praying with us, someone behind me put his hand in my pocket. It was stuffed with napkins from my meal at the hotel. The pickpocket thought he was getting money, but I was keeping my money in a money belt, and the towel that I was wearing covered that. Two boys from the tour company were watching our group of 10 or 12 people. One was near the preacher and one was farther away. I pushed the preacher, thinking that people were trying to get beyond me. He turned around and asked, "What's wrong?" The preacher gave the boys a signal to take care of the man. They gave him a push and he fell down. The people sitting around us started kicking dirt in his face, shouting and beating up on him. Then the police came. They didn't have guns, but they poked him with their sticks as they led him away.

One of the people in our group tried to touch the grave while he was praying. That is not allowed, and the guard hit him on the hand with his stick. I saw that and thought, "Oh my God, that boy is going to lose his hand." When we left, I asked him how his hand was. He replied, "It was nothing, Hajj." I thought maybe the stick was not wood, but he said it was. He thought at first that his hand was cut, but it was not.

We went to another grave of Mohammed's family opposite the mosque where we honored his grave. People were buying wheat to feed the doves. The wheat grew about one foot high in the fields. There were thousands of doves swooping up and down, all blue and white, but no bird droppings around the graves—only wheat. It was amazingly clean around the graves, even though it was a very big place with so many doves. Again the preacher came, and we prayed with him. Whatever he said, we repeated after him. Then he asked if we wanted to go back to the hotel, or go shopping for souvenirs in the nearby shops.

I wanted to see the stores, so I went with my friend and found a shop that sold about 10 kinds of dates. We listened to the shop-keeper, who was an old man. Sometimes he spoke Turkish, sometimes he spoke French, sometimes he spoke Arabic, and sometimes he spoke Persian! He could answer his customers in any language.

He turned to me and asked, "Hajj, you are watching me like a stranger. Where are you from?" I had my nametag on; it had my name, country flag, and address, and the telephone numbers of the Lebanese Embassy and my hotel. I replied, "I came to buy some dates. I enjoyed your conversations with the customers." He laughed and said that he used to come to the store with his father, and he only learned the name of the product, the price, and the way to exchange money in all the different languages. I asked, "Okay, what do you advise me. I want to take some dates home to my family." He said, "Look, my son. You look like a nice boy. I enjoy you. I like you. I have a case of dates stuffed with nuts. Normally I sell them for 60 riyals, but I will give you the case for 50 riyals." I said, "I believe you, because I saw you sell a case to other people for 60 riyals. But can I have two cases?" He responded, "You can have as much as you want. I like you. You look like a nice Lebanese man."

About 350 riyals equaled $100. I gave him my 100 riyals and he gave me two cases. But now I wasn't sure how to carry two cases, which together weighed about 20 pounds. I thought, "Oh, God will help me." I picked one up, and the shopkeeper put the other on top. I started walking. My friend came up to me, "Hajj, Hajj, do you need help?" He took both cases from me. I said, "Let me carry one, you carry one." He said, "No, Hajj. I will carry both of them for you."

We continued on our travels with the tour group, visiting all the graves. We stopped at the grave of Hamza, the uncle and protector of the Prophet. He was a great hunter of animals, and was one of the first followers. He used his hunting skills to protect the Prophet's family from the clansmen in Mecca when they were planning on killing Mohammed and his family.

The next day, we started our drive, arriving in Jeddah one day later. We were told that we had to wait 18 hours at the airport to get our plane. We were housed in tents with air conditioning. There were 300,000 people, so they organized the transportation by countries, and displayed each country's flag so that everyone knew where they were supposed to be. There was a 747 jumbo jet taking off each day, transporting Lebanese people back to their country. There was a little market with a variety of foods.

My friend, Ali, and I made a little place for ourselves near an aisle while we were waiting. Opposite us were Turkish people waiting for their plane. I saw a middle-aged woman, in her forties, lying on her back with an older woman, maybe her mother, sitting near her. Meanwhile, I told Ali that I was going to take a little nap on the carpet. After an hour, I woke up and looked around. I noticed that the Turkish woman was still lying on her back, and had not moved. Most people were moving around, happy, visiting friends, and getting ready to go home. But no one was around those two women. There was no man to help them.

I pointed it out to Ali. He said, "Why do you care? They are Turkish!" (We don't like the Turkish in Lebanon. They stayed in our country for 500 years, and then they handed it over to the British.) I said, "Okay." We sat down and chatted, we went outside, and we went to the canteen to get sandwiches, water and juice. When we got back, that woman was still the same; she hadn't moved. I didn't like it. Something was pushing me to get involved. I said, "Look, Hajj Ali. I am going to call somebody." I thought I should call the Saudis because they were the hosts organizing our stay there. Ali said, "Sit down. Don't mix with them. It is not your business." I replied, "No, it *is* my business. Something is wrong with this woman."

It had been four more hours, with no movement by the woman. I went over to the older woman, sitting beside her and asking, "Do you speak Arabic?" She shook her head no. "Do you speak English?" She shook her head no. "Do you speak French?" She shook her head no. Okay. I just left her alone, and I went to look for the person who was responsible for that group. I saw a big man with a walkie-talkie. I asked, "Are you here to help any Hajj who needs help?" He replied, "Yes, sir. What can I do for you?" I said, "Not for me." I explained about the woman who was lying on her back. He called a young man over who was his helper, and told him to go with me. I explained that we had been there for five or six hours, and the woman had not moved. I told him that I had not noticed any man around to help her.

The boy was so clever. When he saw the woman, he said, "Oh my God. This woman is in danger." Some Saudis were passing by with an empty cart. He stopped them. He told the people around her to get back. He had the Saudis lift her onto the cart, and took her to an emergency field office.

After about a half hour, the man with the walkie-talkie and his assistant came over to me. The asked me my name. I said, "Hajj Habib Fakih." The name Fakih is a popular name. The Finance Minister in Saudi Arabia at the time was also named Fakih. They thought we were related. They thanked me for helping that woman, and said that her family had not arrived yet to take care of her. The man said, "You saved that woman, Habib. God bless you." I asked what happened to her. He said, "I think the sun beat her. The doctor said that she would have only lived another half hour—an hour, at most. Thank you for saving the woman." Evidently, she had suffered heat stroke.

I don't know if it was just curiosity, but something was telling me to check on that woman. Maybe it was God. We were in the hands of God—this was the country of God. Maybe He wanted to save that woman because she was still young. Ali said, "Hey, Habib. How many good things have you done here?" I responded, "Well, God likes me. I worry about people, and people worry about me. I like to do good."

We continued to wait until the plane was ready for us. People were milling around, and the pilot came out and said, "We have a big plane that can take 500 people, but it looks like there are only 200 people here, so don't worry. We need to clean the plane, load the gas, and get the plane ready for the trip." But people did not listen. They still kept pushing each other to get to the front. I just took my bag. Ali suggested, "Let's push to get the better seats." I said, "Go on. Let them push." I pointed out, "Are any of the seats going to reach Lebanon before us?" Ali said, "You are a calm man. You are really American!" We finally got on the plane. Up we went, arriving in Beirut about two hours later.

A couple weeks after I arrived for the pilgrimage, and while I was in the middle of the Hajj, Siham, Mona, and Lila all flew over with plans to meet me when I returned from the Hajj. It was in April, and there was a lot of fighting between the Israelis and the Lebanese resistance forces. The Israelis occupied about one-third of the south at that time, but when I went it was moderately calm—just a few skirmishes. By the time my family came, they could not even land the Jordanian airline in Beirut. They had to be diverted to Jordan. At first they were going to have to stay overnight, because the Israelis were going to bomb the Beirut airport. But eventually they were able to get into Lebanon. Mona and Lila met me at the airport, hugging me after my pilgrimage. Their cousin had his car to take us home. Sami, my son-in-law, was working at the airport. I was *very* tired when

I arrived. The weather and atmosphere were different. The air was very fresh—not air-conditioned, and not hot.

We arrived at my daughter Suad's house, but I was so tired. Suad asked, "Are you hungry, Daddy?" I said, "No, I would like a bath." She had the bath ready for me and I got in. I didn't know what happened to me after that. I woke up at 10:00 or 11:00 the next morning, and thought, *Where am I?* Suad explained that after I had gone to take my bath, the family was waiting for me to get out so we could have a dinner together. "When you weren't in the bathtub," she said, "we looked for you and found you lying on the bed. So we changed you and covered you up."

My big sister lived about a mile and a half away. She was having the Hajj ceremony at her house. Traditionally, they cook a whole sheep and celebrate the family member returning from making the Hajj. In Ashura, another later ceremony that lasts ten days, people honor the time when the grandchild of Mohammed was killed. They discussed Islam and all the values that Mohammed's children sacrificed themselves for.

When back in Lebanon, I started having trouble with my knees, because of all the walking and standing that we did at the shrines we visited. I went to the family doctor, and he gave me tablets and a jelly to apply to my knees. Mona and Lila had returned to the US with their mother, Siham. I wasn't getting better after a week on the medicine, so I called Mona and had her make an appointment so I could see my doctor when I returned.

Meanwhile, my cousin wanted to take me to where the Israelis had blown up the United Nations building. The building was flattened, but you could still see the old milk bottles, diapers and toys of the children who had been killed. All the people were buried there. One interesting story was that a four- or five-year-old child went to his uncle's store and got some candy. His uncle asked him, "Where are you going?" The child, whose father worked in the fields, answered, "I am going to my mother in the U.N. building, where it is safe to hide from the Israeli bombs." His uncle said, "Okay," and gave the child candy for his brothers and sisters, noticing that the child's shirt was red. The boy left, to go to his mother.

That day the Israeli helicopters came and aimed a rocket at the U.N. building, destroying it and the women and children hiding in it. People came to help clean up the destruction. Soldiers from the United Nations brought large plastic bags in which to put the bodies. The uncle came from his store to look for his nephew and family, to whom he had just given candy. The body bags were white, not black like in the US. The uncle spotted some red color through the white plastic. He went to the soldier and asked to look inside the bag, saying, "Please, I want to see inside; it may be my nephew. I want to kiss him and say goodbye to him. Can I do this; please, I beg you?" The soldier let him open the bag and he held his nephew, getting blood all over his body. He held him in a position like he did when the boy was alive. The uncle started screaming and crying. He was crying uncontrollably—then he felt like the boy was moving on his shoulder. He didn't believe it. He waited a little bit, and felt him move again. The uncle shouted to the soldier, "This boy is alive!" The soldier said, "You're kidding!" The boy was taken to the hospital by ambulance. They cleaned his face of blood. He opened his eyes and was given medicine. He lived—but his mother was one of the 105 people killed.

Before coming back to the US, I made a trip to a small village in South Lebanon called Zuwaya, where a friend of mine from Sierra Leone was then living. It was about 15 years since I had seen him and his wife. Luckily for me, they made some of my favorite African food that day. When they were in Sierra Leone they learned to cook the native foods from the local cook they hired. It was so delicious. They told me that the cook had gotten cancer and died. He was still young, so I was very sorry for him. That trip had a mix of sadness and happiness. I left Lebanon a few days later to return to the US.

When back in the US, I went to my doctor and showed him the pills and jelly that I was using. He looked and said, "This medicine is very good. You must have good doctors in Lebanon." I said, "Well, it has already been seven days and I am not improving." Then I realized that, although the medicine was the right kind, because of the war, it had expired. I asked him if he could write me a prescription for the tablets. He agreed and told me that I could get the jelly off the shelf in the store. In two days I recovered. The family had another celebration for me now that I was back in Portland. They made a banner, "Welcome Home from the Hajj!" My hair was still very short, from being shaved, and I brought along the clothes that I had worn. I spent a few days telling my family and friends of all my experiences during the Hajj.

One day a man came from L.A. to tell me he wanted to marry Mona. He had met her in L.A. when she was visiting her sister, Elham. I didn't like this guy. He seemed a little bit greedy. He worked as a construction engineer and made good money. He wanted a woman with a car and a house and everything else. I didn't have that; I only had the woman! No car or house. I told him, "Go work first. When you have a car and a house and a little money left to get married to pay for the ceremony, then you come back." He went off.

Mona's cousin was married to a construction engineer. He was a good boy and engineer. He had many unmarried Lebanese friends who were looking for good wives. My niece described Mona to her husband. She said her cousin lived in Portland, was well-educated, lovely, and worked and made money. Everyone wanted to marry her because she made money! One of the young men, Kamal, was interested in meeting Mona. He knew Lila and her husband, Ahmad, who were living in Portland at the time. They asked me to meet Kamal at their home. I offered to see him, "No problem. I will see anyone."

Mona had discussed this with me. "Look, Papa. You look at the person. If you say he is good, then we will marry. If you say he is no good, I am not going to marry him. I will marry any person you tell me to, because I believe you. If you say someone is good, I am going to depend on you. I don't know anybody and I can't do anything by myself. I want you to help me." Mona trusted me because it happened two or three times in our family: The person I said was good was good. The person that I predicted would be no good was no good.

So I went with Lila and Ahmad to meet Kamal. He was from Lebanon, and was a good, educated person. He told me that he was just starting out, and could rent a house. He said he was getting older, and wanted to settle down and have a family. He said that he respected my family. I liked him because he was very honest and liked my family. He had a brother who was a general in the Lebanese army. He was from a very good family. I had dinner with them when I visited Lebanon. They were very nice. His older brother worked in an office, managing retirement finances. Kamal explained that his father died when he was very young, and his mother took care of the whole family, with help from uncles and cousins. They all did very well. One of Kamal's sisters worked in a bank and married a banker. Another sister was married to a businessman. Another sister was married to a person involved in undercover security.

Mona asked, "Is this man good, Papa?" I said, "Yes, he is good." We started making the arrangements. Mona said, "No, Papa. We need three months. We need to talk to each other, we need time to understand each other. You say he is good. But now it is my turn!" I jokingly responded, "Why do you want to wait three months? I wanted you to get married and go away!" Mona replied, "Papa, you waited 27 years. Now you are impatient with three months?" I said, "Yes, I have patience. Take as long as you like."

Every day Kamal called Mona and they talked. Mona told him to be sensible; he was wasting money on daily phone calls. She reminded him that he might be spending *their* money. They started planning their marriage for August 9, 1997. Kamal spoke with his family members about coming to the wedding—a brother who was an engineer in Saudi Arabia, a sister who worked in the bank, and his sister who was married to the security officer. Kamal talked to his mother so that she could arrange for a visit to attend the wedding. He had other brothers living near him in L.A. The whole family rented a big van, and they all arrived in Portland for the wedding.

We made the engagement ceremony at our new house in Portland. The dinner was held at the DoubleTree Inn in Jantzen Beach, Portland. Lila and I arranged to have dinner for 250 guests. It was a very nice marriage party. After the celebration, Mona had to move to L.A. with Kamal. Mona spent a lot of time with me in the store after school in Africa when she was a little girl. She could always feel when I was happy or worried. The house felt very empty after she left; I missed her so much. But she is very happy with her husband. He has a good job and now they have two little boys. Mona has a very good job in a hospital, working in radiology.

During this time, my brother Mo had been buying Dunkin' Donuts franchises. He had stores in Eugene, Tigard, Hillsboro, 122nd Avenue, Portland, Raleigh Hills and Seattle. The upper echelon management had given Mo a good deal on stores that were not managed well and were run down. Mo came in to improve their management, fix them up, and then sell the franchises. I first got the Raleigh Hills store. Then Mo wanted me to take the Tigard store because it was close. He wanted to give it to me and not make any profit for himself. I would just have to pay Dunkin' Donuts Corporation about $1,000 per month for the franchise fees. I took the Tigard store, but it did not do as well as the Raleigh Hills store. It did not have the volume. I had my kids working in it to save money.

Mo then asked me if I could look after his other stores—the ones in Seattle and the others in the Portland area and Eugene. I would leave early in the morning to check on my stores, and then I would go to his stores. Every few days I drove up to Seattle to check on that store's manager. I would return after 6:00 p.m. every day. It got very tiring.

For all this traveling, I bought a brand new Ford. I put gas in it and drove many miles. One day, I parked the car. When I wanted to leave, it would not start! I called the Ford service department. I came to find out that I had not put any oil or water in the car, though I had been driving it for about three months. There hadn't been time! I told the service people that I took it to the garage for gas and oil. They didn't believe me, but they honored the guarantee anyway by replacing it with a nice white Tempo—which I gifted to Haidar when he was ready to marry.

Mo was going to be opening a big kitchen in L.A. to make donuts to supply 50 or 60 of the 7-Eleven and ampm stores. He would be too busy to oversee the Northwest stores. Mo flew to Portland and told me that he had an arranged to hand back the stores in Oregon and Washington to the territory manager for the Dunkin' Donuts. He suggested that we all go down to L.A., buy a new van, and make donut deliveries to all the convenience stores. He wanted me to hire a manager and said that he didn't want Hassan or me to do any hard work. I said, "Well, brother, first thing, let's see if this store is going to work out. I am not going to hand over my Raleigh Hills store. But if they want Tigard, let them close it—Tigard is losing money."

We would not be able to walk away without making payment according to the agreement that we had with Dunkin' Donuts Corporation. Their representative explained, "Habib, we have a contract for $70,000-$80,000 rent for 20 years for this place. You owe us some money. We would have to charge you $35,000, but you can keep Raleigh Hills." I liked the Raleigh Hills location, and the business was improving every month. The company representative was not very friendly in these discussions. I said, "Look, if you want to throw me away, I am not going to agree with you. I have a sick woman at home. I just came from California. I worked with you guys for so many years. If you want to do me bad, I am not going to accept it."

He replied, "Okay, Habib. You want to keep the Raleigh Hills store. We have to arrange for the losses. We agree to take 2/3 of the loss on Tigard, but you have to take the other 1/3 of the loss. Then we will arrange for you to have the 7-Eleven stores' donut business. We will take good care of you. Don't worry, if you do what we tell you." I responded, "Well, do I have any choice in this?" He said, "No, no choice." I said, "Well, if I have no choice, how can I pay you what I owe you?" He explained, "We will make it easy for you. We will bring you cases for transporting to the 7-Eleven stores. We will help you; you can make payments out of the Raleigh Hills store." Altogether the amount I owed came to $180,000. They took away the Tigard stores, and my brother handed all the Northwest territory stores over to the corporation. They promised him that they would give him the L.A. stores.

My brother was happy. He said, "Habib, give them all the stores and come back to L.A. empty handed." I said, "No, Mo. Before I can return to L.A. with all my children and a sick woman I would have to see if Dunkin' Donuts is going to do what they promised. If it looks good, then I would call Dunkin' Donuts. If they don't force me to pay the money, I would be able to return to L.A. I have no choice."

A few months later, Mo asked Dunkin' Donuts when he was going to get his L.A. territory. Dunkin' Donuts told Mo that the manager who had made the arrangements with Mo had been fired. The arrangements had all been verbal; there was no written agreement. So Mo lost all the stores, except one in L.A. He started to do some other work with another company. A little later he and his brother-in-law opened their own donut shop, called Sesame Donuts. If anybody in the family wanted to open a donut store, it would be named Sesame Donuts.

I only believe what I can see with my eyes, and hold in my hand. Meanwhile, my family and I were in Portland, working hard in the Raleigh Hills Dunkin' Donuts. We started thinking about having a Sesame Donuts store. Said did a lot of research, and worked with our lawyer to determine if we could use the Sesame Donuts name in Oregon. We had to do a lot of work branding the name, copyrighting the logo, and forming the corporation. It cost a lot of money for the lawyers to complete it. An East Indian man started talking to us about the business. In spite of the work we had done to protect the name, he wanted to open a Sesame Donuts store, and thought that he could do it as long as it was not located in Portland. We liked the idea of him opening a store, but said, "How about $5,000 or $10,000 to use the name. We did a lot of work setting up and registering the business." Said told him that the name was protected. He replied, "I can get the same name. I don't think your lawyer did anything except for Portland." Said agreed casually and said, "Yeah, I think it was just Portland." He suggested, "Why do you need this $5,000 or $10,000 anyway?" Said responded, "I really don't need it, but I want it, because we just spent a lot of money to set up the business." He said, "Well, no. I'll call the guys in the state office and work on it for myself."

Right after we finished talking with him, Said immediately phoned our attorney and asked him to change the trademark legal documents for the company name to cover all of Oregon, and Washington also—as the man also had family in Washington. The attorney said that the whole state would cost $97. I said, "Yes, do the whole state. Right now! And fax it!" We knew the man was not going to do any work that day, because it was about three o'clock in the afternoon. In a few minutes the attorney said it was done; the changes were made.

The next morning at about eight o'clock, the Oregon State Business branch registered the company as an "S" corporation. About three days later, the Indian man called Said. "Your lawyer registered the whole state of Oregon," he said. "Not just Portland!"

"You're kidding! We told him to only register Portland. Oh, man. Sorry."

He replied, "Well, anyway, you can go talk to your lawyer so that we can use the name." Said told him, "Yeah, whenever you are ready, you come back." We could have ordered volume discounts and put ads in the paper, but he never came back, because he didn't want to help pay for setting up the corporation. He eventually set up a store that he named Yum Yum Donuts.

Over time, we had many people working for us—some Lebanese, some Iraqis. Some of the Iraqis did not speak English well, so we tried to use them as delivery drivers. They were very nice, and we tried to pay them well. One Lebanese man was Said's friend, and worked with us for about seven years. He was able to buy a house and a van. In 1998, he had a quarrel with my brother Joe and my son Haidar, while I was visiting my sisters in Lebanon. (It is important to keep Ramadan every year after making the Hajj. I like go back to Lebanon to do it and visit the family.) He and some of the Iraqis left us to open a kitchen and start their own business. At the time, we had a contract to deliver donuts to the 7-Eleven stores. Our old friend talked to the 7-Eleven management, underbid us, and took away our business.

There was also a man from Jordan who had a little bakery, much smaller than our store. He started calling our wholesale customers to try to take away our business. At one point, he even called the health department, hoping to cause trouble for us. He was undercutting us by selling his donuts for 25¢, while we sold them for 33¢ each.

But we understood this; it is an open market and competition is to be expected. Someone, we never found out who, called the Dunkin' Donuts corporate offices and told them that we were not running the place well, that it was dirty, and that we were not paying the franchise fees correctly. The management decided to do an audit. Before that, Said had been going to all the franchise owners' meetings. He had told Dunkin' Donuts that we were being charged too much for advertising. Finally, he got together with several other franchise owners, called *The Oregonian*, and determined that they were paying 45% more for their annual advertising through Dunkin' Donuts than if they had placed the ads directly themselves. Said discussed this with company management, and suggested that the owners place the ads themselves. With their savings over just a few years, he pointed out that Dunkin' Donuts could open another store. But the management did not like the suggestions, and felt that we were trying to undercut the system.

They didn't like us, and told us that they were going to remove the Dunkin' Donuts sign and shut us down. They said, "We are coming to audit you, and take the sign down." We had just signed a 10-year franchise renewal with them, but we said okay, and we took the sign down, as they requested. Then they called back and changed their minds, "No, don't take the sign down. We want to talk." They wanted to sell the store. They thought we would be scared when they told us to take the sign down. They did not expect us to say okay; they thought we would be willing to talk and compromise. The company banned Said and me from coming to the shop, because we were the legal franchisees. So we had to have Haidar, Lena, Joe and other family members running the store until everything was resolved. We had to send Lama in to get money to buy groceries. At the time, we had the ice cream shop, so Said and I worked there, and did some of our work for Sesame Donuts out of the house.

Said wanted to fight the Dunkin' Donuts company, but I wanted to resolve everything and move on, especially since we were not going to be able to be present in the store until the issue worked its way through the courts. In meetings with several lawyers, including a franchise lawyer, our personal lawyer—Arnold Polk—saw that I was very quiet. He was very smart. He finally said, "Wait a second. I think Habib is the one who brought you over here to solve the problem. And you guys are listening to Said so that we can go to war. I don't believe it is in Habib's interest to go to war. We just want to get Habib and Said back into the business so they can do what they do best. We don't have time or money to fight these big companies."

The franchise lawyer said, "Well, I can take these guys to court. I can take their franchise agreement to court. I have a 75% chance of winning." Said said, "Okay, good. We'll take that chance." To him, anything over 50% was a good chance. Then we discussed the costs of the lawyer's work, and he reminded us that there was still a 25% chance of losing. We went back to our original, personal lawyer and discussed the issues with him again—including the option of declaring bankruptcy. What we knew was making donuts. We would have had to find a new, good location, and buy equipment, spending at least $200,000. I made the decision. I said, "Just get those nincompoops out of the way. We want to get back in the store so we can work."

We eventually agreed to a confidential out-of-court settlement, and the store became ours to rename and manage. They sent one of the company representatives into the shop to tell us what we had to take down and give to them. He was surprised when he arrived because everything related to Dunkin' Donuts was gone. Everything was already "Sesame Donuts." Then they accused us, "You see, we knew they had it all planned. The Fakihs had it planned all along!"

We went through some tough times in 1990 and 1991 with Dunkin' Donuts, and it was disappointing after almost 20 years of working with them in L.A., Torrance, Hermosa Beach, and then 13 years in Portland. Imagine how much in franchise fees we paid them over the years! It was about $4,000 a month just in Portland. In the eight years in Hermosa Beach they earned $600,000 or $700,000 from the store. And my brother Mo had made lots of business for them in his territories—buying, running and selling the stores. He had been on a management committee for the company. When Dunkin' Donuts was sold to an English company, everything changed, and all the good people we knew were gone.

During this time, I was paying Dunkin' Donuts the lease fee for the building, and they would then send the payment to the landlord. When the lease came up for renewal, I spoke directly to the landlord. He was such a nice man—from Italy. He called me "brother" and told his son, Jerry, to take good care of me. We made a new lease for 15 years, with a little increase every five years. We talked about the building lease, the maintenance of the parking lot, and the trash. We agreed to a price. He asked me if I still planned to run the store as a donut shop. Now, when he comes in one morning each month for the rent, I give him a cup of coffee. We needed to change the lease to Lena's name, so we arranged that. When people saw the new sign and asked who was running the store, we would tell them that Lena and Haidar were the new owners. We had to keep everything under Lena and Haidar's names from a legal standpoint, until the settlement was finalized.

After all the legal wrangling, I went to Lebanon for two months to observe Ramadan. When I returned, Said was still working to finish the settlement and get the final documents in order. We started to get bills from the lawyers. This cost $10,000; that cost $10,000; this cost $7,000—so many bills! We used all of our money and credit cards. The requirements for the settlement funds started coming in. We were afraid we would lose the house and have to live in a tent in the park! We talked to a loan officer, Trista, who was married to a Muslim boy. She converted to Islam when she got married. We introduced her to Lena and they became good friends. One day she came to the store and told us that we could refinance the house. I asked if she could refinance the store. She said, "I can do that." I said, "How about the credit cards?" She said, "I can do that, too." She combined all the payments into one payment per month. She was so nice, and I was so happy.

I tried to go to Lebanon each year for Ramadan. When Siham was healthier, I took her. One time she fell down while we were there. Each problem affected her health more and more after the first stroke. It seemed like whenever I went to Lebanon, something happened. Either Siham got sicker or fell down—whether she stayed in Portland or was in Lebanon with me. She missed me when I was gone. Sometimes when I looked at her, I felt sad. We had been married for almost 50 years. That is not a small thing. I had hopes that when the children were grown, we could buy a camper and drive to L.A. and San Diego to visit them, spending a week along the way, seeing different parts of Oregon and California. It would have been time then to enjoy ourselves. We could let the kids work in the store. We established businesses with them and for them. I had been able to do more for them than what my parents could do for me and the rest of their children.

The wars in Lebanon forced me to leave school early to earn money to help my family survive. I was never a teenager. I only had time to make money to buy bread for my family. But I would not change anything. Thank God for my life. If I were asked how I wanted to change anything, if I could come back and start over, I would say, "I would like to come back as myself. No change. Because I love it. The times when I feel sad, I love them. The times when I have troubles, I love them. I fought for it. The times when I was worried, I loved, because they make me feel always loved, and I like to take care of everything myself and feel that I accomplished everything. I never gave up."

Looking back, I have finished most of my jobs up to now. I am in my seventies and did my best. God has helped. It would take 15 years to pay all the loans off, and now the job belongs more to Said and Haidar. When I left Lebanon, I had only my airline ticket, and a little French and American money with me. I worked hard in Nigeria. In those 60 years, I got a nice wife and made a family. Now I have 15 grandchildren. I am so proud of them, and proud of myself for what I did. I never did anything bad, I never hurt anybody—and if I hurt anybody by accident, I know God will help me. I try to do something good each time I go to Lebanon. If someone asks me for help, I help them.

We were like the immigrants in US history when we moved to L.A. We left a very nice home in Africa and moved to America with nothing. We worked hard and started businesses and are finally successful. I started traditions in the family. The first Thanksgiving in

Portland, we were living in the Laurelwood apartment. We were very tired from just opening the store. We didn't have very much money, and most of the family was still in L.A. But we decided to celebrate Thanksgiving, and give thanks. We bought two chickens, gave thanks, and ate them on a little table. I still have that small table, and now, every Thanksgiving we give thanks to keep the tradition. One year when I was in Lebanon during the holiday, Said told me that his son, Yussef, gave thanks. It is always the oldest son that has that responsibility. It is great to establish and continue that tradition!

All my children have grown up, gotten married, and have their own families. But I still feel like I am taking care of them. I know they respect me. They try to do everything well, in order to show me that respect—even though they know I would not criticize them if they made mistakes. I tried to develop a love for the culture and traditions in their motherland—even though they mostly live in America. I taught them all Arabic. Even Mona, who was born in Africa and lived half her life there and half in America—when she travels to Lebanon, people think she was raised there, because she has the same speech and slang they do. Siham's father raised many of his children outside of Lebanon, but he didn't teach them Arabic. One time when Said was about 10 years old, he started speaking Arabic to his grandfather who replied, "God bless your father! Look, Said speaks Arabic." Siham's father was very nice, and he liked me. He was a tall man with blue eyes—very good looking. Her mother was short and a little bit chubby. She also had blue eyes.

While we were running Sesame Donuts, we thought we might also buy an ice cream store. Besides making donuts, we knew that business because we had run one in the L.A. area. Baskin-Robbins had a pretty good location available. But ice cream and convertible cars aren't as popular in Portland. You start driving and have to put the top up when the rain starts. Ice cream in Portland is like cockroaches. In the summer, the cockroach goes into the fields, works hard and eats the greens. In the winter, when it starts raining, he goes underground and hides. This is just the opposite of ants. During the dry season, ants store food in their tunnels. In the winter, they eat all they save. If you buy an ice cream store, you have to live like a cockroach. In the summertime, be happy and get more money. But in the winter—no sales, no business. Then, like an ant, what you save from the summer, you have to spend during the winter—that is, if you have saved. You still have to pay for the store operations, franchise commission, interest, rent, and the employees. In California if you have an ice cream store, like Baskin-Robbins, you are a king, because the weather is good all year round.

Before I started my own ice cream bar in California, I tried to buy a Baskin-Robbins 31 Flavors, but I missed it. That was a mistake. It was $100,000 or $150,000—the cost of a Dunkin' Donuts store. But now they sell for $500,000 in the L.A. area. I thought that next time I had a chance, I would buy a Baskin-Robbins franchise, but in the Portland area, where I was living. We did buy one, and the family shares the responsibility for running it. When we had orders for ice cream cakes, Lena helped make and design them, before she got too busy with her babies.

In 1999, I returned to London for the first time since I had traveled there from Africa for my operation 30 years before. I stayed with my nephew and niece. They are the children of two of my sisters, and they married. They immigrated to England and work for a hotel company. They jokingly invited me to come whenever I had a chance. Well, the ticket was only about $100, so I decided to take them up on their offer. When I arrived, I showed the London immigration officer my passport, and she asked what I was doing in London. I said, "I am going to visit my cousin. Do you have a problem with that?" She said, "No," and let me go. With an American passport, I felt like I was calling the shots! The police were watching me, but I didn't notice. It was easy—all the signs were in English.

When I arrived, it was raining. But it was sunny the rest of my visit. But the day my nephew took me to the airport, it started raining again. My nephew begged, "Please stay here longer. Look at the change in the weather." For 15 days, they took me all over London. I didn't see the hospital where I had the operation. But I did go to the Queen's Way Hotel, where I had stayed before and after the operation. I told my nephew that I met a girl before I had the operation, and that I made her pregnant. I said, "I want to know the child." He was upset, shouting at me, and asking me what the girl's name was, and whether the child was a boy or girl, and what the child's name was. I kept saying, "I don't know." I had fun teasing them and seeing all the beautiful flowers in the Buckingham Palace gardens. This nephew had a 19-year-old daughter, and my brother, Hassan, in California, had a 27-year-old son. They were engaged to be married in July 2003.

I love my family and my family loves me. I am so happy ... and the story continues as my life continues ... and I still wear my grandfather's hat.

EPILOGUE

OUR BOOK WAS COMPLETED IN 2002, AND SINCE THEN, AS WITH ALL families, there have been transitions and change. Habib is an active 84 years old now. He still loves to go to the store and greet customers with, "A donut a day keeps the doctor away!" He still loves his big American cars, and says he "won't trade his '94 Buick for the new matchboxes they make today!" He and his family celebrate their inclusion in American culture while enjoying their Lebanese traditions. They draw friends from all walks of life and many cultures into their warm hospitality.

Habib's children are settled successfully in their jobs. Some work within the Sesame Donuts business. Sadly, his wife passed away in 2002, but shortly after, a new baby in the family was given her name, Siham—so the wonderful memories carry on. Some of Habib's grandchildren are in college, and some are starting their own families—his great-grandchildren!

The transition from Dunkin' Donuts to Sesame Donuts was a trying time for the family. Habib had to rely on that same intuition and judgment that carried him through so many situations in his younger years. He had to make decisions to stay in Portland, settle with Dunkin' Donuts and the landlord, and establish the Sesame Donuts Corporation. He wrote a poem at that time that laments the difficulties and trials of his earlier life, through his relocations and various businesses, in an effort to support his family. He prayed about what he should do, what decisions about the business would create the best opportunities for his family. But Habib's conclusion to stay in Portland to start his business and raise his family brought success. The business has expanded to several branches of Sesame Donuts in cities surrounding the original Portland location. The shops support many members of Habib's family, paying for college tuitions for the children, providing jobs for others, and actively supporting the community through corporate donations, and participation in various events.

This memoir was originally meant just for the family, but as I was writing it, it became obvious that it was more than a memoir. This is a story with a moral for anyone who reads it. The natural intelligence and logic that Habib had to apply to all the unique situations in which he discovered himself is a lesson in thinking creatively and never conceding to difficulties. It reflects acceptance of other cultures and traditions. It shows the support and strength that a unified family provides during both the best times and the trying times. Habib hopes that his family and other readers find those lessons within these pages, take them to heart, and enjoy successful and happy lives.

*

For readers of Arabic, this is the poem that Habib wrote one day during that stressful period when he was assessing future opportunities for the financial support of his family. The English translation follows.

... لِيش يا زَمَانْ

لَمِين رَح إشْكي هـمِّي لغَيْرَك يَا زَمَانْ

مِنْ زِغري وإنتي مْحَطَّط عليَّ ولَاحقتني بكلّ مكانْ

خليتني أُهجر على فلسطين قبل ما إتعلم وإفهم القرآنْ

بعدها أخذتني، ودَّيتني على آخر البلدان

اللَّي هي أفريقيا اللَّي كانت حلمي من زمان

عطيتني ويسَّرتها وخليت أهلي بالأمان

ولكن بعدها جبتني وقلتلي لوين بعدك رايح يا انسان

لحد هون بكفي، ورجعتني على لبنان

ولاكِن ليش ما تركتني حتى رجعتني تاني للهوان

وكانت رحلتي لسيراليون اللي فيها أُخت كلها حب وحنان

صمَّمِت حتى خلصتها من واحد عجوز وجبان

كذَب عليها تيتزوجها على إنو هوَّي قريب من الإخوان

بعد ما سافرتْ، علِقِتْ هونيك بين الغابات والوديان

اتعارك معك على الخير والشر وطالب من الله الغفران

حتى وصَّلتني على أميركا وجمعتنا بالعيلة والإخوان

واليوم شو بعد بدَّك مِنِّي عن حُب أو كره بآخر هالزمان؟

ولَّا فِكْرَك تِتْخَلَّصْ مِنِّي وتْرَجِّعني على لبنانْ؟

بقلم: الحاج حبيب فقيه

WHY, OH LIFE?

Complain to whom, but to you, oh time and destiny
You have pursued me since boyhood, and kept following me
 everywhere
You made me wander into the land of Palestine before I could learn
 and understand the Koran
Then after you took me and delivered me to lands far and beyond
Land that is Africa, of which I dreamt when I was young
God sustained me, and my brethren until we felt secure and needed
 no one
But then, you asked, Where to, oh Man?
Enough! Stop here! Then you sent me back to Lebanon
But then you never let me be, you came back to bring adventures
 unknown
I traveled to Sierra Leone to a beloved, compassionate sister
There I set my mind to rid her of an old and cowardly man
He misled her into love and marriage of which he has but none
There I was stranded in the jungle and valleys of wild Africa and
 beyond
Battling for goodness to overcome evil, asking God for forgiveness
Finally my destiny was America
You reunited me with family and friends to start anew from nothing
And today, today, what is it you demand of me?
Is it of love or hate at my old age?
You still pursue me at the end of time
Alas! Do you plan to be rid of me and send me back to Lebanon?

Habib Fakih
Summer 1999

CPSIA information can be obtained
at www.ICGtesting.com
Printed in the USA
JSHW010357101221
21075JS00001B/4